TAKE THEM AT THEIR WORDS

TAKE THEM AT THEIR WORDS

SHOCKING, AMUSING AND BAFFLING QUOTATIONS FROM THE GOP AND THEIR FRIENDS, 1994–2004

Bruce J. Miller

with

Diana Maio

INTRODUCTION BY SIDNEY BLUMENTHAL

Cartoons by Mike Luckovich

Academy Chicago Publishers

Published in 2004 by
Academy Chicago Publishers
363 West Erie Street
Chicago, Illinois 60610

© 2004 by Bruce J. Miller
Introduction © 2004 by Sidney Blumenthal
Cartoons by permission of Mike Luckovich and Creators Syndicate, Inc.

Printed in the U.S.A.

Library of Congress Cataloging-in-Publication Data
on file with the publisher

For Jordan and Anita
And for Julia

ACKNOWLEDGMENTS

Special thanks to Mark Crispin Miller whose invaluable help made this project easier. Thanks also to Tom Bielenberg, Vicki Bonson, Theresa Hawthorne, Mark Jung, Jonathan Kurtz, Eric Miller, Marilyn Mulholland, Sarah Olson, Arthur and Lois Solomon, Krishna Vemulapalli and Mary Willard.

"I WILL MAKE A BARGAIN WITH THE REPUBLICANS. IF THEY WILL STOP TELLING LIES ABOUT DEMOCRATS, WE WILL STOP TELLING THE TRUTH ABOUT THEM."

—*Adlai Stevenson (1900–1965)*

Contents

PREFACE

In 1994 "conservative" Republicans gained control of the House of Representatives, electing Newt Gingrich Speaker, and drawing up a "contract with America" that (like subsequent GOP platforms) proudly proclaimed their uncompromising radicalism. Gingrich made Rush Limbaugh an honorary House member, and invited sympathetic talk radio hosts from across the United States to broadcast live from the capitol. Selected Republican Congressmen agreed to meet talk hosts once a month for breakfast or lunch.

As I drove throughout the Midwest to call on clients, I heard the words of Limbaugh and a host of "baby Rushes" relayed everywhere from the most powerful radio transmitters in the country. The public airwaves had been annexed. Amongst Republicans of the 104th Congress—especially the Freshmen who were the foot soldiers of Gingrich's radical rebellion—the talk radio ethic was adopted like a resolution passed on a quick voice vote.

While slander against the Clintons and the Democrats generally was not limited to broadcasting or Capitol Hill, it was the birth of outrage against this onslaught that led me in 1996 to publish a booklet entitled, *When Right Is Wrong: Shocking Quotations from the Republican Revolution*. The few hundred copies I produced rapidly disappeared from the shelves of a small group of booksellers to whom I had given copies, and who sold them for $3.00 each.

When Jordan and Anita Miller of Academy Chicago Publishers came across a battered copy of *When Right Is Wrong* while weeding out books from their personal library, they saw the utility of this little booklet and asked me to expand and update it.

In 1996 I did not foresee the expansion of right-wing radio (with Clear Channel holding 1200 stations), the creation of a Murdoch-owned news channel that would dominate the presentation of political issues on cable, or that the Republican Radicals would flood the market with their mendacious books. Nor could I have imagined that this massive propaganda machine would be employed to justify unnecessary war and policies that threaten the very rights our men and women in uniform have defended so fiercely throughout our history. While some Republican Congressmen have modified their language since the failure of the "Contract with America," the rhetoric of the party's activists and propagandists has become more vile and violent than ever.

This book offers a wide-angle snapshot of the moral values Republicans and their allies proudly embrace. A vast right-wing consensus is clearly visible. My hope is that people unaware of the extreme and dangerous nature of G.O.P.-inspired rhetoric will now give it serious attention, and help vote them out of power.

It may well be that some of the quotations offered here are tame compared with the comments of bloggers and others at the grass-roots level who have taken Republican hate-speech to heart. On C-Span's "Washington Journal" one day last fall, I heard an agitated caller say, "Democrats are always committing mass murder!" It is likely that this man had been reading Ann Coulter or someone like her.

The relationship between violent acts and the radical rhetoric of talk radio is a troubling one with many examples to cite. Francisco Martin Duran, the Colorado resident who fired at the White house with a rifle on October 29, 1994, had listened often to Chuck Baker's program on KVOR in Colorado Springs. In fact, Duran had called the office of Sen. Ben Nighthorse Campbell on August 23 of the same year to protest the assault weapons ban in the crime bill. "This is very bad" he said during the call, "I will go to Washington and take someone out." Baker was a favorite of militia groups.

After the Oklahoma City bombing on April 19, 1995, many hosts became defensive and denied their words were inflammatory, even as Spencer Hughes of KSFO in San Francisco defended Timothy McVeigh.

In November, 2002, Senate Minority Leader Tom Daschle (D-SC) expressed concern about threats he had received after repeated personal attacks on him by Rush Limbaugh and others. Indeed, a year later Sen. Daschle and other Democrats were sent letters laced with deadly anthrax.

The many local talk radio shows remain vitally important to the GOP. In a *New York Times* front-page story on December 29, 2003, Jim Rutenberg pointed out that the Bush administration "is aggressively working the expansive hustings of Republican-friendly talk radio, priming the grass roots faithful for battle next year."

While Republican rhetoric is, at worst, an incitement to violence, at best it is narrowing the platform of debate, alienating the public from our political system, and working against productive compromise.

BRUCE J. MILLER
CHICAGO, IL
JANUARY 2004

INTRODUCTION

The firing of A cable TV talk show host in July, 2003, may have seemed at first glance to be a minor event. Shock jocks crossing the line of good taste, after all, are a cliché and stories of their rise and fall are as regular as the weekly Arbitron ratings. But the unceremonious dispatch of one Michael Savage (born Michael Weiner) indicated more about the turn of contemporary politics, media and language in the age of George W. Bush, who had pledged to "change the tone," than simply the degree of Savage's self-promoting nastiness. It was one of a series of telling incidents occurring in the summer of 2003, including Fox News' lawsuit against its critic Al Franken and the publication of Ann Coulter's *Treason*, clarifying the dominant conservative tone.

"You should only get AIDS and die, you pig," Savage had screamed at a contrary caller, shortly thereafter prompting MSNBC to remove him from his place in front of its cameras. But the cable network, operated by NBC News, a division of General Electric, had been warned from the moment of his hiring that he was a practitioner of the malicious. His outbursts were well-documented: homosexuals were "perverts," Asians "little soy-eaters," and immigrants came from "Turd World nations."

Savage's tone was notorious from his radio show, syndicated to more than 300 stations by the Talk Radio Network Inc. And TRN was embroiled in defending its investment by filing suit against four individuals who had criticized or parodied Savage on the Internet—protecting his speech by intimidating and attempting to suppress others'. But MSNBC trailed badly in the ratings behind the conservative network, Fox News, and sought to capture some of Fox's audience by featuring its very own right-wing hosts.

When Savage's show was announced, MSNBC was impassive to protests. Conservative groups, meanwhile, rallied to his support. Conservative Women of America, staunchly advancing the agenda of the religious right, made Savage's program one of its causes, urging its followers to send letters to the network: "Thank MSNBC for seeing that conservative talk show hosts like Savage, with millions of listeners, represent a vast viewer audience—and one far greater than that of liberal pro-homosexual special interest groups in Washington, D.C."

After five months on the job, Savage's trademark tongue got him dismissed, but it hardly ended his career. He still remains host of his radio show, broadcast on hundreds of stations. He had just gone one insult too far for a mainstream network that had hired him in the first place on his reputation for slurs that it hoped would attract an audience share from Fox.

Savage was not a pioneer in his field, but an imitator, one shrill voice among many on the right that have proliferated to dominate the medium with their vituperation since the end of the Fairness Doctrine in 1987. His language was not much different from that of Rush Limbaugh, the most successful conservative media figure, with 15 million daily listeners of his radio program, and who was awarded a spot as a sports commentator on ESPN, less for any predilection for athletics than for his market niche as a presumptive spokesman for discontented white men. In his lexicon, women's rights advocates were "femi-Nazis," 12-year-old Chelsea Clinton was the "White House dog," and on African-Americans: "They are 12 percent of the population. Who the hell cares?"

Nor was Savage's method of debating much different from that of Bill O'Reilly, the second biggest conservative media star, host of the largest rated show on Fox News, who cuts off and berates guests who disagree with him in a theater of humiliation. When Al Franken, the comedian and author, confronted him on a panel at the May 2003 Book Expo America with the fact that he had falsely claimed a journalism prize, O'Reilly's response was to shout, "Shut up! Just shut up!"

Three months later, in August, Fox News filed suit against Franken and the publisher of his forthcoming book, *Lies and the Lying Liars Who Tell Them: A Fair and Balanced Look at the Right*, for using the phrase "fair and balanced," which Fox claimed it had the sole right to use. Its suit called Franken "a parasite," "unstable" and a "C-level commentator" who is "not a well-respected voice in American politics," while touting Fox News as "world famous" and Bill O'Reilly as a "national celebrity." In the light of numerous decisions by federal courts and the Supreme Court protecting satire and parody as free speech, Fox News's suit could only be interpreted as a means of vindictive bullying, a legal complement to its talk shows—and just talk.

Talk like Savage's, or Limbaugh's or O'Reilly's, has become routine, even systematic, certainly a big business. According to the Senate Democratic Policy Committee, the top five radio station owners that control 45 powerful, 50,000-watt or more radio stations broadcast 310 hours of nationally syndicated right-wing talk, but only a total of five hours of countervailing talk—three of which include, almost as a peculiar courtesy, the Democratic foil on conservative Sean Hannity's show.

The extraordinary compendium of statements made by Republicans that have been assembled by Bruce J. Miller and Diana Maio in *Take Them At Their Words* illustrates that the vilifying language of the right is not confined to fringe elements. Here, for example, is Senator Phil Gramm, Republican of Texas, speaking of "hunting Democrats with dogs." This sort of belligerent posturing is not some underground phenomenon, but available daily in any city or town on the radio dial, or on TV, or in the pages of conservative publications, or in the Congress. Who can forget the chivalry displayed when Hillary Rodham Clinton was elected in 2000 to the Senate from New York? "I tell you one thing," remarked then Senate Republican Majority Leader Trent Lott, "when this Hillary gets to the Senate, if she does, maybe lightning will strike and she won't."

In 1990, then-Republican House Whip Newt Gingrich (later Speaker of the House) hired a pollster to devise a lexicon of demonization. In a memo that Gingrich circulated, "Language: A Key Mechanism of Control," Republicans were instructed that "words and phrases are powerful" and that the list that had been test-marketed should be "memorized."

Apply these to the opponent, their record, proposals and their party:

decay . . . failure (fail) . . . collapse(ing) . . . deeper . . . crisis . . . urgent(cy) . . . destructive . . . destroy . . . sick . . . pathetic . . . lie . . . liberal . . . they/them . . . unionized bureaucracy . . . "compassion" is not enough . . . betray . . . consequences . . . limit(s) . . . shallow . . . traitors . . . sensationalists . . . endanger . . . coercion . . . hypocrisy . . . radical . . . threaten . . . devour . . . waste . . . corruption . . . incompetent . . . permissive attitudes . . . destructive . . . impose . . . self-serving . . . greed . . . ideological . . . insecure . . . anti-(issue): flag, family, child, jobs . . . pessimistic . . . excuses . . . intolerant . . . stagnation . . . welfare . . . corrupt . . . selfish . . . insensitive . . . status quo . . . mandate(s) . . . taxes . . . spend(ing) . . . shame . . . disgrace . . . punish (poor . . .) . . . bizarre . . . cynicism . . . cheat . . . steal . . . abuse of power . . . machine . . . bosses . . . obsolete . . . criminal rights . . . red tape . . . patronage

More than a decade after Gingrich's guidance, these words still echo 'round the clock. They are used to craft talking points for millions of followers, who have accustomed themselves to taking such cues. Out of this vocabulary, an entire mental universe has been conjured of sick, pathetic liberals, traitors against the flag and family, who would betray the country by imposing

their permissive attitudes, bringing shame and disgrace, causing collapse and crisis.

The origins of this garish imagination of fear lie deeper than
the recent escapades of Newt Gingrich, running back to the
Salem witch trials of the 17th century, the Know Nothings of
the 19th century, and Father Charles Coughlin and Senator Joseph McCarthy of the 20th. In 1964, when the first contemporary right-wing candidate, Barry Goldwater, was nominated by
the Republican Party, the historian Richard Hofstadter wrote
an essay on "the paranoid style in American politics." He em-
phasized style because it had become the essence of this brand
of politics: "Style has more to do with the way in which ideas
are believed than with the truth or falsity of their content." But
this did not mean that the right-wingers of Hofstadter's time
did not engage in elaborate displays of "pedantry" and accu-
mulations of "evidence." They piled up "evidence" to create a
thoroughly coherent if fictitious black-and-white picture in
which enemies within conspired and only those who had a special night-vision to identify these satanic hosts could resist them
in the name of patriotism.

The same year that Hofstadter published his piece on "the
paranoid style," an obscure conservative named John Stormer
published the "carefully documented story of America's retreat
from victory" in the face of the liberal/internationalist/Com-
munist conspiracy. It was entitled *None Dare Call It Treason*.
The book, timed to coincide with the 1964 presidential campaign, was turned into a bestseller by the John Birch Society, a
far-right-wing group, which boasted that it had distributed six
million copies within eight months of its publication. (To this
day, the Birch Society sells Stormer's book on its website.)

Nearly 40 years later, in 2003, the bestselling book on the
right was entitled *Treason*, by Ann Coulter. "Liberals have a
preternatural gift for striking a position on the side of treason,"
she wrote. "Everyone says liberals love America, too. No they
don't. Whenever the nation is under attack, from within or with-

out, liberals side with the enemy." Positioned discreetly next to her book on *The New York Times* bestseller list was a tiny dagger signifying bulk sales from unknown sources. Coulter's argument was a conservative perennial, down to the spirited defense of Joseph McCarthy. Both Stormer's and Coulter's works cited mounds of "evidence." Both warned ominously against liberal betrayal. The principal difference between *None Dare Call It Treason* and *Treason* was not in sophistication, nuance, erudition, persuasiveness, or literary quality, but in the expanded capacity of conservatives to disseminate the word far and wide through their own alternative media and in the elevation by the mainstream media of the extremist as entertainer.

Take Them at Their Words is more than a brilliant and endlessly amusing sampling of quotations from the Right. It is a volume that reveals an unabashed worldview that today holds sway in the White House, the Congress and much of the media. You may read and laugh, but, remember, they mean it.

SIDNEY BLUMENTHAL

PART I

LOVE THY NEIGHBOR

"I want you to let a wave of hatred wash over you. Yes, hate is good."

—RANDALL TERRY

FAMILY VALUES

See, I'm not among those who think that the show ["Ellen"] should be hanged, drawn and banned. If someone's idea of great comedy is a TV show based on the premise that a homosexual is just like the rest of us, then who am I not to go along with the joke? . . . But is television yet ready for a fully layered character who is respected for her stand against divorce or for the traditional, intact family? A reverse-Maude, who in the face of the narrow-minded bigotries of the political left, finds the courage to stand against a permissive culture that has spread the seeds of violence, substance abuse, sexually transmitted disease and moral impoverishment that afflict our society?

   —*Dennis Byrne,* member of the editorial board of the *Chicago Sun-Times*, "The Deification of Ellen," 4-29-97.

These people who work in those buildings are not innocent victims. If they work in the Federal Building, they're the very people that are typing the letters, that are making the phone calls, that are getting your land taken away from you, that are calling you up on Internal Revenue Service, that want to confiscate all of your guns. These are the same people who womp up charges against you. These are the very same people that are all involved, every one of them.

   I don't care whether they're any more than a clerk or the high muckety-muck or the guy out there who's got BATF painted on his back, and he's the one who's knocking your door down. These people are not innocent victims. These are people that operate and move the system against you and I. These are people that have sold out to the system. These are the people that are against you and I.

> —*John Dayl*, talk show host for KFYI, Phoenix, AZ, 7-21-96, on the bombng of the Federal Building in Oklahoma City. "Extra! Update: Contra Crack," FAIR (Fairness and Accuracy In Reporting), 9-24-96.

I've asked for God's forgiveness, and I've received it.

> —*Rep. Helen Chenoweth*, a strong supporter of "family values," commenting on her protracted affair with a married man. David Neiwert, "Lives of the Republicans, Part Two," Salon.com, 9-16-98.

Some day I hope I will have the courage to be as much a man as he [Paul Hill] was.

> —*Anti-abortion crusader Dan Holman*. Patrick Condon, "Judge restricts anti-abortion activist who praised killer," *Chicago Tribune*, 10-30-03.

I haven't killed anyone yet, but I believe they [physicians who perform abortions] deserve to die.

> —*Ibid.*

My heart leaps for joy every time one of them gets popped. You won't find me weeping over the grave of an abortionist.

> —*Ibid.*

Brit Hume: When things go badly, as many people would feel they have been in Iraq with the continuing casualties and struggles and difficulties, do you ever doubt?
George Bush: I don't think they're going badly. I mean, obviously I think they're going badly for the soldiers who lost their lives, and I weep for that person and their family. But no, I think we're making good progress. As I said I pray for calmness

when the seas are storming, and I—you know, my faith is an integral part of being who I am, and I'm not going to change.
> —*Fox News Channel*, "Raw Data: Text of Bush Interview,"
> 9-22-03, p.4.

It's not going to affect my work or the committee's work. I think it is very inappropriate to get into somebody's personal life and obviously that's what [Larry Flynt] wants to do.
> —*Rep. Bob Barr*, one of 13 House Managers prosecuting the impeachment case against Bill Clinton before the Senate, on Flynt's threat to reveal embarrassing information about legislators' sex lives. CNN.com, 1-13-99.

I'd just like to tell you that Bob Livingston appreciates your belief in home values, family values.
> —*Rep. Bob Livingston (R-LA)* in a 1987 campaign speech to 8000 people. Joseph Mallia, "U.S. strikes Iraq; Before affairs, Livingston espoused 'family values'," *Boston Herald*, 12-18-98.

I have hurt you deeply. I must set the example that I hope President Clinton will follow. . . . I will not stand for Speaker.
> —*Rep. Bob Livingston*, addressing his wife and announcing his resignation from Congress because of revelations about his extramarital affairs. Rebecca Carr and Ken Foskett, "GOP's Livingston stuns House with Resignation," *Portland Press-Herald*, 12-20-98.

. . . You can't prepare in life to deal in life with the enormity of what I'm dealing with and what I put other people through. Saying I'm sorry to some people is rhetoric. There's no way that I know how to express the sadness and the sorrow and the grief that has been brought to Mr. Robertson's family. None.
> —*Rep. William Janklow (R-SD)* referring to Randy Scott, the man he killed, by the wrong name. Scott was killed

when Janklow ran a stop sign while going 71 m.p.h. in a 55-m.p.h. zone. Cara Hetland, "Janklow says he 'couldn't be sorrier' for accident that killed motorcyclist," Minnesota Public Radio, 9-22-03. Four days later Janklow pleaded not guilty. "Janklow Pleads not guilty to charges in fatal crash," *Sioux City Journal*, 9-27-03.

Really, if I had an opportunity to shoot Britney Spears, I think I would.
—*Kendel Ehrlich, wife of Maryland Gov. Robert Ehrlich (R),* on the way women are portrayed by the entertainment industry. David Nitkin, "First lady's comment draws criticism; She joked about shooting Britney Spears at forum," *Baltimore Sun,* 10-8-03.

In many ways I admired people—it depends for what. I admired Hitler, for instance, because he came from being a little man with almost no formal education, up to power. And I admire him for being such a good public speaker and for his way of getting to the people and so on. But I didn't admire him for what he did with it.
—*Arnold Schwarzenegger.* David Kirkpatrick, "Schwarzenegger Releases Data on Hitler Comments," *New York Times,* 10-4-03.

I want you to just let a wave of intolerance wash over you. I want you to let a wave of hatred wash over you. Yes, hate is good.
—*Randall Terry of Operation Rescue,* an anti-choice organization. "Demagoguery in America," *The New Republic,* 8-1-94.

Turn them over to the taxidermists. Wouldn't they [Department of Human Services workers] all look good in a taxidermy shop?
—*Talk Show Host Chuck Baker,* KKCS 1460-AM, Colorado Springs, talking about county workers who investigate cases of child abuse and neglect. Baker also suggested residents use the "Make My Day" law against DHS workers. This

law "allows residents to use deadly force to protect themselves in their homes if they feel they are in danger." Pam Zubeck and Warren Epstein, "Radio remarks draw scrutiny; Local host reportedly called for force against social workers," *The Gazette*, 9-14-01.

We're here because we care about kids.
—*Sen. Rick Santorum (R-PA)* speaking about welfare reform. Press conference, C-SPAN, 7-30-96.

Making people struggle a little bit is not necessarily the worst thing.
—*Sen. Rick Santorum*, a member of the Finance Committee, voicing opposition to increased funding for child care, while voting in favor of the Bush-backed bill to increase the number of work hours required for families on welfare. Elizabeth Shogren, "Tighter Rules Likely for Welfare Families; A Senate panel approves a bill that would force more recipients to find jobs, work longer hours," *Los Angeles Times*, 9-11-03.

But if there is a brave new world of tomorrow, they will enact the Bob Grant Mandatory Sterilization Act. [Imitating an African-American accent] "I don't have no job, how'm I gonna feed my family?" I wonder if they've ever figured out how they multiply like that. It's like maggots on a hot day. You look one minute and there are so many there, and you look again and, wow, they've tripled!
—*Bob Grant*, longtime employee of New York City's WABC, who now works at WOR 710-AM, giving his opinion of "welfare mothers." The former Republican mayor of New York, Rudolph Giuliani, had been a frequent guest on the Bob Grant Show, as had Christine Todd Whitman, the former head of the EPA under George W. Bush, when she was Republican Governor of New Jersey. "Dial Hate," *New York Magazine*, 10-24-94, p. 29.

It looks like Mr. Newt was right, which they'll be saying more and more as time goes on, just like they did with Dan Quayle.
—*Rush Limbaugh*, discussing a news story published in a San Diego newspaper in January 1996, about the success later in life of those people who grew up in orphanages. Newt Gingrich advocated orphanages to help replace welfare payments. Channel 23 TV, St. Paul, MN, 8-21-96.

It [The Personal Responsibility Act] prohibits AFDC [Aid to Families with Dependent Children] payments and housing benefits to mothers under age 18 who give birth to out-of-wedlock children. The state has the option of extending this prohibition to mothers aged 18, 19, 20.
—*Contract With America, The Bold Plan By Rep. Newt Gingrich, Rep. Dick Armey, and the House Republicans to Change the Nation*. NY: Times Books, 1994. p. 70.

. . . the Department of Education put out dollar after dollar to feed the trough that was one of the most amazing wastes of money you could ever see. Just look at Head Start, excuse me, Title I, take a look at that. Take a look at the billions of dollars sent out through Title 1 that has netted absolutely zilch in terms of how kids are doing, for the past thirty years there was nothing but a feeding frenzy, big-time trough behavior and that's still what we're dealing with out there in the field.
—*Reid Lyon*, Chief, Child Development and Behavior Branch, National Institute of Child Health and Human Development, NIH, and an advisor on child health and education research to George W. Bush. From Lyon's speech at the "major policy forum with U.S. Secretary of Education Rod Paige," held by the Coalition for Evidence-Based Policy, Washington, D.C., 11-19-02. Excelgov.org.

The Clintons have a cat, but their nanny has a dog.
—*Rush Limbaugh*, during a tirade against the Democratic National Convention, 8-28-96. Limbaugh had referred to

Chelsea as the "White House dog" in 1993. Apparently, he
liked the remark so much he decided to repeat it.

So, they could come up with other disability dolls and I would
like to suggest, I think, probably one of the most valuable that
we could have, uh, would be the Lung Cancer Barbie. I think
the Lung Cancer Barbie could be terrific, uh, the Lung Cancer
Barbie would come with accessories like little cigarettes, have
little packs of cigarettes and she'd be dressed in a Joe Camel
sweatshirt. She'd be wearing her Marlboro cap and you could
remove the sweatshirt and her chest would open up and she has
the removable brown lungs. And then of course she comes with
a Barbie Will, leaving everything to Ken. Would this not be a
good lesson for the kids?
   —*Talk Show Host Don Wade* expressing his opinion of the
      handicapped Barbie doll. "Don Wade and Roma," WLS
      890-AM, Chicago, 5-22-97.

But I found it astounding to find how the main networks are
carrying what the United States is doing overseas . . . it basically
is look how badly the U.S. is doing now in Iraq. Look how the
United States blew up this thing, look how the U.S. blew up
that. Bombs hit the wrong place trying to bomb Saddam Hussein
in that restaurant? Oh yeah, we were 50 feet off, oh yeah, he
got away. Look, we killed a lot of people. Look at the hospitals
looted. They blame the United States. Look at the wounded
children; let's get a close-up of the amputated arms and legs
wounded by U.S. bombs. More children, sob stories. I mean it's
terrible that they did die, but I didn't see any media going in
and looking at the poor little children who had been tortured
by Saddam Hussein, but now that there's collateral damage oh,
now we can't get enough of wounded children.
   —*Ibid.*, 4-16-03.

Chelsea is a Clinton. She bears the taint; and though not pros-
ecutable in law, in custom and nature the taint cannot be ig-

nored. All the great despotisms of the past—I'm not arguing for despotism as a principle, but they sure knew how to deal with potential trouble—recognized that the families of objectionable citizens were a continuing threat. In Stalin's penal code it was a crime to be the wife or child of an "enemy of the people". The Nazis used the same principle, which they called Sippenhaft, "clan liability." In Imperial China, enemies of the state were punished "to the ninth degree": that is, everyone in the offender's own generation would be killed and everyone related via four generations up, to the great-great grandparents, and four generations down, to the great-great-grandchildren, would also be killed.

  —*John Derbyshire*, "Be Very Afraid, Clinton's Legacy," *National Review Online*, 2-15-01.

From a listener in Vallejo, says "I saw footage of those maggot-infested protesters yesterday stopping a car downtown and looting the belongings of the poor citizen in the car, I have had enough I am ready to act we need to rise up and confront these snot-nosed punks, I mean whip their asses, if these spoiled punks step in front of my truck and tell me to stop, I'm running their coward asses down like the dogs they are and then I will get out and urinate on their wounds."

  —*Lee Rodgers* reading an e-mail purportedly sent from a listener angry about the anti-Iraq-war protests in San Francisco. "Lee Rodgers and Melanie Morgan Show," KSFO-AM 560, San Francisco, 3-21-03.

Work is not expensive if you focus on people who are close to employability. It is expensive if you have huge day care requirements, if work is used as an excuse for vast new expansions of the welfare state, training, day care, etc. But if you focus on, say, two-parent families, then you do not need day care.

  —*Rep. James Talent (R-MO)*, speaking in support of reforming welfare without allocating funds to help move people into the work force. *Congressional Record*, H3504, 3-22-95.

We call for the removal of structural impediments which liberals throw in the path of poor people: over-regulation of start-up enterprises, excessive licensing requirements, needless restrictions on formation of schools and child-care centers catering to poor families . . .
—*Republican Party Platform*, adopted 8-12-96, p.25.

I was talking to my daughter last night. I was worried because I had not heard from her. I left a message for her Sunday . . . She called back last night [Wednesday] about 10:30, and she said, "Oh gosh, I'm really sorry, everything is fine, but I had just been volunteering full time at the school and Travis' Little League directors meeting was tonight, I had just gotten home from the directors' meeting, and we have been working with our twin daughters having a pen pal program with another school and were planning a party for the children who were coming over to meet for the first time."

My gosh, I thought, how does she have enough hours in the day, and she is a full-time mom. What if she were working and trying to do those wonderful things she is doing to support her son's Little League, or our twin granddaughters' activities in Brownies, which she hosts every week at her home? . . . But, Mr. President, if she were working full time, she would have the stresses that would make it impossible. Impossible. Every mom would like to be able to do those things.

We are trying to relieve some of that stress with this bill [Senate Bill #4]. We are going to try to give hourly employees the ability to say, "I would like to host a Brownie troop every other Friday. Could I work 9 hours every other day of the week and take every other Friday off so I can host a Brownie troop for my daughter." That is what we want for the hourly employees of this country.

. . . You see, the difference between 1938 laws [Fair Labor Standards Act] and today is that I think employers realize how important it is that they have happy, productive employees . . .

I have heard the opposition [to Senate Bill #4]. They say, "Oh, but this will just allow employers to coerce employees. All the rights are with the employers." Well, of course the employer is running the business. Many times it is the small business man or woman that has gone out and borrowed the money, that works 80 hours a week trying to make it go, to contribute to our economy. It is not easy being in business in America with all of the taxes and regulations and litigation that a person in business must face.

> —*Sen. Kay Bailey Hutchinson* (R-TX), speaking in support of the so-called "Family Friendly Workplace Act," sponsored by Sen. John Ashcroft (R-MO), would have removed the legal obligation of employers to pay overtime, and, according to Sen. Kennedy (D-MA), the bill would have allowed employers to work employees up to eighty hours in a single week without paying overtime. *Congressional Record*, S4508–4511, 5-5-97.

Mainstream America is depending on you—counting on you— to draw your sword and fight for them. These people have precious little time or resources to battle misguided Cinderella attitudes, the fringe propaganda of the homosexual coalition, the feminists who preach that it's a divine duty for women to hate men, blacks who raise a militant fist with one hand while they seek preference with the other, and all the New-Age apologists for juvenile crime, who see roving gangs as a means of youthful expression, sex as a means of adolescent merchandising, violence as a form of entertainment for impressionable minds, and gun bans as a means to lord-knows-what. We've reached that point in time when our national social policy originates on Oprah. I say it's time to pull the plug.

> —*NRA Vice-President Charlton Heston* speaking at the Free Congress Foundation's 20th Anniversary Gala, 12-7-97. VPC.org.

Uday and Qusay, now that they're toast, a lot of the lesser known Hussein family are coming to the attention of U.S.-led coalition forces. Among the brothers, Souffle, the restaurateur, Gooday, the half-Australian, Hooray, the sports fanatic, Sachet, the gay brother, Kunte and Kinte, the twins from the African mother . . . Ojay, the stalker-murderer, Goulet, the singer-entertainer, Ebay, the internet czar . . . X-ray, the radiologist . . . Reggae, the half-Jamaican brother, Toupee, the one with the bad hair, and, of course, we don't want to overlook the sisters . . . Douche, the clean sister . . . Safeway, the grocery-store owner, Ole, the half-Mexican sister, Cudlay, the prostitute . . .

> —*Joseph Farah*, host of Worldnetdaily Report, a radio program produced by Worldnetdaily.com, 8-20-03.

I made a commitment during the campaign to designate a rest stop in his [Howard Stern's] honor and I've done it and that's that. I am not condoning what he says or does or anything more than that. And it shouldn't be looked on as anything more than that.

> —*Gov. Christine Todd Whitman (R-NJ)*, defending her decision to erect a 3-foot high monument featuring an 11-by-8-inch aluminum plaque reading, "Howard Stern Rest Stop—Dedicated 1995" at the rest area off the southbound lanes of I-295. "Critics Assail Stern Honor," *Trenton Times*, 1-28-95.

CRACKS IN THE MELTING POT

The blacks from the low-income areas are less likely to convict. I understand it. It's an understandable proposition. There's a resentment for law enforcement. There's a resentment for authority. And as a result, you don't want those people on your jury.

* In selecting blacks, you don't want the real educated ones. This goes across the board. All races. You don't want smart people. If you're sitting down and you're going to take blacks, you want older black men and women, particularly men. Older black men are very good.

* Blacks from the South. Excellent . . . If they are from South Carolina and places like that, I tell you, I don't think you can ever lose a jury with blacks from South Carolina. They are dynamite.

* My experience, young black women are very bad. There's an antagonism. I guess maybe because they're downtrodden in two respects. They are women and they're black . . . so they somehow want to take it out on somebody and you don't want it to be you.

* You do not want smart people. I wish we could ask everyone's IQ. If you could know their IQ, you could pick a great jury all the time. You don't want smart people because smart people will analyze the hell out of your case. They have a higher standard. They hold you up to a higher standard. They hold the courts up to a higher standard . . . They take those words "reasonable doubt," and they actually try to think about them.

* You don't want social workers . . . Teachers, you don't like. Teachers are bad, especially young teachers . . . If you get like a white teacher teaching in a black school that's sick of these guys,

maybe that may be one you accept . . . Bad luck with teachers, bad luck with social workers. Bad luck with intelligent doctors.

> —*Jack McMahon*, Republican candidate for Philadelphia district attorney, produced this videotape in which, while working as a prosecutor, he advised prosecutors in his department on how to pick sympathetic juries. McMahon commented that he did not recall details of the tape. L. Stuart Ditzen, Linda Loyd and Mark Fazlollah, "Avoid poor black jurors, McMahon said," *Philadelphia Inquirer*, 4-1-97.

Just as ethnic identity, militancy and loyalty are tearing Quebec from Canada and Scotland from England, so ethnic militancy among blacks and Hispanics in America is tearing at the fabric of national union.

> —*Patrick J. Buchanan*, "Roiling the Right," *New York Post*, 5-7-97.

[P]robably nothing.

> —*Jeb Bush* in reply to a question during his losing 1994 campaign for Florida governor. He was asked what he would do for blacks if he won the election. Joy-Ann Reid, "When Jeb Bush Speaks, people cringe," Salon.com, 10-5-02.

Free at last, free at last, thank God almighty, free at last.

> —*Mississippi Governor-elect Sonny Perdue*, celebrating his victory which ended 130 years of Democratic governors in that state. Mia Taylor, "Activists offended at Perdue's quote of MLK," *Atlanta Journal-Constitution*, 11-7-02.

[T]he Courts are not super personnel managers charged with second guessing every employment decision made regarding minorities. . . The federal courts must never become safe havens for employees who are in a class protected from discrimination, but who in fact are employees who are derelict in their duties.

> —*Judge Charles W. Pickering, Sr.,* a lifetime appointee on the federal trial court in Mississippi. Nominated by Bush to

the United States Court of Appeals, 5th circuit. *Seeley v. Hattiesburg*, No. 2:96-CV-327PG (S.D. Miss. 2-17-98).

Just turn Ashley [Lowndes County Sheriff Ashley Paulk] loose and let him arrest every Muslim that comes across the state line.
> —*Sen. Saxby Chambliss (R-GA)*. Tom Baxter, "America Responds: Tone on Mideast matters, even here," *Atlanta Journal-Constitution*, 12-2-01.

If I see someone [who] comes in that's got a diaper on his head and a fan belt wrapped around the diaper on his head, that guy needs to be pulled over.
> —*Rep. John Cooksey (R-LA)*. "Cooksey exercises terrible judgment," *Baton Rouge Advocate*, 9-22-01.

Conrad, how can you live back there [in Washington] with all those niggers?
> —*Sen. Conrad Burns (R-MT)* telling a newspaper editor about a rancher who asked him this question on the campaign trail. He said he told the rancher it was "a hell of a challenge." "Conrad Burns Tells a Story," *Washington Post* editorial, 10-26-94.

Quit looking at the symbols. Get out and get a job. Quit shooting each other. Quit having illegitimate babies.
> —*State Rep. John Graham Altman (R-SC)* addressing African-Americans who supported the proposal of Republican Gov. David Beasley to remove the Confederate battle flag from the dome of the capitol. Kevin Sack, "Confederate Flag Divides GOP in South Carolina, House Rejects Governor's Plan to Move It," *New York Times*, 1-24-97.

Racial witch-hunters are people who devote their lives to finding offense and then labeling the offenders a "racist." There are also ethnic, religious and sexual witch-hunters, all of whom do exactly the same thing with only the adjectives changing. Make one comment that can be construed as anti-minority and the witch-hunters fire up their torches and launch their mission to destroy your reputation. If you don't believe me, ask Mr. Lott, Senator Rick Santorum, Dr. Laura, Pat Buchanan and dozens of other public figures who have run afoul of the politically correct demonizers.

> —*Bill O'Reilly, Who's Looking Out For You?*, NY: Broadway Books, 2003, p. 178.

My picture is in the public domain. It gets published in newspapers every day.

> —*Haley Barbour*, Republican candidate for Mississippi governor and former Chairman of the Republican National Committee, discussing the use of his photograph on the website of the racist and anti-Semitic Council of Conservative Citizens. Emily Wagster Pettus, "Barbour won't ask CCC to take photo off website," Associated Press, 10-18-03.

Headline: Orangutan escapes at zoo, runs for county executive. Fascinating stuff. [Voice over jungle music with monkey sounds.] Freakin' monkeys loose up at the zoo again. That's really fine, really fine. Yeah, yeah, and he's running for county executive. What is with that? I think we better go now.

> —*Talk Radio Host Bob Lonsberry*. WHAM 1180-AM, Rochester, N.Y., alluding to the campaign of African-American Mayor William A. Johnson Jr. for Monroe County Executive. Joseph Spector and Rick Armon, "Radio host punished for words; WHAM suspends Lonsberry for reputed remarks about mayor," Democratandchronicle.com, 9-23-03.

Yellow Monkeys.

> —*J.R. Gach*, a talk radio host from Albany who took over Bill Cunningham's 9 p.m.–midnight shift at WLW-AM 700, repeatedly used this phrase while talking about Japanese fishermen accidentally killed when a U.S. submarine surfaced. John Kiesewetter, "WLW host used racial slur," *Cincinnati Post*, 2-15-01.

Talk Radio Host Rich Michaels called public school teachers
"greedy bastards," and referred to the television program "Eye
to Eye" with Connie Chung as "Slant Eye to Slant Eye." These
and other racial and ethnic slurs prompted a boycott of WGR-
Radio, Buffalo, N.Y.

> —*Peter Simon*, "Teachers Call For Advertising Boycott Over
> Remarks By Radio Talk Show Host," *Buffalo News*, 1-24-95.

[Little Joe, the gorilla that escaped from Franklin Park Zoo,
was] probably a Metco gorilla waiting for a bus to take him to
Lexington.

> —*Talk Radio Host John Dennis*, "Dennis & Callahan Show,"
> WEEI 850-AM, Boston. Metco (Metropolitan Council for
> Educational Opportunity) is a desegregation program that
> enrolls Boston students in suburban schools and provides
> transportation. Sasha Talcott, "WEEI host off air for re-
> mark, Racist comment brings criticism, suspension," *Bos-
> ton Globe*, 10-3-03.

We can assimilate Europeans over here, but we can't assimilate
10, 20, 30 million Mexicans . . . [Mexicans are] spreading across
southern Colorado like a Kansas grass fire.

> —*Radio Host Chuck Baker*, KKCS 1460-AM, Colorado
> Springs. Warren Epstein, "Mayor lends name to effort to
> muzzle radio talk show," *The Gazette*, 9-19-97.

Our governor tonight has asked you to give all to those who
will give you nothing. It reminds me of a man, Neville Cham-
berlain, who traveled over 50 years ago to Munich, Germany,
with the best of intentions and made a peace with militants.
They told him the words he wanted to hear, and he surrendered
a heritage, thinking he had guaranteed peace in his own time—
only to find that the eventual outcome was conflict on all fronts
. . . For us to surrender at the dome is to eventually surrender
across South Carolina, where we will not even be free to ex-

hibit our heritage for fear of condemnation or attack. This will amount to cultural genocide.

—*State Sen. Glenn McConnell (R-SC)*, responding to Republican Gov. Beesley's proposal to move the Confederate battle flag from the Statehouse dome to the Statehouse grounds. *Charleston Post and Courier*, 11-27-96.

. . . the editorial writers and the politicians who have relentlessly criticized the Confederate flag should be ashamed of themselves . . . In my judgment, moving the flag would be a victory for the extremist groups. They would immediately start planning their next crisis, their next outrage, their next demand. That's what they do. Controversy is their business. It is not possible to appease the merchant of hate. And it is a mistake even to try.

—*South Carolina Attorney General Charlie Condon (R)*, responding to Gov. Beesley. *Ibid.*

They are 12 percent of the population. Who the hell cares?

—*Rush Limbaugh* to a caller who said black people need to be heard. Steven Rendell, Jim Naureckas, and Jeff Cohen, *The Way Things Aren't: Rush Limbaugh's Reign of Error,* NY: The New Press, 1995.

If [Madonna] were a young lady, 30 years old, of Jewish heritage and hated Judaism as much as she is a young Italian American, former Catholic, hates Catholicism and Christianity, she would be branded as an anti-Semitic Semite and would be a pariah and would never be signed to a contract by anybody at Time-Warner.

—*Rep. Bob Dornan (R-CA)*, on the House floor, June, 1992. Lloyd Grove, "Out of the mouth of . . . Bob," *Washington Post*, 11-23-96.

I think what we've had here is a little social concern in the NFL. The media has been very desirous that a black quarterback do well. They're interested in black coaches and black quarterbacks doing well. I think there's a little hope invested in McNabb, and he got a lot of credit for the performance of his team that he really didn't deserve. The defense carried this team.
    —*Rush Limbaugh* talking on ESPN about Philadelphia Eagles quarterback Donovan McNabb. Ed Sherman, "Limbaugh resigns over remarks," *Chicago Tribune*, 10-2-03.

The management there {at ESPN} was vigorously defending what had happened, they saw really nothing wrong with it, and really nothing was, it's such a tempest in a teapot, particularly, in the sense that we live in a country where there are, supposedly there is a first amendment and you can offer opinions, but you can't, you know, in certain places and at certain times you can't offer an opinion. My opinion it was not a racial opinion it was an opinion about the media.
    —*Rush Limbaugh* discussing his resignation as a commentator on ESPN. MSNBC, 10-2-03.

The truth is that people of minority groups, whether they're African American, Hispanics, Asians or whoever, have been denied opportunity in the past in the United States. And there is, without question, an incredible effort on the part of the media and Hollywood screenwriters etc., to elevate these minorities into positions of prominence, at least if nothing else in fictional stories. You look at Morgan Freeman who is a tremendous actor. He started off playing a chauffeur in *Driving Miss Daisy* and then they elevated him to head of the CIA and then they elevated him to President and in his last role they made him God. I just wonder, isn't Rush Limbaugh right to question the fact, is he that good an actor or not? And was there a preference given? The same thing with the quarterback, did they give him a break? And are the media giving him a break or not?
    —*Pat Robertson*, "700 Club," CBN, 10-2-03.

"Because I've got the greatest physique in the world, I'm sharp, I'm super talented." Then he stood up, walked down the hall, looked over his shoulder and said: "And I'm white."
—*Rick Wayne*, a black bodybuilder from St. Lucia, recalling a 1970s conversation with Arnold Schwarzenegger. Don Nissenbaum, "Arnold Schwarzenegger As . . . The Contender," *San Jose Mercury News*, 8-24-03.

That's right. I thought he [Arnold Schwarzenegger in his first debate] did a good job. I—California is not Mississippi. And you're not going to get the kind of people that I really like . . .
—*Robert Novak,* "The Capital Gang," CNN, 9-27-02.

Pat Buchanan is an American patriot who believes that every single American of whatever race, color, creed, or background, including Jewish-Americans, has constitutional rights . . .
—*Pat Buchanan.* "Politics; In their own words," *New York Times*, 2-24-96, p. 8.

As late as 1959, 78 percent of all black families were intact and less than 2 percent of black children were reared in households in which the mother was not married. This was before civil rights legislation, before the Voting Rights Act, and before the war on poverty. Blacks were still being lynched in the South, but black families were mostly together and provided a strength for their children that is no longer there.
—*Cal Thomas, The Things That Matter Most.* NY: HarperCollins, 1994, p. 61.

The right of individuals to respect our history is a right that the politically correct crowd wants to eliminate, and this is just not acceptable. Take those history standards: the standards make no mention of Lee's military genius! I guess there's too much space devoted to Madonna.
—*Sen. John Ashcroft, Southern Partisan* magazine, 2nd Quarter, 1998.

Two things made this country great: White men & Christianity. The degree these two ingredients have diminished is in direct proportion to the corruption and fall of the nation. Every problem that has arrisen [*sic*] can be directly traced back to our departure from God's Law and the disenfranchisement of White men . . .

> —*State Rep. Don Davis (R-NC)* e-mailed this in a letter to every member of the North Carolina House and Senate, having received the letter himself from "the administrator of an Internet site that asserts that Christianity is a white religion and that the Western world is made up of Christian white nations." Davis defended the mailing: "There's a lot of it that's truth, the way I see it. Who came to this country first—the white man, didn't he? That's who made this country great." Paul Woolverton, "E-mail miffs legislators," *Fayetteville Observer*, 8-22-01.

Let us take a look at how your particular system, the present system, operates. Here is right out of the newspaper: Kids go hungry while parents buy drugs. Three children live in a house of roaches, without food, while the parents spend their monthly welfare benefit on narcotics.

> —*Rep. James Talent (R-MO)*, in support of the Personal Responsibility Act. *Congressional Record*, H3504, 3-22-95.

Jane, come here. Me, Tarzan!

> —*Boston Immigration Judge Thomas Ragno*, speaking to a Ugandan woman seeking political asylum in the United States. *Newsweek*, 8-18-03.

Head Start is a godsend for Mississippi. Some of those kids in it would be better off sitting up on a piano bench at a whorehouse than where they are now.

> —*Candidate for Mississippi Gov. Haley Barbour.* "Remark by Barbour draws fire from Dems," *The Clarion-Ledger*, 5-14-03.

No responsible parent rewards irresponsible children with cash, free food, and an apartment, and the taxpayers should not either.
> —*Rep. Jon Christensen (R-NE)* on welfare reform. *Congressional Record*, H3424, 3-22-95.

The 10th Mountain Division with whom I served in Italy, and the black troops of the 92nd Division who served nearby, were the proof for me, once again, of the truth I am here trying to convey . . . when the blood of the sons of immigrants and the grandsons of slaves fell on foreign fields, it was American blood. In it you could not read the ethnic particulars of a soldier who died near you. He was an American.
> —*Republican Presidential Candidate Bob Dole,* from his speech to the Republican National Convention, 8-15-96. *New York Times,* 8-16-96. In a letter to the *Times* published 8-21-96, Ellen Holly wrote: "The 92nd Division was a segregated unit. What's more, when black soldiers who gave their lives for their country in that war were brought home in body bags, there were many who were refused burial in their local cemeteries on the grounds that they were not white. The 'ethnic particulars' of black soldiers were very much read on domestic soil."

In the spring of 1992, a unanimous Supreme Court struck down so-called "hate crime" laws that many states and cities had passed in an attempt to conform themselves to those who wish to force us to think of people and issues the way they do. The laws imposed special penalties on people who uttered words or behaved in ways that offended certain racial, gender, ethnic, or "sexual orientation" groups. The case involved a St. Paul teenager who had been charged with burning a cross in the backyard of a house owned by a black family . . . The decision dealt a serious blow to the political correctness movement, which had been moving unchecked across the country, imposing speech codes and "hate crime" laws wherever it went.
> —*Cal Thomas,The Things That Matter Most.* NY: HarperCollins, 1994, p. 61,

If they didn't observe Martin Luther King Day there'd be trouble
from the savages . . . They're not satisfied with every third street
being ML King boulevard . . . named after that scumbag Marty.
   —*Bob Grant.* Alan Dershowitz, "Bob Grant Finally Gets His
   Due," *Buffalo News,* 4-22-96.

His kind do have that problem [of forming words]. Maybe they
weren't intended to speak a civilized language. . . .
   —*Bob Grant* talking about a black caller. *Ibid.*

On the evolutionary scale you're about 25 generations behind me.
   —*Bob Grant* talking to a black caller. *Ibid.*

Why is it taking so long for the HIV to go to full-blown AIDS
for crying out loud? I'm making novenas . . . If the guy would
go into full-blown AIDS and deteriorate in front of our eyes
and croak then maybe, maybe he could make a contribution.
   —*Bob Grant* on Magic Johnson. *Ibid.*

Does the C of CC oppose racism? The word *racism* was con-
cocted by a communist ideologue in the 1920's. The purpose of
racism was to instill guilt and shame in the minds of white people
and to inflame racial hostility among blacks.
   —*From the website of the Council of Conservative Citizens.*
   Republican Sen. Trent Lott and Rep. Bob Barr have ad-
   dressed meetings of this group.

Aside from doing a rain dance and making it rain—we'll assign
that to Senator Campbell—I'm not sure what you can do.
   —*Sen. Bob Bennett (R-UT),* suggesting that Sen. Ben
   Nighthorse Campbell, the only Native American in the Senate, might help alleviate a drought in the Western states
   with a rain dance. Some American Indian advocacy groups
   were offended by the remark, saying that a rain dance is a
   sacred ceremony and shouldn't be derided. Robert Gehrke,
   "Bennett assailed for quip," Associated Press, 3-23-03.

I want to say this about my state: When Strom Thurmond ran for president, we voted for him. We're proud of it. And if the rest of the country had followed our lead, we wouldn't have had all these problems over all these years, either.
> —*Sen. Trent Lott (R-MS)* speaking at Thurmond's 100th birthday party on 12-5-02. Ben Bryant, "Burned by Remark, Lott Apologizes," *Sun Herald*, 12-10-02.

. . . If you want to know what America used to be—and a lot of people wish it still were—then you listen to Strom Thurmond.
> —*Rush Limbaugh* television broadcast 9-1-94. Steven Rindell, Jim Naureckas and Jeff Cohen, *The Way Things Aren't, Rush Limbaugh's Reign of Error*, NY: New Press, 1995, p. 48.

His patriotism, courage and lifetime dedication to South Carolina and his nation will always be remembered.
> —*George W. Bush* praising Sen. Strom Thurmond on his 100th birthday. Jim Abrams, "Thurmond Celebrates 100th Birthday," Associated Press, 12-5-02.

I resent personally the efforts to try to sling mud at Trent Lott because he was trying to praise Strom Thurmond. He may have chose [*sic*] a word that was too vulnerable to his critics. And they leap on it like a puppy dog on a biscuit.
> —*Sen. Jesse Helms.* Associated Press, 12-11-02.

What the Lott incident shows is that Republicans have to be careful about letting Democrats into our party. Back when they supported segregation, Lott and Thurmond were Democrats. This is something the media are intentionally hiding to make it look like the Republican Party is the party of segregation and race discrimination, which it never has been. In 1948, Thurmond did not run as a "Dixiecan," he ran as a "Dixiecrat" his party was an offshoot of the Democratic Party. And when he lost, he went right back to being a Democrat. This whole brouhaha is

about a former Democrat praising another former Democrat
for what was once a Democrat policy.
    —*Ann Coulter*, "Democrats: A Lott of Trouble," Townhall.com,
    12-19-02.

Our children began to be fearful of black kids, so we decided
that something had to change, and we were fortunate enough
to be able to make the choice.
    —*Erie County [New York] Executive Joel Giambra* explain-
    ing to a conference on school choice why he moved his kids
    from a public school to a private Christian school.
    "Giambra's Imprudent Words; When Speaking About Race,
    Public Leaders Need to Weigh Their Comments," *Buffalo
    News*, 3-12-03.

The NAACP should have riot rehearsal. They should get a liquor store and practice robberies.
    —*Rush Limbaugh*. Eric Alterman, "Little Limbaughs and the
    fire next time," *The Nation*, 9-27-99.

I can't take these screaming savages. Whether they're in that
African Methodist Church, A.M.E church, or whether they're
in the streets, burning, robbing, looting, I've seen enough of it.
    —*Bob Grant*, then with WABC-NYC. Herb Norman, "The
    talk of the town: The saga of Bob Grant," *Journal of Popu-
    lar Culture*, Summer 1998.

I think there should be a literacy test and a poll tax for people
to vote.
    —*Ann Coulter*. "Hannity & Colmes," Fox News Channel,
    8-17-99.

. . . If they [North Korea] have got two weapons already, and
I've heard estimates of two, I don't know what they have exactly, but some people say they do have a couple, and Saddam

Hussein has none, to me you've got to go in and prove your point in Iraq and then you look over at Kim Jong Il and go, you really want a piece of this zipper head.
   —*Dennis Miller.* "Hardball," MSNBC, 1-31-03.

Folks, it has hit the fan in California, but luckily there will probably be no power later this summer in California to run the fan with. And you know something else? The California-Mexico border is now leakier than Mark Geragos on a diuretic drip. I remember thinking that the other day as I observed a traffic jam in the illegal alien lane of the San Diego freeway. Next stop—simply put, it seems like a no-brainer to me and I think most of you, we need to kill all the terrorists before they can kill us. And you know something? If the phrase "war on terror" violates your delicate sensibilities, you're just going to have to buck it up and think of it as preemptive health care, OK?
   —*Dennis Miller.* "Hannity & Colmes," Fox News Channel, 6-27-03.

[Jim Sasser is] sending Tennessee money to Washington, to Marion Barry . . . While I've been transplanting lungs and hearts to heal Tennesseans, Jim Sasser has been transplanting Tennesseans' wallets to Washington, home of Marion Barry.
   —*Bill Frist* in a 1994 campaign speech. Joshua Micah Marshall, TalkingpointsMemo.com, 12-20-02.

Black ministers should not be involved in politics . . . I thought there was separation of church and state . . .
   —*Talk Radio Host Bill Cunningham.* WLW-AM, Cincinnati, 2-20-95.

We were at war. They [Japanese-Americans] were an endangered species. For many of these Japanese-Americans, it wasn't safe for them to be on the street. [Japanese-Americans] prob-

ably were intent on doing harm to us . . . just as some of these
Arab-Americans are probably intent on doing harm to us.
> —*Rep. Howard Coble (R-NC)*, Chairman of the Judiciary
> Subcommittee on Crime, Terrorism and Homeland Secu-
> rity, on a radio call-in program, 2-4-03. *Sacramento Bee*,
> 2-5-03.

You know, and this can be misconstrued, but honest to goodness [my husband] Ed and I for years, for 20 years, have been
saying, "You know, look at who runs all the convenience stores
across the country." Every little town you go into, you know?
> —*Rep. Sue Myrick (R-NC)*, speaking to the conservative Heri-
> tage Foundation about Americans' lack of readiness to deal
> with future terrorist attacks. Jim Morrill, "Myrick faces
> heat for comments," *Charlotte Observer*, 3-06-03.

I always see two Jewish communities in America, one of deep
intellect and one of shallow, superficial intellect . . . Liberals are
in my estimation just not bright people. They don't think deeply;
they don't comprehend; they don't understand . . . They have a
narrow educational base, as opposed to the hard scientists . . .

Conservatives have a deeper intellect and tend to have "oc-
cupations of the brain" in fields like engineering, science and
economics. [Liberals, on the other hand,] tend to flock to "oc-
cupations of the heart," [defined as jobs in the arts.] "They're
going to be liberals . . . because they want to feel good . . . as
people grow, they become more conservative because they gain
a better sense of "reality." Liberals have a "romanticized" notion of a world they pretend exists.
> —*House Majority leader Dick Armey (R-TX)* addressing a
> mostly Jewish audience in Florida supporting Katharine
> Harris's congressional campaign. Associated Press, 9-24-02.
> *Bradenton [FL] Herald*, 9-22-02.

My friends don't want me to mention Kurt's name, because of all the recent Nazi stuff and the U.N. controversy, but I love him and Maria does too, and so thank you, Kurt.
> —*Arnold Schwarzenegger* speaking in 1986 about Kurt Waldheim, the Austrian President and Secretary General of the United Nations who had been forced to resign because of his hidden Nazi past. Timothy Noah, "Arnold's Nazi problem," *Slate*, 8-7-03.

. . . the real damage to race relations in the South came not from slavery, but from Reconstruction, which would not have occurred if the South had won.
> —*William S. Lind* of the Free Congress Foundation, in an article distributed in an 1999 e-mail newsletter to supporters by Bill Back, vice-chairman of the California Republican Party, during Back's campaign for chairman. He apologized for including the article. Asked about this incident, White House spokeswoman Claire Buchan said: "The California Republican Party will decide who will lead them. We are not involved in the race for state party chair." Thomas B. Edsall, "White House Silent on Racial Controversy," *Washington Post*, 1-5-03.

Whether or not you dig it as a personal philosophy, "diversity" makes a poor legal concept. It was not intended to be precisely defined, but instead woozy and fluffy and soft-focus. It makes a fabulous bumper sticker: "Celebrate Diversity." But it makes a poor legal concept to enshrine at the heart of the U.S. Constitution, which is where Swingin' Sandra's vote put it last week . . . [Supreme Court Justice Sandra O'Connor voted to allow colleges and universities to continue affirmative action]

. . . But, I, Michael Savage, am the true Godfather of Proposition 209 as this book will confirm. I wrote "The Death Of The White Male" in 1977. It began as a poem, a plea from the heart to then President Jimmy Carter. You see, I was in trouble.

I had just earned my Ph.D. from the University of California, Berkeley. I had 2 young children to support. My life-long dream to teach was "put on hold" by the ACLU and their evil socialist scheme for racial gerrymandering called affirmative action.

I wrote to the President because I was suddenly an outcast. Despite my Ph.D. from one of the nation's top universities (at that time). Despite my having written many critically acclaimed books, and having won numerous awards they would not employ me. For one cardinal sin.

I am a White Male. You see, the liberals had destroyed my future to make a future for less qualified people. My babies were crying . . .

> —*Michael Savage* in a letter posted on his website, Homestead.com, 8-14-03.

We have in our city . . . in our nation, not hundreds of thousands but millions of sub-humanoids, savages, who really would feel more at home careening along . . . the dry deserts of eastern Kenya, people who, for whatever reason, have not become civilized.

> —*Bob Grant*, then with WABC-NYC. Herb Norman, "The talk of the town: The saga of Bob Grant," *Journal of Popular Culture*, Summer 1998.

Why is it that every time there is an incident that involves a black man, a white man, or a black and white, why is it that we always say racism? Why can't we just say this is a human being who's been abusive to another human being? Why do we always have to scream racism?

> —*John Kasich*, former GOP congressman from Ohio, filling in for Bill O'Reilly on "The O'Reilly Factor," Fox News Channel. After showing the video of Inglewood police officer Jeremy Morse beating 16-year-old Donovan Jackson, Kasich put the above question to civil rights lawyer Leo Terrell. John Powers, "On Spiking the punch," *LA Weekly*, 7-19-02.

I've always said Affirmative Action is an inherent insult. It is
demeaning, under the guise of being compassionate and helpful.
—*Rush Limbaugh*, 5-12-03.

The majority upholds the Law School's racial discrimination not
by interpreting the people's Constitution, but by responding to a
faddish slogan of the cognoscenti. . . . I respectfully dissent from
the remainder of the Court's opinion and the judgment, however,
because I believe that the Law School's current use of race violates the Equal Protection Clause and that the Constitution means
the same thing today as it will in 300 months . . .
   —*Supreme Court Justice Clarence Thomas*, from his dissenting
   opinion in the University of Michigan Law School affirmative action case, 6-23-03. WashingtonPost.com.

I applaud the Supreme Court for recognizing the value of diversity on our nation's campuses.
   —*George W. Bush*, praising the Supreme Court decision on
   affirmative action that contradicted the Bush administration's
   position on the issue. Bob Kemper, "Democrats hope court
   rulings bruise Bush," *Chicago Tribune*, 6-24-03.

As long as he can fuzz it up just enough, he is OK.
   —*Norm Ornstein* of the American Enterprise Institute, referring to the affirmative action decision, and Bush's declaration of victory although he had been defeated. *Ibid*.

It's outrageous that the majority of these racial preferences was
formed by Republican appointees. Conservatives will want to
make sure that anyone appointed to the court in this administration is a strong and sure opponent of racial preferences.
   —*Clint Bolick* of the Institute for Justice, on the 5-4 Supreme
   Court decision allowing universities to consider race as a
   factor in admissions. Neil A. Lewis, "Some on the Right
   See a Challenge," *New York Times*, 6-23-03.

. . . It is time to face the reality that, according to no particular plan, America is being degraded, disunited and endangered by a powerful flow, wave after wave, legal and illegal, of poor, unskilled and uneducated people into our country, many of whom have no interest in becoming Americans or learning the English language. Unable to join the American mainstream, they will fester in ethnic ghettos, work for sub-standard wages, reproduce, vote the straight Democrat ticket and provide cover for terrorists. As they say down Mexico way, "loco, completamente loco!"
　　—*Linda Bowles*, "Border Blowback," Townhall.com, 11-14-01.

It would be a travesty to have someone who spent 22 years in the Air Force voted out of office by noncitizens. If it's just 500 who voted, it's not massive, but it's horrible voter fraud in a tight race.
　　—*Rep. Bob Dornan (R-CA)* after learning that his Democratic opponent, Loretta Sanchez, was beating him in the 1996 congressional election. "New District Demographics May Be Dornan's Downfall," *USA Today*, 11-14-96.

Now that the Bush tax cuts have already started to kick in and boost the economy, it was beginning to look as if the Treason Lobby would have nothing to run on.
　　But the Democrats have discovered a surprise campaign issue: It turns out that several of them have had a death in the family. Not only that, but many Democrats have cracker-barrel humble origins stories and a Jew or lesbian in the family. . . . In addition . . . the Democrats' other big idea—too nuanced for a bumper sticker—is that many of them have Jewish ancestry. There's Joe Lieberman: Always Jewish. Wesley Clark: Found Out His Father Was Jewish in College. John Kerry: Jewish Since He Began Presidential Fund-Raising. Howard Dean: Married to a Jew. Al Sharpton: Circumcised. Even Hillary Clinton claimed to have unearthed some evidence that she was a Jew . . . And

that, boys and girls, is how the Jews survived thousands of years of persecution: by being susceptible to pandering.

Clark said that when he discovered he was half-Jewish, he remembered growing up in Arkansas and feeling "a certain kinship" with Jewish families in the dry-goods business. (I, too, have always felt a certain kinship with Calvin Trillin.)

The Democrats' urge to assert a Jewish heritage is designed to disguise the fact that the Democrats would allow the state of Israel to perish as Palestinian suicide bombers slaughter Jewish women and children. Their humble-origins claptrap is designed to disguise the fact that liberals think ordinary people are racist scum. Their perverse desire to discuss the deaths and near-deaths of their children is designed to disguise the fact that they support the killing of more than a million unborn children every year. (Oh, by the way, what did their milkman and millworker fathers think about abortion?)

If the Democrats start extolling you—get a gun.

—*Ann Coulter*, "The Party of ideas," 11-20-03. Anncoulter.org.

It's hard to imagine now, but by the late 1980's AM radio was nothing short of a dying medium . . . Sure, there were a scattering of great stations and great personalities out there-among them people like Barry Farber and Bob Grant in New York whom I listened to avidly. But they were the exceptions.

—*Sean Hannity, Let Freedom Ring, NY: Reganbooks, HarperCollins, 2002, p. 259.*

BARNEY FAG & LESBIAN SPEAR-CHUCKERS

Ideally, it would have been nice to have a few phalanxes of
policemen with machine guns and mow them down.
> —*Talk Radio Host Bob Grant,* WABC, New York, discuss-
> ing New York's annual Gay Pride parade. *Boston Globe,*
> 4-29-95.

[Mr. Hormel] has been a leader in promoting a lifestyle. . . .
And the kind of leadership he's exhibited there is likely to be
offensive to . . . individuals in the setting to which he will be
assigned.
> —*Sen. John Ashcroft* on the nomination of James Hormel
> for ambassador to Luxemburg. 1-30-01. Senate.gov.

[James Hormel] has made statements that have convinced me
and others that he's much more concerned about his own gay
agenda than he is in representing the interests of the U.S . . . I
would feel the same way if it were David Duke or anybody
whose agenda is more important than the country.
> —*Sen. James Inhofe (R-OK).* Stacey McCain, "Dueling Agen-
> das," *Washington Times,* 5-20-98.

Chris Matthews: Are you being hotted up by this effort by [Re-
publican National Committee Chairman Ed] Gillespie to razz
you up about the issue of this Reagan movie? Would you watch
it anyway? Would you watch a movie like that about . . .
Janet Parshall: No. No. No, no, no. I wouldn't watch it . . . The
producers, by the way, folks—let's be honest here—two homosexual activists. Do you think this is going to be revisionist history or it's going to be the real story?

Matthews: Why would two homosexual activists. . . . Why would they choose to revise history per se?

Parshsall: Because they made up conversations that didn't take place because they didn't like Reagan's stand on AIDS when it came out. But, remember, he did put together an AIDS commission, but they still want their pound of flesh. They don't like the way he did it.

Matthews: God, you've got in Shylocks and everything here.

   —*Talk Radio Host Janet Parshall* on the then as-yet-unaired two-part CBS TV mini-series, "The Reagans." "Hardball," MSNBC, 10-31-03.

And the morality of the state can be at a stark contrast with traditional Christian morality and with the values Christian parents try to impart to their children. In the state of Massachusetts alone: A public school freshman health textbook in Silver Lake, said, "Testing your ability to function sexually and give pleasure to another person may be less threatening in your early teens with people of your own sex . . . you may come to the conclusion that growing up means rejecting the values of your parents." (Reportedly, students were not allowed to take this book home.)

   —*David Limbaugh, Persecution—How Liberals Are Waging War Against Christianity*, Washington, D.C.: Regnery, 2003, p. 78.

Homosexuality—The Party believes that the practice of sodomy tears at the fabric of society, contributes to the breakdown of the family unit, and leads to the spread of dangerous, communicable diseases. Homosexual behavior is contrary to the fundamental, unchanging truths that have been ordained by God, recognized by our country's founders, and shared by the majority of Texans. Homosexuality must not be presented as an acceptable "alternative" lifestyle in our public education and policy, nor should "family" be redefined to include homosexual

"couples." We are opposed to any granting of special legal en-
titlements, recognition, or privileges including, but not limited
to, marriage between persons of the same sex, custody of children by homosexuals, homosexual partner insurance or retirement benefits. We oppose any criminal or civil penalties against
those who oppose homosexuality out of faith, conviction, or
belief in traditional values.
  —*From the 2002 Republican Party of Texas Platform.*
  TexasGOP.org.

Do homosexual priests rape choirboys? Not in medialand. There,
Catholic priests abuse children—a phrase that's so gender-in-
clusive, and manages to twist one's attention onto the Catholic
church, not the homosexual men who have made inroads into
the clergy so they can prey on the innocence of children.
  —*Craige McMillan.* WorldNetDaily.com, 3-14-02.

We fully intend to use this [opposition to gay marriage] as a
litmus test for offices from president to street sweeper. We would
see people staying home in droves if he [Bush] does not show
strength on this.
  —*Sandy Rios,* President of Concerned Women for America.
  Katherine Q. Seelye, "Conservatives Mobilize Against Ruling on Gay Marriage," *New York Times,* 11-20-03.

The gay and lesbian movement is another good example. Many
homosexuals are hugely talented artists and executives . . . also
dear friends. I don't despise their lifestyle, though I don't share
it. As long as gay and lesbian Americans are as productive, law-
abiding and private as the rest of us, I think America owes them
absolute tolerance. It's the right thing to do. But on the other
hand, I find my blood pressure rising when Clinton's cultural
shock troops participate in homosexual-rights fund-raisers but
boycott gun-rights fund-raisers . . . and then claim it's time to
place homosexual men in tents with Boy Scouts, and suggest

that sperm donor babies born into lesbian relationships are somehow better served and more loved. Such demands have nothing
to do with equality. They're about the currency of cultural war—
money and votes—and the Clinton camp will let anyone in the
tent if there's a donkey on his hat, or a check in the mail or
some yen in the fortune cookie.

> —NRA Vice-President Charlton Heston addressing the Free
> Congress Foundation 20th Anniversary Gala. VPC.org, 12-
> 7-97.

The homosexual blitzkrieg has been better planned and executed
than Hitler's.

> —Rep. William Dannemeyer (R-CA). "Demagoguery in
> America," The New Republic, 8-1-94.

Overnight, you'll have the court saying . . . homosexual marriage is a protected right. I would call it a blitzkrieg of the homosexual juggernaut. It's not an erosion. It's a frontal assault
on decency and morality.

> —Randall Terry on the recent Supreme Court decision ban-
> ning anti-sodomy laws. Russ Bynu, "Abortion opponent
> Randall Terry seeks comeback opposing gay marriage,"
> Atlanta Journal-Constitution, 8-16-03.

I would warn Orlando that you're right in the way of some serious hurricanes, and I don't think I'd be waving those flags in
God's face if I were you. This is not a message of hate; this is a
message of redemption. But a condition like this will bring about
the destruction of your nation. It'll bring about terrorist bombs;
it'll bring earthquakes, tornadoes and possibly a meteor.

> —Pat Robertson on the rainbow flags put up by gay organi-
> zations in support of sexual diversity. "Robertson Warns
> Orlando On Gays Broadcaster: City Faces Disaster For
> Helping Group," Washington Post, 6-10-98.

The Bible says that because of certain abominations such as homosexuality, a land shall vomit out its inhabitants. . . . [According to Paul], when values are turned upside down and moral anarchy appears, men burn with lust for other men and women burn for women, and they will receive in their own bodies the punishment for their actions. From a biblical standpoint, the rise of homosexuality is a sign that a society is in the last stages of decay.
   —*Pat Robertson. Ibid.*

God hates homosexuality.
   —*Jerry Falwell,* no date. Hatecrime.org.

Every lesbian spear-chucker in this country is hoping I get defeated.
   —*Rep. Bob Dornan.* Lloyd Grove, "Out of the Mouth of . . . Bob," *Washington Post,* 11-23-96.

If the world accepts homosexuality as its norm and if it moves the entire world in that regard, the whole world is then going to be sitting like Sodom and Gomorrah before a Holy God. And when the wrath of God comes on this earth, we will all be guilty and we will all suffer for it.
   —*Pat Robertson.* "700 Club," CBN, 9-6-95.

[Vice President Gore] recently praised the lesbian actress who plays "Ellen" on ABC Television . . . I believe he may even put children, young people, and adults in danger by his public endorsement of deviant homosexual behavior . . . Our elected leaders are attempting to glorify and legitimize perversion.
   —*Jerry Falwell.* "Hostile Climate," People for the American Way, 1998, p. 9. Hatecrime.org.

Someone must not be afraid to say, "moral perversion is wrong." If we do not act now, homosexuals will "own" America! . . . If you and I do not speak up now, this homosexual steamroller

will literally crush all decent men, women, and children who
get in its way . . . and our nation will pay a terrible price!
—*Jerry Falwell. Ibid.*, 1997, p.15. Hatecrime.org.

The continuing flap, which was intensified early on by President Clinton's efforts to pay back a loyal special interest group,
is an unnecessary and dangerous attack on what remains of the
country's foundational principles. The military is the last public
embodiment of traditional morality. If homosexuals succeed in
winning approval for their lifestyle (the real goal of this campaign), there will be no stopping them. They will claim that if
they can openly fight and die for their country, they should be
allowed to legally marry, adopt children, and receive the full
approval of the culture.
    —*Cal Thomas, The Things That Matter Most*, NY:
    HarperCollins, 1994, p. 92.

Satan uses homosexuals as pawns. They're in, as you know, key
positions in the media, they're in the White House, they're in
everything, they're in Hollywood now. Then, unfortunately, after
he uses them, he infects them with AIDS and then they die.
    —*Anthony Falzarano.* "Janet Parshall's America," PFAW.org,
    2-27-96.

When lawlessness is abroad in the land, the same thing will
happen here that happened in Nazi Germany. Many of those
people involved in Adolph Hitler were Satanists. Many of them
were homosexuals. The two things seem to go together.
    —*Pat Robertson.* "700 Club," CBN, 1-21-93.

[Homosexuals] want to come into churches and disrupt church
services and throw blood all around and try to give people AIDS
and spit in the face of ministers.
    —*Ibid.*, 1-18-95.

Well, it's not a question of discriminating against homosexuals. It's a question of giving people special rights under the law because of the way they do sex acts.
—*Ibid.*, 2-11-98.

If the militant homosexuals succeed in their accursed agenda, God will curse and judge our nation. . . . The goal of the homosexual movement is to "mainstream" unspeakable acts of evil . . . Their cries for tolerance are really a demand for our surrender. They want us to surrender our values, our love for God's law, our faith, our families, the entire nation to their abhorrent agenda.
—*Randall Terry* campaign literature from his 1998 run for Congress in New York.

The GOP has done more for gay rights than the Democratic National Committee ever did.
—*Maurice Bonamigo*, trying to start a chapter of the Log Cabin Republican group in Palm Beach, FL. Ron Hayes, "Man Organizing Gay GOP Group Disputes Idea of Being 'Turncoat'," *Palm Beach Post*, 7-29-02.

If the Supreme Court says that you have the right to consensual [gay] sex within your home, then you have the right to bigamy, you have the right to polygamy, you have the right to incest, you have the right to adultery. You have the right to anything. All of those things are antithetical to a healthy, stable, traditional family and that's sort of where we are in today's world, unfortunately. It all comes from, I would argue, this right to privacy that doesn't exist, in my opinion, in the United States Constitution.
—*Sen. Rick Santorum (R-PA)*. "Santorum Says Homosexual Acts a Threat," Associated Press, 4-22-03.

The basic liberal philosophy is materialistic, is relativistic, to the point of, you've got candidates for president saying we should

condone different types of marriage. That is, to me, the death knell of the American family.
—*Sen. Rick Santorum. Ibid.*

. . . Sen. Rick Santorum predicted two months ago that if the court struck down anti-sodomy laws, challenges would soon follow to laws prohibiting bestiality, polygamy and all sorts of other sexual practices. We will now see him proved right . . . Prostitutes, call your lawyers.
—*Cal Thomas*, "Courting Disaster, Sodomy ruling bodes ill," *Milwaukee Journal-Sentinel*, 7-1-03.

Given the Supreme Court's 6-3 ruling Thursday that Texas anti-sodomy law violates the constitutional privacy right, lap danc-ing—like prostitution for that matter—looks like a fundamen-tal constitutional right . . . Once consent—"choice"—supplants marriage as the important interest served by cloaking sexual activities as constitutional rights, by what principle is any con-sensual sexual adult conduct not a protected right? Bigamy? Polygamy? Prostitution? Incest? Even—if we assume animals can consent, or that their consent doesn't matter—bestiality? . . .
—*George Will*, "Now that court says sodomy's OK, all lim-its are off," *Chicago Sun-Times*, 6-29-03.

Sen. Santorum is exactly right. If courts can strike down laws against sodomy, then there is little reason to believe that laws against bigamy, prostitution and incest will stand.
—*Robert Knight*, Director of CWA's Culture & Family Insti-tute, CWA press release, "CWA Condemns 'Gay Thought Police' for Attacks on Sen. Santorum," 4-22-03.

The Log Cabin Republicans (LCR) have shown once again that they don't see any room in the "big tent" for people who object to homosexual behavior on religious grounds. I would remind the Republican leadership that millions of voters who make up the GOP base agree with Santorum—not the "gay" thought police . . . The Philadelphia branch of the Log Cabin Republicans has joined other "gay" pressure groups in calling on Sen. Santorum to step down from leadership. This ought to show the Republican leadership that they cannot espouse family values while embracing groups that are more loyal to deviant sexual behavior than the Republican cause.

—*Sandy Rios*, President of Concerned Women for America.
CWA press release, 4-22-03.

The court continues pillaging its way through the moral norms of our country. If the people have no right to regulate sexuality, then ultimately the institution of marriage is in peril, and with it, the welfare of the coming generations of children. By unlocking one of society's last social seat belts, the court has guaranteed only one thing: More fatal collisions lay just down the road.

—*Tom Minnery* of Focus on the Family, responding to the Supreme Court's decision striking down sodomy laws. Karen S. Peterson, "Sodomy ruling gives hope to many," *USA Today*, 6-27-03.

Most of my life when the word Holocaust was referred to, it referred to the Jewish suffering and deaths that occurred during the Nazi occupation. It has just been within the recent two or three years that it has been brought forward that homosexuals also suffered like that . . . There is information out there on both sides . . . What I am trying to prevent is the holocaust of our children getting STDs, AIDS and other various other diseases that is going to affect their lives for the rest of their lives . . . If you want to sit around here and wait until America becomes another African continent then you do that, but I'm not about to do that.

—*State Rep. Arlon Linder (R-MN)* speaking on the floor of the Minnesota House of Representatives in support of his bill (HF341), which would remove gays and lesbians from protection under the state's Human Rights Act. Rachael E. Stassen-Berger, "Colleagues ask Linder for Apology," *St. Paul Pioneer Press*, 3-11-03. The *Minneapolis Star-Tribune*, 3-1-03: "previous complaints against [Linder] involved alleged misconduct while chairing a committee meeting, equating a Jewish House member's views with those of the 'irreligious left' and describing Buddhism as a 'cult.'"

[The Supreme Court] magically discovered a right of privacy that includes sexual perversion.
  —*Jan LaRue*, chief counsel for Concerned Women for America. Joan Biskupic, "Decision Represents an enormous turn in the law," *USA Today*, 6-27-03.

I have this fear that this zone of privacy that we all want protected in our own homes is gradually—or I'm concerned about the potential for it gradually being encroached upon, where criminal activity within the home would in some way be condoned . . . And I'm thinking of—whether it's prostitution or illegal commercial drug activity in the home . . . to have the courts come in, in this zone of privacy, and begin to define it gives me some concern.
  —*Senate Majority Leader Bill Frist (R-TN)* on the ABC-TV show "This Week," discussing the Supreme Court's overturning of a Texas law banning private acts of sodomy between consenting adults. The decision overturned similar laws in 12 other states. William C. Mann, "Frist Endorses Idea of Gay Marriage Ban," Associated Press, 6-29-03.

People who engage in homosexual behavior have the same rights as other citizens, but should not be given additional rights based on their willingness to perform peculiar and often medically dangerous sex acts.
  —*Robert Knight*, "Why Nashville Should Reject the 'Sexual Orientation' Law," CWFA.org, 3-4-03.

The sexual preference of Tinky Winky, the largest of the four Teletubbies characters on the series that airs in America on PBS stations, has been the subject of debate since the series premiered in England in 1997.

The character, whose voice is obviously that of a boy, has been found carrying a red purse in many episodes and has become a favorite character among gay groups worldwide.

Now, further evidence that the creators of the series intend for Tinky Winky to be a gay role model have surfaced. He is purple—the gay-pride color; and his antenna is shaped like a triangle—the gay-pride symbol.

Furthering Tinky's "outing" was a recent *Washington Post* editorial that cast the character's photo opposite that of Ellen DeGeneres in an "In/Out" column. This implies that Ellen is "out" as the chief national gay representative, while Tinky Winky is the trendy "in" celebrity.

These subtle depictions are no doubt intentional and parents are warned to be alert to these elements of the series.
   —*Jerry Falwell*, "Parents' Alert, Tinky Winky Comes Out of the Closet," *National Liberty Journal*, 2-99.

Michael Savage: So you're one of those sodomists. Are you a sodomite?
Caller: Yes, I am.
Savage: Oh, you're one of the sodomites . . . You should only get AIDS and die, you pig. How's that? Why don't you see if you can sue me, you pig. You got nothing better than to put me down, you piece of garbage. You have got nothing to do today, go eat a sausage and choke on it.
   —*Michael Savage*, host of talk radio and the MSNBC TV show "The Savage Nation," which was cancelled after the above exchange. David Bauder, "MSNBC Fires Savage on Anti-Gay Remarks," Associated Press, 7-7-03.

For the record, Mr. President, let me say that I do not hate anybody, but I have been accused of it in editorial after editorial. I
do not hate homosexuals. I do not even know any homosexuals. But what I do not like is for the Congress of the United
States to bow and scrape to homosexual pressure and give them
Federal funds and rights and privileges that other Americans
are denied. That is what I do not like.

>   —*Sen. Jesse Helms (R-NC). Congressional Record*, S10705,
>   7-26-95.

We believe homosexuality is not normal and should not be made
an acceptable "alternative" lifestyle either in public education
or in public policy. We oppose special treatment by law based
on nothing other than homosexual behavior or identity. We
therefore oppose actions, such as "marriage" or the adoption
of children by same-sex couples, which attempt to legitimize
and normalize homosexual relationships. We support the Defense of Marriage Act. We also stand united with private organizations, such as the Boy Scouts, who defend moral decency
and freedom according to their own long held and well established traditions and beliefs.

>   —*North Carolina Republican Party Platform*, adopted 5-31-
>   02.

. . . We support the traditional definition of "marriage" as the
legal union of one man and one woman, and we believe that
federal judges and bureaucrats should not force states to recognize other living arrangements as marriages. We rely on the
home, as did the founders of the American Republic, to instill
the virtues that sustain democracy itself. That belief led Congress to enact the Defense of Marriage Act, which a Republican
Department of Justice will energetically defend in the courts.
For the same reason, we do not believe sexual preference should
be given special legal protection or standing in law . . .

>   —*Republican Party Platform 2000*, "Renewing America's Pur-
>   pose. Together."

Pat Buchanan, in a column titled, "Yes, Virginia, there is a religious war," this week wrote of the need for Americans to get involved in this critical war to protect the Judeo-Christian values of our Forefathers. If we continue to sit on our hands, traditional marriage will be lost and multiple denominations will ignore biblical teachings by embracing homosexual rights. Pat [said that] Rev. V. Gene Robinson, now bishop-elect of the Episcopal Church of New Hampshire, is "a flaming fraud." Fifteen years ago, Robinson dissolved his marriage, dumped his wife, abandoned his two little girls and went off to shack up. He thus violated his marriage vows, flouted the teachings of the Anglican faith he was ordained to uphold and entered into a sinful liaison his church has always taught was perverted.

Having failed to conform his life to scriptural command. . . . [Pat continues,] "Robinson now demands that Scripture be reinterpreted to conform to his deviant life style. To see Robinson elevated to bishop is to be reminded that in the French Revolution, the Paris mob used the high altar at Notre Dame Cathedral to canonize the town tramp as their Goddess of Reason . . ."

. . . Christianity, dying in Europe, is under siege in America. A paganism that holds homosexual unions to be "sacramental"—the Rev. Robinson's term—is ascending.

The solution is a vast uprising of Christians in America, people of faith who will sacrificially work to preserve the sanctity of marriage and boldly take a stand for the Judeo-Christian standards that brought about this nation. Join me in taking this stand by signing the Petition of Support for the Federal Marriage Amendment today.

—*Jerry Falwell*, "The Falwell Confidential," Falwell.com, 8-14-03.

The first same-sex marriage in North American history has just taken place. The highest court of Ontario has ruled that the millennia-old definition of marriage of one man and one woman violates Canada's constitution. How did three people change marriage, always understood to be a privilege defined by society, into a right defined by judges? How can three people have the hubris to overturn a pillar of Western civilization without allowing their society to have a say in the matter? There is a one-word answer to these questions. Liberalism. There is no arrogance like liberal arrogance. Nowhere in the conservative world is there anything to match it.

> —*Dennis Prager*, syndicated columnist and former Reagan appointee. "No arrogance like liberal arrogance," Creators Syndicate, 6-24-03.

I realized the other day that our inspectors are looking in the wrong place for weapons of mass destruction. These weapons are not in Baghdad; they're in Washington, in the hands of the sexual liberationist lobby. And they're deploying them against America's most respected Christians in public life. Their most recent target is Senator Rick Santorum of Pennsylvania (R). A few weeks ago, Santorum committed the ultimate crime in the eyes of those hoping to redefine the way the law treats sexual behavior: He told the truth. And media and political leaders have been piling on him ever since. And Santorum is not the only one. Bill Bennett is another. The goal of his detractors is not simply to discredit Bennett, but to destroy him. From now on, every time you see Bennett's name in print, you're going to see the words *reformed gambler*—just as every time you see Santorum's name, you're going to see the words *gay basher*. It's an attempt to eliminate their voices from serious public policy discussion by ad hominem and untrue ridicule. The same thing will happen to almost any other public figure who dares to make a truth claim. Truth claims are deeply offensive to the titans of secular orthodoxy—so much so that it's not enough to dispute arguments through civil discourse, or to have an honest disagreement. No, truth-tellers have to be destroyed.

> —*Charles Colson*, "Santorum and the Sex Lobby," CBN.com, 6-19-03.

This great American institution [Boy Scouts of America] has come under attack from homosexual activists—who may well set their sights on *your* church next.
—*Jay Sekulow*, direct mail, March 2000, PFAW.org.

Can you imagine, that in public schools of America today, students are being taught that homosexual conduct, which in many states is still deemed illegal, is not only a viable alternative lifestyle, but is actually equal to heterosexual relationships?
—*Ibid. Danbury News-Times*, 1-2-97.

It's a religious belief to me that homosexuality flies in the face of biblical teachings. Now, where I have difficulties is in determining whether it's a genetic predisposition or whether it is a choice. Either way, though, in contradistinction to people of color, people of color can't do anything about their color, but I do believe gay people have a choice to live within the legal rules or not . . . It's up to them, that they do have a choice, where an African-American has no choice with regard to the color of their skin. So that's why we have civil-rights laws to protect African-Americans from discrimination.
—*Sen. Orrin Hatch (R-UT)*. John Heilprin, "Hatch Says He's Misunderstood, But Some Say His Anti-Gay Bias Is Clear," *Salt Lake Tribune*, 8-13-99.

NOW is saying that in order to be a woman, you've got to be a lesbian.
—*Pat Robertson*, "700 Club," CBN, 12-3-97.

Imagine we identify the gene—assuming that there is one, this is hypothetical—that will tell us prior to birth that a baby is going to be gay. Just like a baby is going to be redheaded and freckled and maybe tend to be overweight and so we tell the parents that, and the parents say "Nope, don't wanna give birth to that child, [it's] not gonna have a fair chance. Who wants to give birth to an overweight, freckle-faced redhead?" Bam. So we abort the kid. Well, you add to this, let's say we discover the gene that says the kid's gonna be gay. How many parents, if they knew before the kid was going to be born, [that he] was going to be gay, they would take the pregnancy to term? Well, you don't know but let's say half of them said, "Oh, no, I don't wanna do that to a kid." [Then the] gay community finds out about this. The gay community would do the fastest 180 and become pro-life faster than anybody you've ever seen. . . . They'd be so against abortion if it was discovered that you could abort what you knew were gonna be gay babies.

>   —*Rush Limbaugh.* Joe Kovacs, "Rush Limbaugh: Abortions
>   kill liberal causes Radio host also says homosexuals would be
>   pro-life if 'gay' gene proved," Worldnetdaily.com, 1-23-03.

Newt is always able to handle a harangue going on around him better than I am. I like peace and quiet. And I don't need to listen to Barney Fag (pause), Barney *Frank,* haranguing in my ear because I made a few bucks off a book I worked on. I just don't want to listen to it.

>   —*Dick Armey (R-TX),* House Majority Leader. Jim
>   Drinkard, "GOP leader uses slur for gay colleague Armey
>   calls Frank "Barney Fag," *San Francisco Examiner,* 1-27-
>   95. Armey was responding to reporters' questions about a
>   book he was writing; questions prompted by Newt
>   Gingrich's recent controversially lucrative book deal.

I do not want Barney Frank to believe for one moment I would use a slur against him. I had a trouble with alliteration. I was stumbling, mumbling . . . Barney Frank is a friend of mine. I don't use the word in personal conversation. I would not use such an expression and I don't approve of anyone who does this.

>   —*Dick Armey (R-TX). Ibid.*

Yes, I am Dick Armey. And if there is a dick army, Barney Frank
would want to join up.

   —*Dick Armey* responding to humor columnist Dave Barry's
   question, "Are you really Dick Armey?" at a cocktail party
   during the Republican National Convention. Ben White,
   Beth Berselli, "Armey Upsets Gays With Off-Color Joke,"
   Washington Post, 8-5-00.

Mr. Speaker, that there is absolutely nothing that we do that is
more important than protecting our families and protecting the
institution of marriage. I have said, too, that this current situation that is taking place in Hawaii, where the Supreme Court is
about to rule that same sex marriages are in order, is a frontal
assault on the institution of marriage and, if successful, will
demolish the institution in and of itself with that redefinition.
How can we possibly, once we begin to redraw the border, the
playing field of the institution of marriage to say it also includes
two men, or two women, how can we stop there and say it
should not also include two men and one woman, or three men,
four men, or an adult and a child? If they love one another,
what would be the problem with that? As long as we are going
to expand the definition of what marriage is, why stop there?
Logically there would be no reasonable stopping place.

   —*Rep. Steve Largent (R-OK)* discussing H.R. 3396, the Defense of Marriage Act. *Congressional Record,* H7276, 7-
   11-96. Largent made an unsuccessful run for Governor of
   Oklahoma in 2002.

One of the most astounding things that I heard was in our committee, one member indicating that he did not really know the
difference for legal purposes between a man and a woman or
between a male and a female. I daresay, Mr. Speaker, that we all
know that. And the fact of the matter is that marriage throughout the entire history of not only our civilization but Western
civilization has meant the legal union between one man and

one woman. For us to now be poised as a country, and this is an issue that will be presented, to sweep that away would be outrageous. The American people demand this legislation.
     —*Bob Barr (R-GA)*, on H.R. 3396, the Defense of Marriage Act. *Congressional Record*, H7275, 7-11-96.

For those homosexuals who are not into the politics of gay rights and who desire help, Dr. Spitzer's findings offer hope. And hope is one of the greatest gifts a psychiatrist can give a patient.
     —*Cal Thomas*, "New Study: Gays Can Go Straight," Tribune Media Services, 5-10-01.

HOLY WAR

... Then, at around five o'clock in the evening a cry of joy rang out from the Schindler family. Both the House and the Senate in Florida had overwhelmingly passed what they called the Terri Bill—a bill that had come from nowhere. Governor Bush was standing by to quickly sign it so that Terri could LIVE! DEATH had been defeated at least for the moment, and a power that was not their own had caused the lawmakers to act righteously and CHOOSE LIFE! "The king's heart is in the hand of the Lord, as are the watercourses; he turns it whichever way He wills" (Prov. 21:1). The gates of Hell had been pushed back! God Almighty had intervened and everyone knew it! ...

> —*Tom and Linda McGlade*, "Terri Schiavo—God's
> Living Parable to a Dying World!" 10-31-03.
> Operationsaveamerica.org.

As chief justice of the state of Alabama, it is my duty to administer the justice system of our state, not destroy it. I have no intention of removing the monument. . . . To do so would, in effect, result in the disestablishment of our system of justice in this state. This I cannot and will not do.

> —*Alabama Supreme Court Chief Justice Roy Moore* announc-
> ing he would defy a Federal District Court order to remove
> a 20-ton monument of the Ten Commandments from the
> state judicial building. Todd Kleffman, "Moore won't move
> display," *Montgomery Advertiser*, 8-15-03.

Judge Roy Moore will be going to trial November 12, 2003. The trial will take place in the very court where he presided as Chief Justice before being suspended from his duties by several

"Christian" associate justices—the Supreme Court of the state
of Alabama. He is being charged with contempt of court for
not abiding by Federal Judge Myron Thompson's "illegal" court
order to remove the Ten Commandments Monument from the
rotunda of the Alabama Supreme Court building.

This is an outrage! We cannot not sit passively by while this
utter injustice is taking place in the God-hating courts of this
land. We must stand with the man who is standing with Jesus.

We must be there to support Judge Roy Moore! We are
asking, no pleading with you to do whatever is necessary to
allow your theology to become biography in the streets of Montgomery, once again. We know that you have been all over this
country fighting the Gospel battle but, you were born for a time
such as this. The trumpet has sounded. Bill Pryor, the Attorney
General of the State of Alabama, will be leading the prosecution. Remember, Mr. Pryor ran for office based on the fact that
he would stand by Judge Roy Moore and his right to display
the Ten Commandments in the Alabama Supreme Court building. Mr. Pryor confesses Christ, but Mr. Pryor has been less
than truthful in carrying out the duties of his office.

It is imperative that we stand with our brother!

See you in Montgomery, Alabama, November 11-13, as we
storm the gates of hell once again. Colossians 4:17.

Judge Roy Moore Needs Us Now!

—"We must go back to Montgomery," Nov. 11–13, 2003.
  Operationsaveamerica.org.

I think the most important thing to note in this case is the issue,
and according to the federal judge who tried this case, he
said, "the issue is can the state acknowledge God?" That's the
issue in this case. It's not about a monument. It's not about
politics or religion. It's about whether or not the state of Alabama can acknowledge God. And indeed we must if we're to
uphold the justice system in the state of Alabama.

—*Judge Roy Moore.* "The Abrams Report," MSNBC, 8-21-03.

Christian Nation—The Republican Party of Texas reaffirms the United States of America is a Christian nation, which was founded on fundamental Judeo-Christian principles based on the Holy Bible. We also affirm the right of each individual to worship in the religion of his or her choice.
> —*Texas State GOP Platform 2002.* TexasGOP.org.

Well, you know what I knew—that my god was bigger than his. I knew that my god was a real god and his was an idol.
> —*Lt. Gen. William G. Boykin*, Deputy Undersecretary of Defense, on a 1993 U.S. Army battle against a Muslim warlord in Somalia. "Rumsfeld Says Anti-Islam Aide Is "'Outstanding'," *New York Times*, 10-17-03.

Why is this man in the White House? The majority of Americans did not vote for him. Why is he there? And I tell you this morning that he's in the White House because God put him there for a time such as this.
> —*Lt. Gen. William G. Boykin*, on George W. Bush. *Ibid.*

Mr. Speaker, I rise today to introduce a Constitutional amendment to ensure that students can choose to pray in school. Regrettably, the notion of the separation of church and state has been widely misrepresented in recent years, and the Government has strayed far from the vision of America as established by the Founding Fathers.
> —*Rep. Jo Ann Emerson (R-MO)*, addressing the House. *Congressional Record*, E37, 1-7-97.

The greatest danger that we have faced, the greatest danger we face today lies not in the guns of any enemy. It lies not in the strength of any foreign power. The greatest danger that we face today is those who wish to tell us, in the name of freedom, that we must turn our backs on God!
> —*Alan Keyes,* 2000 candidate for the Republican Presidential nomination, at a rally in support of Judge Roy Moore's

refusal to remove a replica of the Ten Commandments from his courthouse. "WorldView," CNN, 4-12-03.

Let the eagle soar / like she's never soared before / from rocky coast / to golden shore / let the mighty eagle soar. / Soar with healing in her wings / as the land beneath her sings: / "Only God, no other kings," / let the mighty eagle soar. / This country's far too young to die / Though she's cried a bit for what we've put her through / she's soared above the lifted lamp / that guards sweet freedom's door / in the dews, the damps, the watch fires / of a nation torn by war / oh she's far too young to die / you can see it in her eye / she's not yet begun to fly / it's time to let the mighty eagle soar.
—*Song lyrics by Attorney General John Ashcroft*, written during the Thanksgiving holiday, 1997. "Senator's New Tune has political ring," *St Louis Post-Dispatch*, 9-3-98.

The *L.A. Times*, it's an anti-Christian publication, as is the *New York Times*.
—*Mel Gibson*. Peter J. Boyer, "The Jesus War," *The New Yorker*, 9-15-03.

Why are they calling her [Anne Catherine Emmerich] a Nazi? Because modern secular Judaism wants to blame the Holocaust on the Catholic Church. And it's a lie. And it's revisionism. And they've been working on that one for a while.
—*Ibid*. Gibson carries an Emmerich relic in his pocket. She was a 19th-century Augustinian nun who had visions and, according to Boyer, "is proceeding toward beatification." Emmerich was virulently anti-Semitic.

If the people who control the networks in Hollywood were 59 percent Christian and if they were only 1 percent as anti-Semitic as the networks currently are anti-Christian, there would be a massive public outcry.
—*Donald Wildmon*. "Demagoguery in America," *New Republic* editorial, 8-1-94.

Pat Robertson: Just like what Nazi Germany did to the Jews, so liberal America is now doing to the evangelical Christians.
Jerry Falwell: Modern U.S. Supreme Courts have raped the Constitution and raped the Christian faith and raped the churches.
>   —*Ibid.*

God told me to strike at al Qaeda and I struck them, and then he instructed me to strike at Saddam, which I did, and now I am determined to solve the problem in the Middle East. If you can help me I will act, and if not, the elections will come and I will have to focus on them.
>   —*President George W. Bush* speaking to Palestinian Prime Minister Mahmoud Abbas. Gene Lyons, "It Ain't Stealing When You Admit It," *Arkansas Democrat-Gazette,* 7-9-03.

We condemn attempts by the EEOC [Equal Employment Opportunity Commission] or any other arm of government to regulate or ban religious symbols from the workplace . . .
>   —*Republican Party Platform*, adopted 8-12-96, p.15.

. . . I think Christianity is dead in the United States of America. For a group of atheistic cowards to go to the heart of the Bible Belt and hide behind a law degree and order, "rip down the Ten Commandments! hee hee hee hee hee" like rats from NYU and Columbia, shall I paint you a picture? And the Christians do nothing? Then you deserve to lose your church . . . you deserve to lose your religion, you deserve to lose your heritage. That's what I say. If you won't defend your own religion then you deserve to lose it! . . .

It's out of state lawyers from Columbia and NYU who are doing this to you, you Christian morons . . .

They're doing it because they want to show that if they can take the Ten Commandments down in the Bible Belt they can do anything to you anywhere in this country at any time. They could put up phony hate-crime laws that if you look at a gay person or someone the wrong way you'll go to jail just for looking the wrong way. What, do you think I'm kidding you? Do you think I don't see where this is all going? You think I don't see the big picture? I do, you may not, but I do! I have it bottled up in me like a genie all day long! How a small band of Christ-haters, degenerates by the way in my opinion, can do this and get away with it, is simple, because you're doing nothing. Prayer will help you to no end. Prayer is worth nothing, so you can take your bibles and you can throw 'em back in the drawer ... It's all going in one direction, to establish judicial tyranny, and to destroy the liberty of you the people, first in the state government, and to take away your acknowledgement and your ability to revere God Almighty.

    —*Michael Savage* on his radio program, "The Savage Nation," 8-22-03.

I want to address this nettlesome notion of the separation of church and state. . . . When you hear people talking about the supposed "separation of church and state," what they usually mean is "The Establishment Clause of the First Amendment requires a separation." But it doesn't. Aside from the fact that the Establishment Clause has been erroneously extended to apply to the states as well as Congress, let's look how far the scope of "establishment" has been stretched on both the state and federal levels. It's darn near criminal.

    —*David Limbaugh*, syndicated columnist and brother of Rush.
    "The myth of church-state separation," Townhall.com, 8-30-03.

We will continue to work for the return of voluntary prayer to our schools . . . We encourage state legislatures to pass statutes which prohibit local school boards from adopting policies of denial regarding voluntary school prayer.

    —*Republican Party Platform*, adopted 8-12-96, p.22.

Jerry Falwell: And I agree totally with you that the Lord has protected us so wonderfully these 225 years. And since 1812, this is the first time that we've been attacked on our soil and by far the worst results. And I fear, as Donald Rumsfeld, the Secretary of Defense, said yesterday, that this is only the beginning. And with biological warfare available to these monsters—the Husseins, the Bin Ladens, the Arafats—what we saw on Tuesday, as terrible as it is, could be miniscule if, in fact—if, in fact—God continues to lift the curtain and allow the enemies of America to give us probably what we deserve.

Pat Robertson: Jerry, that's my feeling. I think we've just seen the antechamber to terror. We haven't even begun to see what they can do to the major population.

Falwell: The ACLU's got to take a lot of blame for this.

Robertson: Well, yes.

Falwell: And, I know that I'll hear from them for this. But, throwing God out successfully with the help of the federal court system, throwing God out of the public square, out of the schools. The abortionists have got to bear some burden for this because God will not be mocked. And when we destroy 40 million little innocent babies, we make God mad. I really believe that the pagans, and the abortionists, and the feminists, and the gays and the lesbians who are actively trying to make that an alternative lifestyle, the ACLU, People For the American Way—all of them who have tried to secularize America—I point the finger in their face and say "you helped this happen."

Robertson: Well, I totally concur, and the problem is we have adopted that agenda at the highest levels of our government. And so we're responsible as a free society for what the top people do. And, the top people, of course, is the court system.

—*Jerry Falwell and Pat Robertson* discussing the World Trade Center catastrophe. "700 Club," CBN, 9-13-01.

We have sinned against Almighty God, at the highest level of our government, we've stuck our finger in your eye. The Su-

preme Court has insulted you over and over again, Lord. They've taken your Bible away from the schools. They've forbidden little children to pray. They've taken the knowledge of God as best they can, and organizations have come into court to take the knowledge of God out of the public square of America.
    —*Pat Robertson* discussing 9-11 with Jerry Falwell. *Ibid.*, 9-13-03.

In order for me to believe that God was sending America a message, I would need to be shown that the people who died Tuesday were all members of the NOW gang, or abortionists, civil libertarians, et cetera.
    —*Rush Limbaugh*, 9-18-01.

. . . a couple of thousand years [ago] Pilate stepped before the people in Jerusalem and said, "Whom would ye that I release unto you? Barabas? Or Jesus, which is called the Christ?" And when they said "Barabas," he said, "But what about Jesus? King of the Jews?" And the outcry was, "We have no king but Caesar."
    There's a difference between a culture that has no king but Caesar, no standard but the civil authority, and a culture that has no king but Jesus, no standard but the eternal authority. When you have no king but Caesar, you release Barabas—criminality, destruction, thievery, the lowest and the least. When you have no king but Jesus, you release the eternal, you release the highest and the best.
    If America is to be great in the future, it will be if we understand that our source is not civic and temporal, but our source is godly and eternal . . . I thank God for this institution and for you, who recognize and commit yourselves to the proposition that . . . to live with respect to the Creator promises us the greatest potential as a nation and as individuals. And for such we must reacquaint ourselves daily with His call upon our lives.
    —*Sen. John Ashcroft (R-MO)* speaking at Bob Jones University, 5-8-99. ABCnews.com.

The secularists are gloating. They got a court order to remove the Ten Commandments monument from the rotunda of the Alabama Judicial Building and another court order to suspend Alabama Supreme Court Chief Justice Roy Moore who put it there . . . The goal of the secularists and the atheists is to treat religious people like smokers. You can continue to exist only if you are out of sight, out of hearing and out of smell.
— *Phyllis Schlafly*. "Secular humanists rock foundations of Christian nation," Copley News Service, 9-1-03.

Why does there need to be a separation of church and state? I don't understand the reason for that.
— *Erie County Executive Joel Giambra* quoted in a letter from Gary R. Haaf to the *Buffalo News*, "Keeping Church, State Separate Is Essential," 3-25-03. Haaf added, "If Giambra does not understand the reasoning of our founding fathers in ensuring the separation of church and state, perhaps he should pursue his political career in Iran."

. . . Christianity, in principle, cannot accept subordination to the political authorities, for the end to which it directs men is higher than the end of the political order; the source of its authority is higher than the political authority . . .
— *Judge James Leon Holmes*, nominated by the Bush administration on 1-28-03 to the U.S. District Court for the Eastern District of Arkansas, speaking at the annual meeting of the Society of Catholic Social Scientists in Ann Arbor, MI, 10-19-02. IndependentJudiciary.com

In the West, we most often see Islamic people as crazed and irrational. But have we considered that the Muslims might not be irrational when they consider America to be akin to Satan? Let's look at the Satanic Bible. What are the values of Satan? Lust, Greed, Gluttony, Revenge. Hmm. Sounds like American society. Is New York the head of the "Great Satan"? All that is evil in the world can be found in New York: MTV, the United

Nations, the U.N. abortion programs, the Council on Foreign Relations, New Age Church of St. John the Divine, Wall Street greed, Madison Avenue manipulation and of course more confirmed AIDS cases than the rest of America combined. Let's remember the filthy sodomite gay parade last summer in New York. Let's remember all the New York politicians falling all over themselves to praise this sick spectacle. And let's not forget that New Yorkers elected—by a landslide—the openly Marxist, treasonous and abortion-mongering, occultic Hillary to a Senate seat.

> —*Online columnist Anthony LoBaido*, WorldNetDaily.com, on why the terrorists targeted New York in 9-11. James Taranto, "Best of the Web," *Wall Street Journal*, 9-16-01. Taranto blasted LoBaido and called Joseph Farah, editor and CEO of Worldnetdaily, "a purveyor of obscenity." Farah was a driving force behind the Western Journalism Center, which issued newsletters, reports and ads accusing Bill Clinton of murder, among other crimes.

We have seen over the past 30 years that the radical revolution of the left has torn this country apart at the seams. We live today in a country, as the Speaker says, that has 12-year-old children on drugs, 15-year-olds shooting each other, and 18-year-olds graduating from high school with diplomas that they cannot even read. America has lived in a valueless society that our radical policies of the past 30 years have created. In 1994, there was a shift back to the center, and yesterday I believe that Congress passed a simple resolution that helped move us back to the right direction where our Founding Fathers wanted us to be.

> —*Rep. Joe Scarborough (R-FL)* discussing a resolution supporting Roy Moore, the Alabama judge who posted the Ten Commandments in his courtroom. *Congressional Record*, H790, 3-6-97.

. . . Airports scrupulously apply the same laughably ineffective airport harassment to Suzy Chapstick as to Muslim hijackers.

It is preposterous to assume every passenger is a potential crazed homicidal maniac. We know who the homicidal maniacs are. They are the ones cheering and dancing right now. We should invade their countries, kill their leaders and convert them to Christianity. We weren't punctilious about locating and punishing only Hitler and his top officers. We carpet-bombed German cities; we killed civilians. That's war. And this is war.
   —*Ann Coulter,* "This Is War," *National Review Online,* 9-13-01.

Todd Starnes: Tell me about your daily walk with the Lord. Do you have a quiet time or a prayer time by yourself or with your family?

Rod Paige: Absolutely. I begin the day that way. When I get up in the morning and get my coffee I then prepare myself for today, that day. And I begin to prepare myself that day by my Scripture lessons, readings, and my prayer, the whole thing that I call devotion. That takes about 20 to 25 minutes in the morning. And this is the very first thing to do. I never allow anything else to interfere with that. And I start each day with that, even the Sundays when I'm preparing to go to church.

Starnes: Wow. What are you studying right now, anything in particular that maybe the Lord is teaching you or speaking to you about?

Paige: Well, you know, strangely, when I do have devotion in the morning I feel that I'm being spoken to. And a lot of the issues that I have I find decisions, or I'll find solutions come to me during that period of time. At first I used to worry about that and feel that I was unfocused when I'm reading Scripture or just before I begin prayer. But I'm beginning now to feel at home with that, because as I read Scripture not only am I focusing on the Scripture, but sometimes I'm beginning to see more clearly paths that I should take or solutions that—to problems that have been bugging me for some time. So it's not only a good time for what I learn from the Scriptures, but just that quiet time to be by myself and focus on some of these issues is very important.

—*Education Secretary Rod Paige*, in a 3-7-03 interview with Todd Starnes of the Baptist Press, published 4-7-03. BPnews.net.

Again, identify yourself as a Christian, and dare to speak about it, and the elite witch-hunters will come for you. And they will do whatever it takes to silence you.

—*Laura Ingraham, Shut Up And Sing*, NY: Regnery, 2003, p. 124. She refers to the outcry against Sen. Santorum's condemnation of homosexuals.

THE GENDER GAP

How's this for a new principle of law: A captured bank robber can't be prosecuted if he certifies that he needs the money. My gosh, most folks would say, that doesn't make any sense . . . And so it goes for the "compromise" abortion legislation offered by Senate Minority Leader Tom Daschle (D-SD). It would prohibit the abortion of a viable fetus—one able to live outside the womb—except when the continuation of the pregnancy would threaten the mother's life or "grievously injure" her physical health.

—*Dennis Byrne*, "'Compromise' bill in truth one-sided," *Chicago Sun-Times*, 5-14-97.

Ever wonder where the feminists have been during all this??? [The controversy over whether to end Terri Schiavo's life.] I mean, here's a man who is obviously hell-bent and determined to take this woman's life. Not only that, he has involved other men in the act (attorney George Felos, Judge George Greer, and countless others) . . . yet nary a word, that I've heard, from those paragons of women's rights, the feminists.

It reminds me of the old "4-6-8-10, why are all your leaders men?" rant we used to hear them chant while we were at the abortion mills rescuing babies. At the time, I was inclined to answer that with the straightforward, "Because that's the biblical order," etc. . . . which is true, excepting abuses such as Mr. Schiavo's. But now that I know more than I did then about their own background—how most abortionists are men, and both co-founders of NARAL—Perhaps Michael Vice [a pro-life Christian activist in Birmingham] did better with his rejoinder, "2-4-6-10, why are all your *women* men?"

. . . Or, consider 1992 when the court challenged God's ability to mark when life begins and ends. Three Reagan appointees joined the majority in *Planned Parenthood of Southeastern Pennsylvania v. Casey* to uphold a "woman's right to choose." So much for recapturing the Court. Together, *Roe*, *Casey* and their illegitimate progeny have occasioned the slaughter of thirty-five million children, thirty-five million innocents denied standing before the law. . . .

 —*Sen. John Ashcroft*, at the Conservative Political Action
  Conference (CPAC) Annual Meeting, 3-6-97.

The nags at NARAL, NOW, Planned Parenthood, etc., are all in rebellion to biblical order and desire to be men, but men of the worst order. Men who would take their women into an abortion mill to kill their own children. Men who put themselves first, above all else. Men who become tyrannical despots in their own homes. Men who would seek to kill their own wives simply because they are inconvenient. For all their railing against "male chauvinism," they do have a strange and more than a little disturbing penchant for siding, in an actual fight, with the "chauvinistic pig" . . . or doing nothing on behalf of his female victim.

 —*Janet Spear*, "Terri Schindler-Schiavo—Where are the Feminists Crying for her Rights?" Operationsaveamerica.org,
  10-28-03.

About the two 18-year-olds who are charged with having chosen to kill their seven-and-a-half-pound boy, putting his body in a trash bag in the motel's dumpster: Don't young people read newspapers? Don't they know that, thanks to President Clinton, they could have chosen to have a doctor suck their baby's brains out, and Delaware would not have chosen to charge them with murder?

 —*George Will*, "An Abortion Choice," *Washington Post*,
  11-24-96.

Now, if we did this procedure . . . of jamming scissors in the base of the skull and suctioning out the brains on someone who had raped and murdered 30 people, the Supreme Court and every Member of this Senate would say, "You can't do that, you can't do that, that's cruel and inhumane punishment." Oh, but if you are a little baby, if you haven't hurt anybody, if you are nestled up in your mother's womb, warm and safe—supposedly safe—we can do that to you. In fact, it is our right, it is my right that I can do that . . . and you will hear rights, you will hear rights, my right to do this, my right to do that, it's my body, I can do whatever I want, I can kill this baby, it's my baby. Rights.

> —Sen. Rick Santorum (R-PA), on the Senate floor arguing for
> a ban on "partial-birth abortion." *Congressional Record*,
> S4432, 5-14-97.

You know, we have debates here on the floor, and we have committee meetings even to talk about juvenile crime, talk about Generation X, and how they have no respect for our institutions or even each other, that they think everybody is in it for themselves. The cynicism is so rampant. If you want to know why that occurs, tune in to this debate. Children are not oblivious to what is going on in this country when it comes to the issue of abortion. Ask why a child should be any more concerned about shooting their neighbor if members of the U.S. Senate and the President of the United States says [*sic*] we can kill a little baby.

> —Sen. Rick Santorum. *Ibid.*, S4433, 5-14-97.

Why then, can't we as a society, if the child is threatening the mother's health, deliver the child and, if possible, to try to save it? Why does that child have to be killed? There is no medical answer for that, there is no medical reason. But let me submit a reason that I think is critically clear from the debate and, more importantly, from the evidence and, more importantly, from

the words of the doctors who perform these abortions. Why is it done? Why does the child have to be killed? The child has to be killed because that is the goal. That is the goal. That is what the doctor wants to do.
> —*Sen. Mike DeWine (R-OH). Congressional Record*, S4437, 5-14-97.

Arnold Schwarzenegger: Well, first of all, a lot of these are made up stories. I have never grabbed anyone, and pulled up their shirt and grabbed their breasts and stuff like that. This is not me. So there's a lot of this stuff going on that is not true.
Tom Brokaw: So you deny all those stories about grabbing.
Arnold Schwarzenegger: No, not all. But I'm just saying this is not—this is not me. What I am is I'm, you know, someone that sometimes makes outrageous jokes, someone that is out there saying sometimes crazy things that may be offensive because there is a certain atmosphere on the set and all those things.
> —*"Dateline NBC,"* 10-5-03.

He [Arnold Schwarzenegger] shut down the spin machine before his handlers could even get it cranked up, and forthrightly apologized, in a way that Bill Clinton never did. A blockbuster revelation that he was a randy Hollywood dude in his younger days has been expected since he first entered the race, but this blockbuster is probably too little and too late to bust Arnold's block. Besides, getting patted and squeezed is why boobs and bottoms go to Hollywood in the first place.
> —*Wesley Prudin*, editor-in-chief of the *Washington Times*. "A Tight Squeeze for the Terminator," *Jewish World Review*, 10-3-03.

As much as when you see a blonde with great t—and a great ass, you say to yourself, Hey, she must be stupid or must have nothing else to offer, which maybe is the case many times. But then again there is the one that is as smart as her breasts look,

great as her face looks, beautiful as her whole body looks gorgeous, you know, so people are shocked.
    —*Arnold Schwarzenegger.* Robert Salladay, "Schwarzenegger's 2 sides when it comes to women Macho actor exhibits disdain and respect for the opposite sex," *San Francisco Chronicle*, 8-14-03.

Abortion was supposed to free women from the "burdens" of their gender. Women get pregnant. Men don't. So, in order for women to feel as fully free as men, women must be allowed to become "unpregnant" if they wish, for whatever reason. In arguing from such a base, women are reclassifying themselves into something less than men, something less than human, because they are sacrificing their unique biological and psychological roles as mothers on the altar of convenience, based on a lie that they will be better off without the "burden" of an "unwanted" child.
    —*Cal Thomas, The Things That Matter Most*, NY: HarperCollins, 1994, p. 154

Feminist disdain for the family and the sexual revolution have given millions of women the "full potential" of abandonment and poverty and "liberated" countless children from the affection and care of their parents.
    —*Ibid.*, p. 7.

Men in the pro-choice movement are either women trapped in men's bodies like Alan Alda or Phil Donahue, or younger guys who are like camp followers looking for easy sex.
    —*Rep. Bob Dornan* at a February, 1990, anti-abortion rally in Orange County. Lloyd Grove, "Out of the mouth of. . . . Bob," *Washington Post*, 11-23-96.

If we pray down destruction on the head of Osama bin Laden for that violation of innocent life [the 9-11 attacks], we have to

be aware that we pray down destruction as well on a nation that is willing to enshrine in principle a right to administer the selfsame blow to those innocent lives of our offspring that ought to be more sacred in our obligation to God than any others.
    —*Alan Keyes.* Peter Finney, "Twin evils of abortion, 9/11 terror related," *Clarion Herald,* 7-17-02.

. . . The loss of human life on September 11 was enormous. Certainly STOPP would not want to minimize this tragedy in any way, and we urge our supporters to keep the victims of terrorism in New York City, Washington and Pennsylvania in their prayers. But let us remember those in the womb who are also victims of terrorism. Where is the national outpouring of grief for them? Does anyone suppose a baby going through a partial birth abortion or a saline abortion or a suction abortion at a Planned Parenthood clinic suffers any less terror than did the victims of September 11?
    —*"The Ryan Report,"* published by STOPP International, 11-01. ALL.org.

. . . Men are in a state of confusion over the meaning of sex-role identity. We know it is unacceptable to be "macho" (whatever in the world that is), but we're a little uncertain about how a real man behaves. Is he a breadwinner and a protector of his family? Well, not exactly. Should he assume a position of leadership and authority at home? Not if he's married to a woman who's had her "consciousness raised." Should he open doors for his wife or give a lady his seat on the train or rise when she enters the room? Who knows? Will he march off to defend his homeland in times of war, or will his wife be the one to fight on foreign soil? Should he wear jewellery and satin shoes or carry a purse? Alas, is there anything that marks him as different from his female counterpart? Not to hear the media tell it!
    —*Family World News,* 5-97. Pastornet.net.

We thank God that Clayton Lee Waagner has finally been apprehended and that perhaps the truth will be told about the collusion between him, anthrax and the abortion industry. More than anything else, Clayton Lee Waagner, the self-proclaimed "abortion avenger," is an invention of his own warped mind, with the willing help of the abortion industry and its spin machine. The two are, hand in glove, perpetrating one of the most heinous hoaxes in American history. Believe it or not the abortion industry and Waagner are in cahoots! The abortion industry, ever vigilant to keep our eyes off of what it does (brutalizing and killing innocent American baby boys and girls), has found a new friend in Clayton Waagner. Yes, Waagner has become for the abortion industry what Ken Starr became for Bill Clinton—a whipping boy to keep our eyes off of the real crime being committed!

　—*Rev. Flip Benham*, National Director of Operation Rescue and Operation Save America. Press release, "After scurrilous attacks by abortion industry spin machine," 12-5-01. Waagner, an habitual criminal, mailed false anthrax letters to women's health clinics.

I saw this toilet bowl. How many times do you get away with this—to take a woman, grab her upside down, and bury her face in a toilet bowl? I wanted to have something floating there. The thing is, you can do it, because in the end, I didn't do it to a woman—she's a machine! We could get away with it without being crucified by who-knows-what group.

　—*Arnold Schwarzenegger*, on a *Terminator* movie, in an interview with *Entertainment Weekly*, 7-11-03.

The wife is to subordinate herself to her husband . . . to place herself under the authority of the man.

　—*Judge James Leon Holmes*, nominated by the Bush administration on 1-28-03 to the U.S. District Court for the Eastern District of Arkansas. Paul Slansky, "The Back Page," *The New Yorker*, 12-4-03.

I think the abortion issue is the simplest issue this country has faced since slavery was made unconstitutional. And it deserves the same response.
  —*Judge James Leon Holmes. Moline Daily Dispatch*, 12-24-80.

Women—and I don't mean to limit that to the biological sense— always become hysterical at the first sign of trouble. They have no capacity to solve problems, so instead they fret. But despite the fearful fifth columnists whiling away the war naysaying America's response, we will win this war. You just stay warm, girls—the men are fixing the car.
  —*Ann Coulter*, "The Eunuchs are Whining," Townhall.com, 11-1-01.

Bill Press: I am not a voter in the 13th congressional district of Florida. If I were, I'd want to ask you a couple of questions. No. 1, where do you stand on the issue of choice? Do you support a woman's right of choice?
Katherine Harris: I'm personally pro-life.
Press: That means no exceptions?
Harris: There are exceptions.
Press: Such as?
Harris: Lack of a mother.
  —*Former Florida Secretary of State Katherine Harris,* during her successful campaign for Congress. "Buchanan and Press," MSNBC, 10-9-02.

When sin is full grown, said James, it brings forth death. Alas, the terrible sin of slavery reached its full maturity in 1860 when it contributed to a shameful and devastating Civil War. An entire nation was soon bathed in its own blood . . . Now here we go again. Nearly 30 million unborn babies have been killed since the Supreme Court issued its despicable *Roe v. Wade* decision in 1973. That number represents more than 10 percent of the U.S. population, and it is growing by 4,110 per day. Such bloodshed and butchery, now occurring worldwide, is unprecedented in human history, yet we've only seen the beginning. Don't tell me this crime against humanity will go unpunished! Those voiceless little people cry out to the Almighty from the incinerators and the garbage heaps where they have been discarded. Someday, this "unborn holocaust" will rain death and destruction upon our nation. Just wait. You'll see. It is in the nature of the universe. Sin inevitably devastates a people who embrace it.

    —*Dr. James Dobson, When God Doesn't Make Sense*, Wheaton, Ill.: Tyndale House, 1993, pp. 183–184.

We need to argue our case forcefully. We need to convince America by the power of our ideas and by the depth of our passion that abortion deserves no place in any society that would call itself civilized. We condemn Hitler for the slaughter of 6 million Jews. We condemn Stalin for the murder of 20 million Russians. We condemn Pol Pot for the extermination of 1 million Cambodians. But we raise nary a peep about the 1.5 million innocent children who are killed on our own shores every year. My colleagues, I ask you: Where is our conscience? Where is our shame?

    —*Rep. Cliff Stearns (R-FL)* before the U.S. House the day after the 23rd Anniversary of *Roe v. Wade. Congressional Record*, H742, 1-23-96.

. . . given the superficial nature of men's sex drive, the sex act for almost any man can be utterly devoid of any human, emotional, intellectual or romantic meaning. That is why a wife can understand—not excuse, but understand—that her husband can be a good man and slip up. Saints never weaken, men sometimes do . . . A woman who leaves her marriage solely because her husband was sexually unfaithful is most likely making a grievous error. Such women should speak to the women who have called my radio show when I have discussed this subject, to tell me how profoundly they regret having ended their marriages solely because their husband had an affair. (I hold the same position regarding men leaving their marriage solely because of their wife's

affair, but most women's affairs are far more emotionally involved, and therefore marriage-threatening.)
   —*Dennis Prager*, "Vanessa Bryant deserves admiration, not contempt," Creators Syndicate, 7-29-03.

Almost all zero tolerance rulings punish boys. Boys are also the victims of the current fad to eliminate recess and build new schools without playgrounds. It is beginning to look as though these fads cannot be mere stupidity. By banning the games that boys like to play and preventing them from running off their excess energy during recess, this nonsense might be part of a feminist agenda to try to make little boys behave like little girls.
   —*Phyllis Schlafly*, founder of the conservative group Eagle Forum, "Zero tolerance or zero common sense?" 4-22-03. By "zero tolerance," Ms. Schlafly is referring to the stringent policy in some public school systems banning weapons and drugs from school property. Townhall.com.

In a new book of dispatches from the front, feminism's most potent foe exposes the delusions and hypocrisy behind a movement that has cheated millions of women out of their happiness, health, and security . . . Like communism, feminism has been a catastrophe for the people it was meant to help.
   —*From the jacket copy of Phyllis Schlafly, Feminist Fantasies*. Dallas, Tex.: Spence, 2003.

We oppose all encroachments against American sovereignty through treaties (such as the International Criminal Court) and United Nations conferences (such as those aimed at imposing energy restrictions on the U.S., registering privately owned guns, imposing global taxes, or promoting feminist goals) . . . We oppose the feminist goals of federally financed and regulated child care and the feminization of the military.
   —*First and last lines of Eagle Forum's Mission Statement*. Eagle Forum is a conservative "volunteer group" founded by Phyllis Schlafly in 1972. Eagleforum.org.

Caller: God's given me a revelation about the truth about abortions . . . And that is that the women are being deceived into legally donating their baby to be not only experimented with, but to be processed, to be taken apart and processed into parts for vaccinations and other medications, that are not talked about. I mean this is, this is money, greed, like you said, but to have the concept that they are literally, there's—they have a mill, a machine that—and they want to get the babies as old as they can so they have the parts that are more viable, they're worth alot more money.

Johnny Rowland: That's right. That's true.

Caller: And so, and the tissue is worth alot more. And, and I kinda had this vision God was revealing to me I felt like that, one of the things that I'd like you guys to ask is if anybody knows somebody that is actually involved in making these vaccines that would go public? You know, because they've got to have vats where they have to process these baby parts, and these serums and these babies. And then that one vial of a vaccination could have thousands of baby parts of DNA in it.

Johnny Rowland: I don't know, but I tell you what, the further you dig into the abortion industry, the sicker it gets. The more gut wrenching, the more despicable it gets. The—well, anyway, I appreciate you calling.

—*Johnny Rowland's talk radio show "Thinking Right"* on the American Freedom Network, 1340-AM, Johnstown, CO, Heartbeat of the Rockies, 6-8-03.

This law is transparent in that it provides protection for women who chose to carry their pregnancies to term. There are no nuances or hidden agenda for the law. It simply provides protection for the loss of their children . . . Any pregnant woman that is choosing to carry her pregnancy to term would very much agree that what is in her womb is a human person, and to those women that is very significant.

—*Elizabeth Graham*, spokeswoman for Texas Right to Life, praising Texas State Senate Bill 319, defining "an individual" as "an unborn child at every state of gestation from fertilization until birth." David Pasztor, "Senate passes bill that defines a fetus as an individual," *Austin American-Statesman*, 5-23-03.

There is nothing reproductive about killing an unborn child. The gentlewoman [Rep. Patricia Schroeder (D-CO)] wants to elevate reproductive health clinics, anything but what she really means, which is abortion clinics or abortion mills. She wants to elevate that to a very special place where the bill, the block grant program, will specify they get special protection . . . What I have a problem with is elevating abortion clinics to a special status over other places where an awful lot of killing really goes on.

In 1993 there were 1,946 people killed in New York. In the great District of Columbia there were 454 murders. In Chicago, my city, there were 845 murders. How many cab drivers have been murdered in their cabs?

We cannot specify every place, every location, every convenience store, every liquor store, every currency exchange that is going to be threatened by robbery and people with guns that are going to kill people.
   —*Rep. Henry Hyde (R-IL)* voicing his objections to an amendment protecting abortion clinics from violence and criminal acts. *Congressional Record*, H1728, 2-14-95.

[Abortion rights activists] are homosexuals, wimps, and/or Jewish lawyers.
   —*Stan Solomon*, talk show host, WIBC-AM, Indianapolis. *Indianapolis Star*, 6-9-94. The *Star* identified Solomon as "a gun carrying Indiana militia representative," 4-25-95.

I don't care about the circumstances of a child's conception. You want to execute somebody in the case of rape, execute the rapist and let the unborn child live.
   —*Pat Buchanan. New York Times*, 2-24-96, p.1.

I thought the resolution was inappropriate because it only condemned violence against abortion clinics. I want to condemn that violence. I happen to be on the pro-life side of this debate. But I think people who are breaking the law by murdering other individuals are going too far, and they are actually hurting the cause that they supposedly are trying to help, so I think we should condemn that violence.

But I also think we should condemn violence such as occurred in Alabama in 1993. A pro-life minister and talk show host Jerry Simon was shot and killed by a self-described Satan worshipper, Eileen Janezic, stating she did it "to please Satan." That case received almost no publicity. We have seen a lot of publicity concerning the murder where Paul Hill murdered an abortionist in Florida, and maybe rightfully so; it needed some attention. He was certainly wrong.

—*Sen. Don Nickles (R-OK)*, on a resolution offered by Sen. Barbara Boxer (D-CA), condemning violent attacks on abortion clinics. *Congressional Record*, S1057, 1-18-95.

Given the facts of this case, it is entirely appropriate that an advocate be appointed to represent the unborn child's best interests in all decisions.

—*Gov. Jeb Bush (R-FL)* explaining his intervention in the case of a 22-year-old, developmentally impaired woman who became pregnant after she was raped. Dana Canedy, "Gov. Jeb Bush to seek Guardian for Fetus of Rape Victim," *New York Times*, 5-15-03.

The unborn child has a fundamental individual right to life which cannot be infringed. We support a human life amendment to the constitution, and we endorse legislation to make clear that the Fourteenth Amendment's protections apply to unborn children. Our purpose is to have legislative and judicial protection of that right against those who perform abortions. We oppose using public revenues for abortion and will not fund organizations which advocate it. We support the appointment of judges who respect

traditional family values and the sanctity of innocent human life
... We oppose abortion, but our pro-life agenda does not include
punitive action against women who have an abortion.
    —*Republican Party Platform*, adopted 8-12-96, p.16.

Rail as they will about "discrimination," women are simply
not endowed by nature with the same measures of single-minded
ambition and the will to succeed in the fiercely competitive world
of Western capitalism.
    —*Pat Buchanan*, newspaper column, 11-22-83. *USA Today*,
    2-22-96.

Using the coercive power of government to force American taxpayers to fund health-care facilities where abortions are performed would be, I think, a terrible precedent.
    —*Sen. Sam Brownback (R-KS)* speaking against an amend-
    ment allowing military women and dependents to obtain
    abortions at military medical facilities overseas, using their
    own money. "House, Senate pass separate defense spend-
    ing measures," Associated Press, 5-23-03.

If the current liberal, politically correct trends continue, it will
mean an end to the traditional family as the fundamental unit
of society, significant loss of individual freedoms as established
by our Constitution, and possible return to a Dark Age society.
The overwhelming feminization of society is rapidly leading to
a replacement of rule by law, with rule by emotion.
    —*Men's Defense Association*, a conservative group dedicated
    to helping men with divorce and child custody issues, among
    other things. Mensdefense.org. Phyllis Schlafly, lists this
    website as an "Eagle Forum Favorite." 4-24-03.

Their view of women's emancipation puts feminist supporters of
day care in the strange position of pushing to increase the number of children who must lead regimented lives. They lobby for
public schools and businesses to include day care programs for

preschoolers, push for longer school years and mandatory summer school, and want to lower the age of kindergarten. Not only that, they seek greater government intervention in family life to insure that parents are raising their children correctly at home.

> —*Brian C. Robertson*, from his book *Day Care Deception, What the Childcare Establishment Isn't Telling Us*, San Francisco: Encounter Books, 2003, p. 156.

Their Cold Dead Hands

Our members don't want to buy their songs, don't want to go to their movies, don't want to support their careers.
  —*National Rifle Association Executive Vice-President Wayne LaPierre* describing the organization's blacklist of businesses, religious groups, performers, and others. "NRA blacklist is a badge of honor for gun-control backers," *Chicago Tribune,* 10-30-03.

Right to Keep and Bear Arms—The Party calls upon the Texas Legislature and the United States Congress to repeal any and all laws that infringe upon the right of individual citizens to keep and bear arms as guaranteed by the 2nd Amendment to the United States Constitution; and to reject the establishment of any mechanism to process, license, record, register or monitor the ownership of guns. We urge the Legislature to clearly declare that it has the exclusive authority to determine where firearms may or may not be legally carried in the State of Texas, and that no other state governmental entity and no local governmental entity may regulate or prohibit the possession of firearms. We believe it is the responsibility of all gun owners to safely store and operate their firearms.
  —*Texas State GOP platform 2002.* TexasGOP.org.

As long as I am Speaker of this House, no gun control legislation is going to move in committee or on the floor of the House.
  —*House Speaker Newt Gingrich (R-GA),* in a letter dated 1-29-95 to Tanya Metaksa of the National Rifle Association. "Gingrich Note Reveals His Vow to NRA," *Chicago Tribune,* 8-2-95.

Question: How do you explain the low crime rates in democratic societies with strong firearms regulations?

Tanya Metaksa: The same way I would explain low crime rates in other countries which have less firearm restrictions than the countries you are talking about, and less restrictions than the high crime parts of the U.S.—there is no correlation between gun laws and crime rates, one way or the other, for the most part. As noted, though, where gun laws respect the right to self-protection, crime rates are much lower.

Nancy Kearney: To paraphrase many of the questions tonight: why do we need assault weapons?

Metaksa: "Need" is something for each individual to decide for him or herself. The issue is not "need"—certainly not in a free society where liberty is paramount. The issue is rights. If you mean to ask what uses there are for various kinds of firearms, that's another matter. Ask if that is your direction.

> —*Tanya Metaksa*, Executive Director of the National Rifle Association's Institute for Legislative Action in a "Time online" interview. *Time*'s Nancy Kearney was the moderator, 5-30-95. Hoboes.com.

Here's the evidence so far: Three people saw him in front of the building, he didn't react to pictures of dead babies, and he's not talking or cooperating. . . . How is he supposed to react? Is he supposed to break down on his hands and knees and go, "boo-hoo-hoo, it's so horrible what happened"?

> —*Spencer Hughes*, morning host at KSFO AM in San Francisco, defending accused bomber Timothy McVeigh. Kevin Berger, "Hate Radio," *San Francisco Examiner*, 5-1-95.

[Sarah Brady] ought to be put down. A humane shot at a veterinarian's would be an easy way to do it. I wish she would just keep wheeling her husband around, wiping the saliva off his mouth once in a while—and leave the rest of us damn well alone.

> —*Bob Mohan*, talk radio host, KFYI Phoenix, on gun control activists Sarah and James Brady. The latter was Ronald

Reagan's press secretary when he was shot with a handgun
by John Hinckley on 3-30-81. Timothy Egan, "Talk Radio
or Hate Radio: Critics Assail Some Hosts," *New York
Times,* 1-1-95.

That ugly cackler. She [Sarah Brady] pulls her husband around
like a pull-toy on a string. My friends and I say that if that ever
happened to one of us and our wife did that, somebody would
slip into the house one night and slit her throat.
   —*Leroy Pyle,* NRA board member. Osha Gray Davidson,
   Under Fire: The NRA and the Battle for Gun Control, Iowa
   City: University of Iowa Press,1998, p. 275.

I fear there are a lot of people in this country who fear they may
be bombed by the Federal Government at another Waco. I mean,
these people [the Branch Davidians] committed no crimes.
   —*Rep. Ron Paul (R-TX),* on "Washington Journal," C-SPAN,
   2-26-97.

I know that everyone enjoyed visiting with Larry Pratt this past
week . . . And I think Larry is the premiere pro-gun debater that
we have. I mean, he is absolutely, it is such a pleasure to watch
Larry slice and dice anti-gunners. (Laughter) In fact, they don't
want on with Larry. The anti-gunners if they find out, sometimes they won't even show up. They refuse, 'cause they know,
they know, they can't win. Because they have nothing but nonsense about guns being used in crime and all this other stuff and
how dangerous they are to our society. It's nonsense, they know
it's nonsense. Or at least they know they can't argue with our
friend Larry Pratt. So, I tell you what, friends, it's really fun
watching Larry (laughter) literally slice up the anti-gun debate
team, because Larry has the facts.
   —*Johnny Rowland,* host of the show "Thinking Right," 1360
   AM, Johnstown, CO. American Freedom Network radio,
   America_newsnet.com, 6-1-03. Larry Pratt is the spokes-
   person for Gun Owners of America.

But you know what else would've made nine-eleven impossible? If the pilots in those four airplanes had the right to be armed. They should've been armed thirty years ago. It's a no-brainer. It's the quickest, cheapest, most thorough means to protect our skies. And why not? . . . But on September 11th, they didn't have that right. That loss of liberty led to a terrible loss of life. And that led to a terrible loss of privacy in our nation's airports. Walk through any airport today and you see red-faced, teary-eyed women, singled out to endure security wands orbiting their breasts, while electronic squeals detect the metal in their underwire bras.

. . . In the 2000 elections we won a battle, but not the war. Because the gun-ban lobby was laying in wait for bad news—for an assassination, a school shooting, a deranged gunman, a celebrity murder to make bad news their good news. In this respect, they used September 11th as a godsend. Within weeks, the ailing gun-ban lobby was back, marketing terrorism as the new reason to ban your guns. Led by Senators Dianne Feinstein, Charles Schumer, Dick Durbin and Barbara Boxer, even John McCain, these groups began painting a fictional picture of wild-eyed terrorists equipping rogue armies through small town gun shows in the heartland of America.

> —*Wayne LaPierre*, Executive Vice President of the NRA, at the NRA Annual Meeting, 5-3-02. NRAILA.com.

It's time that we join the 35 other states that . . . allow their citizens to protect themselves when they're outside their homes.

> —*Rep. Larry Crawford (R-MO)*, sponsor of H.B. 349, allowing Missourians to carry concealed handguns. Gov. Bob Holden (D) promised to veto it. Holden did veto it, but the legislature passed it over his veto, 9-03. Tim Hoover, "Concealed-carry bill passes House; fight looms over probable veto," *Kansas City Star*, 5-6-03.

If guns are outlawed, how can we shoot the liberals?

> —*State Sen. Mike Gunn (R-MS)*. Larry Engelmann, "Quotable '96; A Year-End Tour Of Words; Atlanta's Olympic Year," *Atlanta Journal-Constitution*, 12-31-96.

If the Bureau of Alcohol, Tobacco and Firearms comes to disarm you and they are bearing arms, resist them with arms. Go for a head shot; they're gonna be wearing bulletproof vests . . . Head shots, head shots.
  —G. Gordon Liddy, 8-94. Boston Globe, 4-29-95. After the Oklahoma City bombing, Liddy corrected this statement, saying that experts had told him heads were a difficult target: "So you shoot twice to the body, center of mass, and if that does not work, then shoot to the groin area." Associated Press, 7-31-96.

We defend the constitutional right to keep and bear arms. We will promote training in the safe usage of firearms, especially in programs for women and the elderly.
  —Republican Party Platform, adopted 8-12-96, p.16.

[The repeal of the assault weapons ban is] necessary to fully restore our citizens' rights to self-protection.
  —Rep. Bob Barr (R-GA), co-sponsor of the bill to repeal the assault weapons ban. "Ft. America? GOP May Be Off the Mark," Chicago Tribune, 4-16-95. Sen. Paul Simon (R-IL) quoted a Violence Policy Center study: "The study finds that at least one in ten law enforcement officers killed in the line of duty will be felled by assault weapons." Congressional Record, S15169–S15170, 10-13-95.

The framers made it clear—very clear—that unless the Constitution explicitly granted a power to the Federal Government, that power would be reserved to the States, to the localities, to civil society, or to the people. I know there are many and this is the frustrating part for me—too many in this body who reject that vision. I have been here going on 9 years, and it is very frustrating for me to watch the Constitution of the United States being trampled time after time. Just a week or so ago, we passed more gun controls and sent it to conference. Gun control, however you may feel about the need for gun control, is unconstitu-

tional because we have a Second Amendment that says we have the right to keep and bear arms. Whatever you may feel about that issue, we did not come here to pass laws about our personal beliefs. We came here to pass laws that support the Constitution of the United States of America.
>   —*Sen. Bob Smith (I-NH)* on the Senate floor. *Congressional Record,* S10276, 8-5-99. Smith was elected to the Senate as a Republican, but left the party in July of 1999 because it wasn't conservative enough. He re-joined the party a few months after an unsuccessful run for the White House as an independent candidate. He was defeated in a primary in 2000 by John Sununu.

Pass your gun laws. I will not beg the government for a license to continue to be a handgun owner. I will not submit to being fingerprinted or photographed or interrogated like a criminal for claiming my birthright as a free American. I will not register a single gun that I own. I will not surrender a single gun that I own. I will not apply for an "arsenal" license because I own more than 20 guns or more than a thousand rounds of ammunition. I will not attend mandatory safety training, nor will I submit to a test to prove that I'm fit to be a gun owner. And Miss [Attorney General Janet] Reno, I have this to say to you: If you send your jack-booted, baby-burning bushwhackers to confiscate my guns, pack them a lunch; it will be a damned long day. The Branch Davidians were amateurs; I'm a professional.
>   —*NRA Board Member Lt. Harry Thomas. Denver Post,* 12-29-95.

The whole process was completely transparent . . . I'm trying to figure out how there can be a conflict of interest if everyone knows.
>   —*Gun-rights Lobbyist Joseph Olson,* who wrote the Minnesota law allowing citizens to carry concealed handguns. The law, which went in to effect 5-28-03, contained a provision naming Olson's company as one of six qualified to train instructors for those seeking gun permits. The company,

The American Association of Certified Firearms Instructors, Inc., is the only for-profit business mentioned in the law. Conrad deFiebre, "Trainer's role in new gun law questioned," *Star-Tribune*, 7-9-03.

Gun control is based on the premise that guns increase crime, and therefore guns should be controlled. Yet that ignores the fact that millions of guns are and have been owned in America that have never been involved in any crime. Ironically, evidence from areas where guns are banned or strictly regulated indicates that generally only criminals have them. If we really want to fight crime, we need to focus on the criminals rather than their tools. That will do more to curb firearm violence than gun control ever could.

  —*Sen. Larry Craig (R-ID)*, "Second Amendment Rights," Craig.senate.gov, 7-12-03.

San Francisco Deputy District Attorney Nathan Ballard is targeting a different industry as Public Enemy No. 1. He's spearheading San Francisco's lawsuit against gun manufacturers, an effort that is spreading across America. "They are practically the only industry that can harm people and go largely unregulated," Ballard says about gun makers. But Ballard has yet to demonstrate that guns are to blame for violence, any more than cars are responsible for drunk driving or Harvard is responsible for Al Gore.

  —*Oliver North*, syndicated columnist and former Iran-contra collaborator, discussing "frivolous lawsuits." "Open Season on Micky D's," Townhall.com, 11-29-02.

It's like saying we're going to limit the right of people to peaceably assemble to one assembly a month.

  —*State Sen. Ed Petka (R-IL)* explaining his opposition to a bill capping an individual's new gun purchases to one per month. The bill was part of Mayor Daley's effort to reduce gun violence in Chicago neighborhoods. Christie Parsons and Ray Long, "Senate Rejects Daley's Gun Plan," *Chicago Tribune*, 5-17-03.

I would urge that the firearms industry hold the line and not cave in to these abusive legal tactics being perpetrated by trial lawyers and by certain cash-strapped cities who, in an effort to disguise their own inadequate responses to the problems within our communities, are looking for a scapegoat.

> —*Rep. Bob Barr* in support of his proposed bill, "The Firearms Heritage Preservation Act," granting the arms industry immunity from lawsuits. George McEvoy, "Barr Taking On Gunmaker Suits With Both Barrels," *Palm Beach Post*, 5-15-99.

You in this room, whom many would say are among the most powerful people on earth, you are shamed into silence! Because you embrace a view at odds with the cultural warlords. If that is the outcome of cultural war, and you are the victims, I can only ask the gravely obvious question: What'll become of the right itself? Or other rights not deemed acceptable by the thought police? What other truth in your heart will you disavow with your hand? I remember when European Jews feared to admit their faith. The Nazis forced them to wear six-pointed yellow stars sewn on their chests as identity badges. It worked. So what color star will they pin on our coats? How will the self-styled elite tag us? There may not be a Gestapo officer on every street corner yet, but the influence on our culture is just as pervasive.

> —*NRA Vice-President Charlton Heston* at the Free Congress Foundation's 20th Anniversary Gala. VPC.org, 12-7-97.

Charlton Heston: I grew up in Michigan on the Au Sable River. I learned to be an American in a one-room schoolhouse. That is why it irritates me to see Gore come here telling us what he knows about guns and unions. Now, he's saying I'm with you guys on guns. In any other time or place you'd be looking for a lynching mob.

Crowd: Let's do it! I've got a rope!

> —*An NRA rally in Walker, MI.* Theresa D. McClellan, "Heston declares war on Gore," *Grand Rapids Press*, 10-17-00.

We are here in Michigan where you had the most heinous shooting and all the president [Clinton] could say was that if we had trigger locks, the nurturing crack dealers would have used them.
    —*Wayne LaPierre*, mentioning the case of a six-year-old girl who was killed by a classmate near Flint, MI. *Ibid.*

If we win we'll have a president where we can work out of their office, unbelievably friendly relations.
    —*Kayne Robinson,* Vice President of the National Rifle Association, before an audience in Los Angeles. "The NRA In The Oval Office?" *Hartford Courant,* 5-22-00.

Take your daughter or son to work today, if you want to support the feminist agenda. But if you're looking to give your daughter a real edge in this dangerous world, then we suggest a new holiday. Make April 24th Teach your Daughters to Shoot Day!
    —*Gary Aldrich*, former FBI agent, and founder of the conservative Patrick Henry Center for Individual Liberty. "Teach our Daughters to Shoot Day," Townhall.com, 4-25-03.

One amendment today said we could not sell guns to anybody under drug treatment. So does that mean if you go into a black community, you cannot sell a gun to any black person . . .
    —*Rep. Barbara Cubin (R-WY)*, attacking amendments to H.R. 1036, the Protection of Lawful Commerce in Arms Act. *Congressional Record*, H2989, 4-9-03. Rep. Melvin Watt (D-NC) objected to these comments, and Cubin was asked to withdraw them but she refused. "Mr. Watt, who is black, asked that she be punished for inappropriate language. But his proposal was defeated, largely on party lines." John Tierney, "House Votes to Limit Lawsuits Against Gun Manufacturers," *New York Times,* 4-10-03.

As a law enforcement official, I know crimes are caused by criminals, not by the gun industry. Indeed, by providing good-qual-

ity firearms at reasonable prices to law-abiding citizens and law-
men, the gun industry helps reduce crime.

  —*William Pryor*, Alabama Attorney General and Bush Ad-
    ministration nominee for the Federal Appeals court in At-
    lanta. PFAW.org, no date.

RESPECTING OUR ELDERS

On the Senate Floor Senator Robert Byrd said, "today I weep for my country"—I hope he didn't soil the sheets—"no more is the image of America one of strong yet benevolent peace-keeper, we flaunt our super-power status with arrogance," he said.

> —*Rush Limbaugh*, promotional excerpt during a web broadcast of the "Lee Rodgers and Melanie Morgan Show," KSFO-AM 560, 3-21-03.

The whole question of the seniors and drugs is, they don't want to pay any money for their drugs, not even those who can afford it. The people's—people go to Miami, they go to play bingo, they do all these things. But what they don't want to do is, they don't want to pay any money for the drugs, and they want the government . . . And they should be a little ashamed of themselves, but at least they're using private industry instead of HCFA, the Medicare thing where, you know, they have a picture of Joe Stalin on the wall there because that's their idol.

> —*Robert Novak*, "Capital Gang," CNN, 3-8-03.

As I write this, the full orchestra of the Philharmonic Symphony gives Handel's Messiah full volume in my head. After seventeen resolutions and twelve plus years, Iraq is not deviating one bit from its past behaviour and the United Nations just can't help but go down the toilet with Saddam. A fitting end to a United Nations that has done nothing but steal money and sovereignty from the free people of the United States and suppress liberty around the world.

If they [Democratic Hispanic members of the U.S. House] have a defense for their actions, they should deliver it to the kids in uniform that could one day have their—shot off to protect these ninnies! Even Tom Daschle, Senate leader, committed to President Bush today . . . he's just waiting for doddering old Bob Byrd, the senile senator from West Virginia, to shut up and sit down so the senate can vote!

> —*E-mail sent by a White House intern to Hispanic leaders.* A White House spokeswoman claimed it was a mistake. Bill McAllister, "White House e-mail calls Byrd 'Senile.' Mistakenly sent message also rips Hispanic leaders," *Charleston Daily Mail,* 10-12-02.

My grandparents' generation thought being on the government dole was disgraceful, a blight on the family's honor. Today's senior citizens blithely cannibalize their grandchildren because they have a right to get as much "free" stuff as the political system will permit them to extract . . . Big government is the drug of choice for multinational corporations and single moms, for regulated industries and rugged Midwestern farmers, and militant senior citizens.

> —*Judge Janice Rogers Brown,* Bush nominee for a seat on the Federal Appeals Court in Washington. Her nomination has been filibustered by the Senate Democrats. "Fifty ways to lose your freedom," speech to the Institute of Justice, 8-12-00.

I would deny [the senior citizen] plaintiff relief because she has failed to establish the public policy against age discrimination "inures to the benefit of the public" or is "fundamental and substantial" . . . Discrimination based on age . . . does not mark its victim with a "stigma of inferiority and second class citizenship" . . . ; it is the unavoidable consequence of that universal leveler: time.

> —*Ibid.* Dissenting opinion in *Stevenson v. Superior Court,* 941P.2d1157, 1177, 1187 (Cal. 1997).

I can say this because I'm not an elected official: the most self-ish group in America today is senior citizens. Their demands on Washington are: "Give us more and more and more." They have become the new welfare state, and given the size and po-litical clout of this constituency, it's very dangerous. One of the biggest myths in politics today is this idea that grandparents care about their grandkids. What they really care about is that that Social Security check and those Medicare payments are made on a timely basis.

   —*Stephen Moore*, co-founder of the conservative campaign fundraising group Club for Growth, in an interview with *The American Spectator*, Nov/Dec 2002.

PART II

GIVE WAR A CHANCE

"Bring 'em on."
—GEORGE W. BUSH

The Art of Diplomacy

After 9/11, NYC has already a big expensive hole downtown. Do they really need another on the East side of the island? Moreover, NYC already has the Mafia, so they are up to their limit in the corruption department, too. So who needs a United Nations? Not us and not the USA.

—*Barbara Stanley*, "United Nations Outs Itself—Dangerous Marxist Money-Hole in NYC," Bluestarbase.org, 3-7-03.

North Korea is a regime arming with missiles and weapons of mass destruction, while starving its citizens. Iran aggressively pursues these weapons and exports terror, while an unelected few repress the Iranian people's hope for freedom. Iraq continues to flaunt its hostility toward America and to support terror.

The Iraqi regime has plotted to develop anthrax, and nerve gas, and nuclear weapons for over a decade. This is a regime that has already used poison gas to murder thousands of its own citizens—leaving the bodies of mothers huddled over their dead children. This is a regime that agreed to international inspections—then kicked out the inspectors. This is a regime that has something to hide from the civilized world. States like these, and their terrorist allies, constitute an axis of evil, arming to threaten the peace of the world.

By seeking weapons of mass destruction, these regimes pose a grave and growing danger. They could provide these arms to terrorists, giving them the means to match their hatred. They could attack our allies or attempt to blackmail the United States. In any of these cases, the price of indifference would be catastrophic.

. . . We will develop and deploy effective missile defenses to protect America and our allies from sudden attack. And all nations should know: America will do what is necessary to ensure our nation's security . . .
—*George W. Bush*, State of the Union Address, 1-29-02.

Tim Russert: How do you respond to those who suggest that the war on terror should have been focused on al-Qaeda, and that the resources that are now applied to Iraq are misapplied, that Saddam was not the threat that he was presented by the administration, and the war should have been focused on Osama bin Laden and al Qaeda?
Donald Rumsfeld: Tim, we said from the outset that there are several terrorist networks that have global reach and that there were several countries that were harboring terrorists that have global reach. We weren't going into Iraq when we were hit on September 11. And the question is: Well, what do you do about that? If you know there are terrorists and you know there's terrorist states—Iraq's been a terrorist state for decades—and you know there are countries harboring terrorists, we believe, correctly, I think, that the only way to deal with it is—you can't just hunker down and hope they won't hit you again. You simply have to take the battle to them.
—*"Meet The Press,"* NBC, 11-2-03.

Japan really knew how to take an ass-kicking and they were honorable about it instead of jumping up and turning around and spitting in our faces.
—*Roe Conn*, referring to Japan's defeat in WWII and condemning Germany's attitude toward the Iraq war. "Roe and Gary Show," WLS-AM 890, 3-25-03

Over half the membership [of the United Nations] are thugs, they are terrorists themselves.
—*Rush Limbaugh*. Audio played on "World News Tonight," ABC, 10-2-03.

... Let me talk about North Korea. I loathe Kim Jong II. I've got a visceral reaction to this guy because he is starving his people. They tell me, we don't need to move too fast [against Kim] because the financial burdens on people will be so immense if we try to—if this guy were to topple. Who would take care of—I just don't buy that. Either you believe in freedom, and want to—and worry about the human condition, or you don't. I don't know if that gives you insight as to how I think . . . there is a value system that cannot be compromised, and that is the values that we praise. And if the values are good enough for our people, they ought to be good enough for others, not in a way to impose because these are God-given values. These aren't United States-created values. These are values of freedom and the human condition and mothers loving their children.

—*George W. Bush*. Bob Woodward, "A Course of 'Confident Action'; Bush Says Other Countries Will Follow Assertive U.S. in Combating Terror," *Washington Post*, 11-19-02.

Reporter: Mr. Boucher, do you have anything on the proposal for the creation of a European Union military headquarters in Brussels independent of NATO, something that has angered the United States . . . ?

State Department Spokesman Richard Boucher: I'm not quite sure what proposal that is. You mean the one from the four countries [Belgium, Germany, France and Luxembourg] that got together and had a little . . . had a little bitty summit . . . Yeah, [Belgium] the chocolate makers. Sorry. No, I . . . I think they've been referred to that way in the press; I shouldn't repeat things I see in the press.

—*Al Kamen*, "Not So 'New' After All," *Washington Post*, 9-5-03.

Every now and then we've got to remind these guys we've got the Big Portabella. I don't say drop one on the people. Wait for

a windless day and drop one out in the desert. Just remind them
that you've got the Big Persuader.

> —*Dennis Miller.* Dave Tianen, "Comic Miller Scores Check-
> mate," *Milwaukee Journal-Sentinel*, 1-16-03.

. . . I'm not sure my friend Michael Ledeen will thank me for
ascribing authorship to him and he may have only been semi-
serious when he crafted it, but here is the bedrock tenet of the
Ledeen Doctrine in more or less his own words: "Every ten
years or so, the United States needs to pick up some small crappy
little country and throw it against the wall, just to show the
world we mean business." That's at least how I remember
Michael phrasing it at a speech at the American Enterprise Institute about a decade ago (Ledeen is one of the most entertain-
ing public speakers I've ever heard, by the way).

> —*Jonah Goldberg*, "Baghdad Delenda Est, Part Two, Get on
> with it," *National Review Online*, 4-23-02.

I think we should be very hard on the French government. I do
not believe that we should back off one inch, and I think when
this war is over we need to rethink how we relate to the United
Nations, and we need to rethink how we relate to France. Because this French government—Chirac—has deliberately and
maliciously tried to undermine us . . .

> —*Newt Gingrich.* "Sean Hannity Radio Show," 3-19-03

I think that's wrong, especially with a country that had mad
cow disease. I think it's a health issue that we ought to at least
let people know this product [French wine] has been manufac-
tured with raw bovine blood.

> —*House Speaker Dennis Hastert (R-IL).* Mike Dorning and
> Jill Zuckman, "Hastert Blisters France on Iraq War Resis-
> tance," *Chicago Tribune*, 2-27-03.

There's a big question as to whether or not, you know, the uh,
there should be any enforcement of any business contracts, oil

contracts made between the regime of Saddam Hussein and countries like France, and Russia, and others that did not support the war, and the answer is no! Heck no! Double heck no! We're not gonna have it.

—*Sean Hannity* on the UN's Oil for Food program, 4-21-03.

And as I stated before, the debate on this issue is just as important as the passage of the amendment. There needs to be some message sent to any country that chooses to put in harm's way American and allied soldiers that there will be a penalty. The message should be, "Do not tread on me."

Now, that does not mean that we do not want them as allies in the future. I would state, and I do not mean to demean Turkey by making this point, but merely to make a point, if my own daughters intentionally did something egregious, I am surely, Mr. Chairman, not going to raise their allowance. I love them. I want their love in the future. And the same goes for Turkey.

—*Rep. Randy Cunningham (R-CA)*, arguing against a provision to pay one billion dollars in aid to Turkey. *Congressional Record*, H2747, 4-3-03.

... the war that should serve to say to a lot of the, these piss-ant countries, "you can think whatever you want about us, but you keep your mouth shut and don't do anything about it or we're going to kick your ass!" ... I do hope by the way, I hope we get that Tariq Aziz, Saddam's butt-boy, I hope we get him alive, because I want to hear him cry like a baby when he's told the deal is over, I really do.

—*Lee Rodgers.* "Lee Rodgers and Melanie Morgan Show," KSFO-AM 560, 3-21-03.

Please, President Bush, for God's sake, in addition to getting us out of that whorehouse on the East River called the United Nations, just have the State Department call Hans Blix, tell him he is persona non grata, get out of the United States and don't

ever even think about coming back, go back to Sweden and raise reindeer or whatever the hell you're gonna do, don't think of ever setting foot on this continent again.
    —*Ibid.*

. . . Jacques Chirac isn't marching in front of some of those Iraqi soldiers, it would be a very satisfying thing to watch, put that on pay TV and I'm in, 50 bucks, a hundred, whatever, to see that S.O.B. get just blown to smithereens . . .
    —*Ibid.*, 3-25-03.

They remind me of an aging movie actress in the 1940's who's still trying to dine out on her looks. The cynical role France is playing proves that you cannot be a great nation unless you have great purpose, and they've lost their purpose.
    —*Sen. John McCain (R-AZ).* "Face the Nation," CBS, 2-16-03.

. . . And I'm tellin' you, we've gotta look at them as the pariahs that they've been and frankly, in the case of Chirac and other forces against liberty and forces against humanity. I mean if they want to contribute food and money and humanitarian assistance, that's fine, but that's it! And I gotta tell you something, there's gonna be a big battle in this country over this . . . Look, I fear our own State Department is gonna, you know, be the voice of these people in our government . . . we're gonna have all this pressure to rebuild these coalitions and once again we're gonna be urged to embrace the United Nations Security Council where the French are going to be able to thwart our efforts, undermine our positions and it's gonna be a grave mistake. You punish bad behavior, you do not reward it, and if we go back to the UN no good is gonna come from that and surely we've got to have learned the danger from that approach in the last several months, and the truth is the French, the Germans, the Russians and Chinese, they don't care about the fate of the Iraqi people, this is all about dollars . . .
    —*Sean Hannity.* "Sean Hannity Radio Show," 4-8-03.

. . . and I think the pressure between Kofi Annan representing the bureaucratic pressure of the UN at its worst, the French and the Germans and the Russians who did everything they could to block this from happening, and the State Department bureaucracy, those three forces are all going to be at work trying to convince the President to give up in diplomacy what he has won militarily . . . and I want to point out that the French have a big economic interest in this because it is their government-owned oil company that has a sweetheart contract with the dictatorship, and I'm not sure we ought to saddle the people of Iraq with sweetheart deals on behalf of the French oil company made by a dictator who didn't care at all about the well-being of his people.

   —*Newt Gingrich. Ibid.*

I read your book. When you get through, you say, "If I could put a nuclear device inside Foggy Bottom, I think that's the answer." I mean, you get through this, and you say, "We've got to blow that thing up."

   —*Pat Robertson*, interviewing Joel Mowbray, author of *Dangerous Diplomacy: How the State Department Endangers America's Security.* "700 Club," CBN. "Robertson remark on TV condemned," *Chicago Tribune*, 10-12-03.

Let it be said before we know the outcome of the war in Iraq that America and the world are inordinately lucky to have George W. Bush as America's president. In fact, I would go further. To the extent that one is ever able to see the hand of God in history—and since biblical times, one has never been given certitude in this regard—I believe that either divine intervention or good luck on the magnitude of a lottery win explains George W. Bush's rise to the position of president . . . George W. Bush is regularly described by American and foreign critics as a "cowboy." They are right, and for this, too, we should thank God. The Europeans and Democrats use that term as an epithet, but for many Americans the image of a lone cowboy fight-

ing bad men is a revered one. Many of us have far more moral
confidence in the Lone Ranger than in Jacques Chirac or Kofi
Annan. The Lone Ranger rides again. Thank God he does.
    —*Dennis Prager*, "The Lone Ranger Rides Again,"
    Townhall.com, 3-11-03.

When it comes to our security, we really don't need anybody's
permission.
    —*George W. Bush*. Thomas Friedman, "Fire, Ready, Aim,"
    New York Times, 3-9-03.

Here's this little pot-bellied Kim Jong II, crying like a little baby
in the crib almost like he doesn't have his two bucks to co-pay
for his prescription, going, waahaa, waahaa, notice me, notice
me, I will nuke you, I will nuke you, I have a bomb!
    —*Rush Limbaugh*, 3-17-03.

The quagmire happens to be with diplomacy. I mean, that's what
you get when you resort to diplomacy. By definition, you find
yourself in a quagmire.
    —*Ibid.*, 4-21-03.

CAKEWALK: ONGOING WAR

Now, I think things have gotten so bad inside Iraq, from the standpoint of the Iraqi people, my belief is we will, in fact, be greeted as liberators.
>   —*Vice-President Dick Cheney*. "Meet The Press," NBC, 3-16-03.

There may be pockets of resistance, but very few Iraqis are going to defend Saddam Hussein.
>   —*Richard N. Perle*. "Hardball," 2-03. Perle, a long-time Iraq hawk was forced to resign as Chairman of the Defense Advisory Board because of a conflict of interest. He remains a member of the board.

I don't agree that you need an enormous number of American troops . . . [Saddam's army] is down to one-third than it was before, and I think it would be a cakewalk.
>   —*Kenneth Adelman*, member of the Defense Policy Board and former UN ambassador during the Reagan administration, talking to Wolf Blitzer about the potential war with Iraq. CNN, 12-6-01.

The cost of the war will be small. We can afford the war, and we'll put it behind us.
>   —*Treasury Secretary John W. Snow* before the House Ways and Means Committee. David E. Rosenbaum, "Tax cuts and war have seldom mixed," *New York Times*, 3-9-03.

He [Rumsfeld] talked about his style of probing his staff to think ahead, to think out of the box, to make sure we're thinking

about problems in every possible way. It's a good thing. We're asking these questions instead of blindly walking down the path.
> —*House Armed Services Committee member Rep. John Kline (R-MN)*, spinning Defense Secretary Donald Rumsfeld's memo of 10-16-03. Rumsfeld questioned the long-term strategy and effectiveness of the current war on terrorism. James Janega, "Rumsfeld memo roils D.C.," *Chicago Tribune*, 10-23-03.

Let me say one other thing. The images you are seeing on television you are seeing over, and over, and over, and it's the same picture of some person walking out of some building with a vase, and you see it 20 times, and you think, "My goodness, were there that many vases? Is it possible that there were that many vases in the whole country?"
> —*Donald H. Rumsfeld,* talking about looting of the Iraqi Antiquities Museum. U.S. Department of Defense website, Defenselink.mil, Department briefing, 4-11-03.

Tim Russert: How did we allow that museum to be looted?
Sec. of Defense Donald Rumsfeld : "How did we allow?" Now, that's really a wonderful, amazing statement . . . But we didn't allow it. It happened. And that's what happens when you go from a dictatorship with repressed order, police state, to something that is going to be different. There's a transition period, and no one is in control. There are periods where—there was still fighting in Baghdad. We don't allow bad things to happen. Bad things do happen in life and people do loot. We've seen that in the United States. It's happened in every country. It's a shame when it happens.
> —*"Meet The Press,"* MSNBC, 4-13-03. Professor of Archaeology Maguire Gibson had contacted State Department officials "months before the war started" warning them of the danger to the Antiquities Museum in Baghdad: "Gibson noted ruefully that the U.S. Military assigned men to chip away the disrespectful mural of Former President George Bush on

the floor of the Al Rashid Hotel, yet failed to save the match-
less legacy of the museum." Jeremy Manier, "U. of C. Pleads
for Iraq Artifacts," *Chicago Tribune*, 4-15-03.

Russert: The Red Cross said hospitals were also looted. Does
that surprise you? I mean, it's one thing for the Iraqis to ran-
sack, loot Saddam's palaces and steal his faucets. It's quite another to loot their own museum and their own hospitals. Did
that surprise you?
Rumsfeld: Surprise me? I don't—disorder happens every time
there's a transition. We saw it in Eastern European countries when
they move from the Communist system to a free system. We've
seen it in Los Angeles here in our own country. We've seen it in
Detroit, we've seen it in city after city when there was a difficulty.
And it always breaks your heart. You're always sorry to see it,
and it isn't something that someone allows or doesn't allow. It's
something that happens. We know there are people—there are
people who do bad things. There are people who steal from hospitals in the United States. So does it surprise me that people
went into a hospital and did something? I guess it doesn't surprise me. It's a shame, it's too bad, and we're trying to get medical supplies in to those hospitals that were robbed, and we are
doing it, and we are having good success at it.
    —*Ibid.*

Looting is an unfortunate thing. Human beings are not perfect.
We've seen looting in this country. We've seen riots at soccer
games in various countries around the world. We've seen destruction after athletic events in our own country. No one likes
it. No one allows it. It happens, and it's unfortunate. And to the
extent it can be stopped, it should be stopped. To the extent it
happens in a war zone, it's difficult to stop.
    —*Sec. Rumsfeld* with Gen. Myers, Defenselink.mil, 4-15-03.

Frank Luntz: . . . But no one ever said this was going to be easy. And no one ever said that—

Chris Matthews: Oh, yes they did. I heard the word "cakewalk." I heard Chalabi; I heard Wolfowitz. All of those guys said those people are going to be cheering us. The phrase "happy Iraqi" was used over and over again. They were going to cheer. It was going to be easy because all we had to do was decapitate the bad guys. They'll be part of us . . .

Luntz: So Chris, you're going to let that fringe in Iraq—and they're not necessarily Iraqis, as you on your own show have shown. You've got some dissidents from Saudi Arabia, from Egypt, from Syria that have come in. You're going to let terrorists determine the future of—

Matthews: No, no. Frank, most countries resist being taken over and occupied. We should have assumed that before going in.

Luntz: No, most countries—Hey, Chris. The people in most countries want to be liberated. They were being occupied by Saddam Hussein.

—*"Hardball,"* MSNBC, 9-16-03.

Well, the independent voter is reacting in the same way that most voters are because they're seeing the same visuals. Chris, I've got to emphasize the pictures are what matter in Iraq. I'm a linguist, and I follow how people communicate. This is one case where words don't matter. If they don't see visuals, positive visuals of things happening—and it's hard to show, I admit it—if they don't see positive visuals, they're going to be hostile to the war.

So this administration, it's not a matter of getting the words right. They've got to find some way to convince the networks and the cable companies to get the pictures right.

—*Republican pollster Frank Luntz.* "Hardball," MSNBC, 10-28-03.

They understand the visual as well as anybody ever has. They watched what we did, they watched the mistakes of Bush I, they watched how Clinton kind of stumbled into it, and they've taken it to an art form.

— *Michael K. Deaver,* Ronald Reagan's chief image maker, talking about George W. Bush's White House communications department. Elisabeth Bumiller, "Keepers of Bush image lift stagecraft to new heights," *New York Times,* 5-16-03.

Again, I will repeat myself, that the more progress we make on the ground, the more free the Iraqis become, the more electricity is available, the more jobs are available, the more kids that are going to school, the more desperate these killers become, because they can't stand the thought of a free society.

— *George W. Bush.* "President Bush, Ambassador Bremer Discuss Progress in Iraq; Remarks by the President and Special Envoy to Iraq, Ambassador Bremer, in Photo Opportunity, The Oval Office," Whitehouse.gov, 10-27-03.

The fact of the matter is that this [increased American casualties] is a sign of the success of our operation, not its failure.

— *Republican strategist Ralph Reed.* "Hardball," MSNBC, 10-28-03.

There are some who feel like that, you know, the conditions are such that they can attack us there. My answer is, "Bring 'em on." We have the force necessary to deal with the situation.

— *George W. Bush* speaking about Iraq to reporters at the White House. Bob Kemper, "Bush Berates Iraqi Insurgents," *Chicago Tribune,* 7-3-03.

What the president was expressing there is his confidence in the men and women of the military to handle the military mission that they still remain in the middle of. Major combat operations have ended, but, obviously, combat has not for those who are there.

— *Ari Fleischer* defending the "bring em on" remark. *Ibid.*

The "Mission Accomplished" sign, of course, was put up by the members of the U.S.S. *Abraham Lincoln,* saying that their mission was accomplished. I know it was attributed somehow to some ingenious advance man from my staff. They weren't that ingenious, by the way.

> —*George W. Bush.* "Bush Steps Away From Victory Banner," *New York Times,* 10-29-03. At the time of this remark, Elisabeth Bumiller commented: "The most elaborate—and criticized—White House event so far was Mr. Bush's speech aboard the Abraham Lincoln announcing the end of major combat in Iraq. White House officials say that a variety of people, including the president, came up with the idea, and that Mr. Sforza embedded himself on the carrier to make preparations days before Mr. Bush's landing in a flight suit and his early evening speech. Media strategists noted afterward that Mr. Sforza and his aides had choreographed every aspect of the event, even down to the members of the Lincoln crew arrayed in coordinated shirt colors over Mr. Bush's right shoulder and the 'Mission Accomplished' banner placed to perfectly capture the president and the celebratory two words in a single shot. The speech was specifically timed for what image makers call 'magic hour light,' which cast a golden glow on Mr. Bush. If you looked at the TV picture, you saw there was flattering light on his left cheek and slight shadowing on his right, Mr. King said. 'It looked great.'" "Keepers of Bush image lift stagecraft to new heights," *New York Times,* 5-16-03.

. . . I'll tell you what's going to happen is, the more people who go into that country and see how serious the situation is, the needs of those people, and they're real needs, they're going to report there's a humanitarian crisis, the implication that it just occurred. It didn't just occur. When they say some city's been— one-third of the city doesn't have sufficient water, compare that with six months ago when maybe half of the city didn't have sufficient water.

> —*Donald H. Rumsfeld.* U.S. Department of Defense website: Defenselink.mil, 4-9-03.

There is an understandable tendency to look back on America's experience in post-war Germany and see only the successes. But as some of you here today surely remember, the road we traveled was very difficult. 1945 through 1947 was an especially challenging period. Germany was not immediately stable or prosperous. SS officers—called "werewolves"—engaged in sabotage and attacked both coalition forces and those locals cooperating with them—much like today's Baathist and Fedayeen remnants.

> —*National Security Advisor Condoleezza Rice*, addressing the 104th national convention of Veterans of Foreign Wars in San Antonio, 8-29-03. To further confuse this imaginary issue, Dr. Rice mistakenly called World War II Allied armies "coalition forces." VFW.org.

—Indeed I suspect that some of you in this hall today, especially those who served in Germany during World War II or in the period immediately after the war were not surprised that some Ba'athists have kept on fighting. You will recall that some dead-enders fought on during and after the defeat of the Nazi regime in Germany . . . One group of those dead-enders was known as "werewolves." They and other Nazi regime remnants targeted allied soldiers and they targeted Germans who cooperated with the allied forces. Mayors were assassinated including the American appointed Mayor of Aachen, the first major German city to be liberated. Children as young as ten were used as snipers, radio broadcast and leaflets warned Germans not to collaborate with the Allies. They plotted sabotage of factories, power plants, rail lines. They blew up police stations and government building, and they destroyed stocks of art and antiques that were stored by the Berlin museum. Does this sound familiar?

> —*Defense Secretary Donald Rumsfeld, Ibid.* Daniel Benjamin, former Clinton NSC aide wrote in *Slate* that "Werewolf amounted to next to nothing" and that "the total number of post-conflict American combat casualties in Germany— was zero." Al Kamen, "Not So 'New' After All," *Washington Post*, 9-5-03.

TREATIES NO, NEW NUKES YES

The Secretary of State,
Washington, May 5, 2003.
Hon. John Warner,
Chairman, Committee on Armed Services,
U.S. Senate.

Dear Mr. Chairman: I am writing to express support for the President's FY2004 budget request to fund the feasibility and cost study for the Robust Nuclear Earth Penetrator (RNEP), and to repeal the FY1994 legislation that prohibits the United States from conducting research and development on low yield nuclear weapons. I do not believe that these legislative steps will complicate our ongoing efforts with North Korea. Inasmuch as work on the RNEP was authorized and funded in last year's National Defense Authorization Act, I believe that North Korea already has factored the RNEP into its calculations and will not vary those calculations depending on how Congress acts on this element of the FY2004 budget request.

Thank you for your important work on these issues and please do not hesitate to ask if I can be of further assistance in the future.

Sincerely,
Colin L. Powell
—*Congressional Record*, S6679, 5-20-03.

What we know from intelligence is that there are a lot of other nations in the world that know one thing: If you get deep enough underground with enough concrete and steel above your head, they can't get you. That is exactly the kind of facility being built by our potential enemies today. There is only one way to get those, and that is through a precise low-yield nuclear weapon. The design of those weapons is certainly in the mind of our scientists. And if they are allowed to think about this, to do some research on it, we think at least we would be prepared, should the Pentagon decide that it wants to ask the Congress for the authority to go forward with the program, to be able to do so. The point has been made adequately, this does not authorize anything. This merely removes a self-imposed prohibition on the United States. No other country in the world is suffering under this same prohibition. . . . It has also been noted that they could be very useful in the destruction of chemical and biological agents or weapons which are not easily destroyed by conventional weaponry and in any event where the fallout can be more dangerous than the weapon just sitting there on the ground. If you put a large conventional explosion on top of chemical or biological agents, you could end up dispersing those agents in a very dangerous way over a far greater area than if the enemy actually tried to use the weapon. But with a precise low-yield nuclear weapon, you might well be able to destroy that biological or chemical agent or weapon. In this new world there may well be reasons to have these weapons. For somebody to suggest it is nuts is simply an uneducated approach to this very serious issue . . .

—*Sen. John Kyl (R-AZ). Congressional Record*, S6677, 5-20-03.

Russian Reporter: There are people who say that the fact of the U.S. withdrawal from the ABM Treaty will lead to another arms race. Is that true?

Donald Rumsfeld: They are wrong. They are not just a little wrong, they are very wrong. The whole history of your adult life proves they are wrong. Since the beginning of Arms Control in the 1960s and '70s the numbers of weapons were going up and up and up. That was an arms race during the era of arms control. President Putin and President Bush have announced they are going to have the weapons go down and down and down from thousands down to 1700 to 2200. Any suggestion by anybody, attributed or unattributed, that some change in the ABM treaty is going to lead to an arms race is just flap—not so. In fact, the next five years will prove what I've just said to be the case.

    —*Donald H. Rumsfeld.* A newsbriefing in Werevan, Armenia. Defenselink.mil, 12-15-01.

To date, more than 50 generals, admirals and senior foreign policy leaders have come out in opposition to the treaty, including, I might add, defense secretaries of every single Republican administration since Nixon . . . if the [Clinton] administration continues to stonewall, and refuses to address senators' concerns on the treaty's verifiability, constitutionality, universality and crushing effect on business, their opposition to making essential changes will ensure the Senate never ratifies the Chemical Weapons Convention.

    —*Sen. Jesse Helms (R-NC)*, Chairman of the Foreign Relations Committee, responding to President Clinton's call for passage of an international treaty outlawing chemical weapons. Thomas W. Lippman, "Sen. Helms Offers List of Treaty Opponents," *Washington Post*, 4-5-97.

The Clinton Administration's proposed Treaty (CTBT) is inconsistent with American security interests.

    . . . A Republican President will withdraw from Senate consideration any pending international conventions or treaties that erode the constitutional foundations of our Republic and will neither negotiate nor submit such agreements in the future.

    . . . The governments of North Korea, Iran, Syria, Iraq, Libya, Sudan and Cuba must know that America's first line of defense is not our shoreline, but their own borders. We will be proactive, not reactive, to strike the hand of terrorism before it can be raised against Americans.

—*Republican Party Platform*, adopted 8-12-96, pp. 33, 34, 35.

It [Chemical Weapons Treaty] is not verifiable and it will not work. It will facilitate the spread of poison gas to rogue nations most likely to use it against American citizens.

—*Sen. Jesse Helms.* William Neikirk, "Key Allies join Clinton on treaty," *Chicago Tribune*, 4-24-97. The treaty was passed in the Senate by a vote of 74-26.

But you're not gonna go out and get these entrepreneurial bad guys out there to sign the chemical weapons treaty, and even if they do they don't mean it . . . like the Russians, how many times did they violate nuclear treaties? This is an exercise in liberal symbolism, liberal feel good-ism, but in terms of—it's like any other law—we have laws against murder but it didn't stop Pedro Medina, but old Sparky did.

—*Rush Limbaugh* on the proposed ban on chemical weapons, 4-7-97. Pedro Medina was executed in Florida in an electric chair referred to by prison guards as "Old Sparky." The apparatus caught fire after the chair was switched on with the prisoner strapped in it.

In pursuit of arms control symbolism, we've reached a chemical pact undertaking to police the world for weapons we know a Japanese cult cooked up in a basement laboratory . . . For such gains American industry will be forced to open its plants to batches of international busybodies, actually working for who knows whom. Worst of all, the treaty specifically provides for "sharing" of chemical technologies; that is to say, in the end the treaty will not be a constraint on chemical weapons, but a vehicle for their proliferation.

—*Wall Street Journal* editorial, "Arms Control Mystique," 4-14-97.

The problem, as Will Rogers used to say, is that the United States has never lost a war or won a treaty. And history shows that a lot of the treaties that have been signed have not advanced the cause of peace, but have actually set them back. . . .

  —*Sen. John Kyl (R-AZ)*, giving his reasons for opposing Senate ratification of the Chemical Weapons Treaty. "Late Edition with Frank Sesno," CNN, 4-6-97.

I think the President [George W. Bush] is wise not to renounce unequivocally that he would never use a nuclear weapon before it has been used on us, particularly when people have the ability to threaten us with biological and chemical weapons that could cause even more loss of life than a single nuclear weapon. We need to keep our poise here. The President is reducing nuclear weapons. He is not expanding our nuclear weapons. The Defense Department and the President have not allowed the politically correct crowd or other groups to pressure him into saying we would never use a weapon before it is used on us.

  —*Sen. Jeff Sessions (R-AL)* defending the Bush Administration's reversal of a longstanding policy against the "first use" of nuclear weapons. The Bush bill requests funds for testing new nuclear weapons. *Congressional Record*, S6582, S6584, 5-19-03.

TREASON, TRAITORS, FREEDOM-FRIED FRENCHMEN

Let me be clear: Liberal ideas are not responsible for the terrorist attacks of September 11, 2001. They are, however, responsible for making America more vulnerable, for creating confusion in our society and among our children about what is right and wrong, and thus for placing our freedom and security at risk . . . It is therefore our job to stop them. Not just debate them, but defeat them.

—*Sean Hannity, Let Freedom Ring*, NY: Reganbooks, HarperCollins, 2002, p. 11.

The Pentagon's Iraqi Most Wanted "Deck of Death" playing cards was a huge hit with Americans. Now, NewsMax.com is raising the ante—with the Deck of Weasels, depicting the 54 worst leaders and celebrities who opposed America and were key members of "The United Nations of Weasels."

This hot new set of playing and informational cards—which will surely be a collector's item—depicts the enemies of America and Iraq's liberation in a satirical way while revealing the evidence of their hatred—their own quotes against America!

No doubt the Deck of Weasels will enrage those included—including Michael Moore, Tim Robbins, Jacques Chirac, Barbra Streisand, Teddy Kennedy, Kofi Annan and many more.

You'll laugh out loud looking at the faces of the world's greatest weasels—each wearing the beret of Saddam Hussein's Republican Guard—now dubbed "Saddam's Weasel Brigade."

Under each photo is each Weasel's quote revealing his anti-American, pro-Saddam ranting!

The Ace of Spades is none other than French Prime Minister Chirac, Saddam Hussein's partner in crime of 30 years, and includes his most infamous quote: "Our position is no matter what the circumstances, France will vote 'no.'" The *Washington Times*' new revelation that France helped Saddam's top goons escape shows just how relevant and useful this deck is.

The Deck of Weasels also includes many other notables, weasels such as NAFTA "partners" Vicente Fox of Mexico and Jean Chrétien of Canada, and others in our own Senate such as Teddy Kennedy and Robert "KKK" Byrd.

The Deck of Weasels is a who's who of celebrity weasels: Martin Sheen, Jane Fonda, Janeane Garofalo, Sean Penn, George Clooney, Susan Sarandon and more.

There will be enough in the Deck of Weasels to keep you laughing for years!

Each suite of the Deck of Weasels reveals America's enemies. The Spades are the most treacherous of the world's foreign leaders. The Diamonds are the most backstabbing U.S. leaders. The (bleeding) Hearts, of course, consist of Hollywood's woefully ill-informed would-be geopolitical "experts." And the Clubs include the worst of the biased media and self-appointed pundits.

And we have the Jokers, with their funny little hats: Jimmy Carter and Jesse Jackson.
   —*A NewsMax.com advertisement*, 9-10-03.

Pete Davis: Thank God Al Gore wasn't in office. Can you imagine what it would've been like if he'd been in there?
Wayne Kitchens: We'd be reading the Koran right now. (Laughter)
   —*Davis and Kitchens*, filling in for Talk Radio Host Kim Peterson, discussing the terrorist attacks on the second anniversary of 9-11. Newsradio WGST 640, Atlanta, 9-11-03.

The hindsight of history has shown that our efforts in the 1960s to end the war in Vietnam had two practical effects. The first was to prolong the war itself. Every testimony by North Viet-

namese generals in the postwar years has affirmed that they
knew they could not defeat the United States on the battlefield,
and that they counted on the division of our people at home to
win the war for them . . . The blood of hundreds of thousands
of Vietnamese, and tens of thousands of Americans, is on the
hands of the anti-war activists who prolonged the struggle and
gave victory to the Communists.

The second effect of the war was to surrender South Vietnam
to the forces of Communism. This resulted in the imposition of a
monstrous police state, the murder of hundreds of thousands of
innocent South Vietnamese, the incarceration in "re-education
camps" of hundreds of thousands more, and a quarter of a century of abject poverty imposed by crackpot Marxist economic
plans, which continue to this day. This, too, is the responsibility
of the so-called anti-war movement of the 1960s.

I say "so-called anti-war movement," because while many
Americans were sincerely troubled by America's war effort, the
organizers of this movement were Marxists and radicals who
supported a Communist victory and an American defeat. Today the same people and their youthful followers are organizing the campus demonstrations against America's effort to defend its citizens against the forces of international terrorism and
anti-American hatred, responsible for the September attacks.

If I have one regret from my radical years, it is that this
country was too tolerant towards the treason of its enemies
within. If patriotic Americans had been more vigilant in the
defense of their country, if they had called things by their right
names, if they had confronted us with the seriousness of our
attacks, they might have caught the attention of those of us
who were well-meaning but utterly misguided. And they might
have stopped us in our tracks . . .

—*David Horowitz*, "Horowitz's Notepad: An Open Letter
    to the 'Anti-War' Demonstrators: Think Twice Before You
    Bring The War Home," FrontPageMag.com, 9-27-01.

That liberalism is a mental disorder that has undermined our families, our society and our national security . . . The country is ever so slowly awakening to what has happened, but I don't know if we are going to be saved. Take a look at what's happening with Iraq. You have outright treason being committed by senators like Barbara Boxer. They might as well be working for Saddam Hussein. You've got people like Wolf Blitzer, who might as well be part of the propaganda machine of Saddam Hussein. If these people had been in power in the 1940s most of your readers would either be speaking German or be lampshades.

—*Michael Savage.* Jarret Wollstein and Christopher Ruddy, "Michael Savage: Stop the Left From Causing Another 9/11," NewsMax.com interview, 2-1-03.

My friend, there is a Fifth Column in America, an enemy within. It's the so-called "peace movement." Sign the e-petition to EX-POSE THE ENEMY WITHIN to editors and producers of the nation's largest newspapers, news magazines, and network newsrooms.

—*FrontPageMag.com*, 4-19-03.

. . . anybody today that buys a French product knowingly, unless you can absolutely avoid it but, if you buy French wine, *you* should be deemed a Benedict Arnold. A traitor. It's un-American right now and I believe it will be un-American for a long, long time to come.

—*Cigar Dave.* "Smoke This!" Radio Show, Miami, 640-AM WGST, Atlanta talk radio, 4-07-03.

In a symbolic effort to show their support for American troops protecting freedom abroad and their displeasure with France's continued refusal to stand with its U.S. allies, U.S. Rep. Bob Ney (OH-18), Chairman of the Committee on House Administration, today responded to a letter circulated by U.S. Rep. Walter Jones (NC-03), and ordered that "French fries" be removed from all restaurant menus in the three House office buildings and be replaced with freedom fries. Chairman Ney directed this change, as well as the new term, "freedom toast," instead of "French toast," in a letter to the House Chief Administrative Officer who supervises restaurant operations in the House. Ney and Jones will hold a press availability at 12 PM TODAY in the Longworth House Office Building cafeteria to make this name change official by changing the menu signs personally.

> —*From the website of the House Administration Committee,* under the headline: "House Office Buildings to Serve 'Freedom Fries' Reps. Ney and Jones Remove 'French' Fries From House Restaurant Menus," House.gov, 3-11-03.

When contemplating college liberals, you really regret once again that John Walker [John Walker Lind, the American Talib] is not getting the death penalty. We need to execute people like John Walker in order to physically intimidate liberals, by making them realize that they can be killed too. Otherwise they will turn out to be outright traitors.

> —*Ann Coulter* at the Conservative Political Action Conference 2002, in Crystal City, VA. PFAW.org, 2-26-02.

Ladies and Gentleman, I understand many of you out there are upset about Peter Arnett, he of the Hammurabi Division of the Democratic party, the Hammurabi Wing of the Democratic party, and many people are terrifically upset about this. Again, what's happened here, I think, is something everyone ought to be rejoicing about, instead of being angry.

> —*Rush Limbaugh* discussing reporter Peter Arnett's controversial interview on Iraqi television during Operation Iraqi Freedom, and Arnett's subsequent firing by NBC, 3-31-03. "The Hammurabi Division" was part of Saddam Hussein's Republican Guard.

They are absolutely committing sedition, or treason.

> —*Michael Savage* talking on MSNBC about anti-war protesters. Jim Rutenberg, "Cable's War Coverage Suggests a New 'Fox Effect' on Television," *New York Times,* 4-16-03.

These leftist stooges for anti-American causes are always given a free pass. Isn't it time to make them stand up and be counted for their views?
— *Joe Scarborough*, talk show host, talking about anti-war protesters on MSNBC. *Ibid.*

One of the great things that's in the news today, that's being absolutely ignored is that humanitarian aid ship, it's a British ship, the *Sir Galahad*, that is pulling into the port. That is gonna unload hundreds and hundreds of tons of stuff. Now, the people who are against this war resent the fact that we are actually good guys, and we're gonna go in there and we're trying to get rid of the bad guys and we want to bring food and medicine and water to these, these, these, horribly mistreated people. They would love to have that ship sink so it would never get there.
—*Don Wade.* "Don Wade and Roma," WLS-AM 890, 3-28-03.

Oh by the way the latest rumor here, Saddam Hussein has already fled the country, he's in California campaigning for Gray Davis.
—*Don Wade. Ibid.*, 7-29-03.

Sen. Edward Kennedy: His appeasement of Saddam may mean the death of the liberal-wing of the democratic party. Moderates like Joseph Lieberman and John Edwards are rising, Ted and his committed Ideologues risk extinction. At this point Senator Kennedy makes George McGovern look like a navy SEAL.
. . . Jacques Chirac: Replaces Michael Jackson as the most detested man in America. Maybe he should visit one of Jackson's plastic surgeons as he faces persona non grata in the USA.
—*Bill O'Reilly.* O'Reilly.com, 4-9-03.

This [a formal declaration of war by congress] would ensure the hands of the military are completely untied and Arnett (and others of his stripe) could have been charged with treason as well as lending aid and comfort to the enemy, been tried by military tribunal in the field and justifiably executed on conviction for the

treasonous scum he is, was and will seemingly always be. Once dead, Arnett could be cremated instead of buried and his ashes promptly flushed down the toilet.
   —*Timothy Rollins*, "Benedict Arnett," *The American Partisan*, 4-2-03.

Mr. Speaker . . . I want to read a letter from Charlie Daniels . . . We know Charlie Daniels is the songwriter who wrote The Devil Went Down to Georgia, among other things. He is great playing the fiddle, and he is a great American. So this is Charlie Daniels' letter, open letter to the Hollywood bunch. I am going to read directly from the letter:

> Okay, let's say just for a moment you bunch of pampered, overpaid, unrealistic children had your way and the USA did not go into Iraq. Let's say that you really get your way and we destroy all of our nuclear weapons, stick daisies in our gun barrels and sit around with some white wine and cheese and pat ourselves on the back, so proud of what we have done for world peace.
>
> Let's say that we cut the military budget to just enough to keep the National Guard on hand to help out with floods and fires. Let's say that we close down our military bases all over the world and bring our troops home, increase foreign aid, and drop all trade sanctions against everybody.
>
> I suppose that in your fantasy world, this would create a utopian world where everybody would live in peace. After all, the great monster, the United States of America, the cause of all of the world's trouble, would have disbanded its horrible military and certainly all of the other countries of the world would follow suit.
>
> After all, they only arm themselves to defend their country from the mean USA.
>
> Why, you bunch of pitiful, hypocritical, idiotic spoiled mugwumps. Get your head out of the sand and smell the Trade Towers burning.
>
> Do you think that a trip to Iraq by Sean Penn did anything but encourage a wanton murderer to think that the people of the USA didn't have the nerve or guts to fight him?

Barbara [*sic*] Streisand's fanatical and hateful rantings about George Bush makes about as much sense as Michael Jackson hanging a baby over a railing. You people need to get out of Hollywood once in a while and get into the real world. You'd be surprised at the hostility you would find out here. Stop in at a truck stop and tell an overworked long-distance trucker that you don't think Saddam Hussein is doing anything wrong.

Tell a farmer with a couple of sons in the United States military that you think the United States has no right to defend itself. Go down to Baxley, Georgia, and hold an antiwar rally and see what the folks down there think about you. You people are some of the most disgusting examples of a waste of protoplasm I've ever had the displeasure to hear about. Sean Penn, you are a traitor to the United States of America. You gave aid and comfort to the enemy. How many American lives will your little fact-finding trip to Iraq cost? You encourage Saddam Hussein to think that we didn't have the stomach for war.

You people protect one of the most evil men on the face of this earth and you won't lift a finger to save the life of an unborn baby. Freedom of choice, you say? . . . Well, I'm going to exercise some freedom of choice of my own. If I see any of your names on a marquee, I'm going to boycott the movie. I will completely stop going to the movies if I have to. In most cases, it certainly wouldn't be much of a loss.

You scoff at our military whose boots you are not even worthy to shine. They go to battle and risk their lives so ingrates like you can live in luxury. The day of reckoning is coming when you will be faced with the undeniable truth that the war against Saddam Hussein is the war on terrorism. America is in imminent danger.

You're either for her or against her. There is no middle ground. I think we all know where you stand. What do you think? God bless America.

Unquote, Charlie Daniels.

—*Rep. Jack Kingston (R-GA). Congressional Record,* H2389, 3-26-03.

You are seeking political advantage in the war on terrorism just exactly as you sought political advantage after the war on terrorism started on September 11. Just as you sought political advantage with the economy plundering [*sic*], just as you sought political advantage with the stock market collapse, just as you sought political advantage with the corporate scandals. You seek political advantage with the nation at war. There is no greater testament to the depths to which the Democratic Party and liberalism have fallen. You now position yourself, Senator Daschle, to exploit future terrorist attacks for political gain. You are worse, sir, than the ambulance-chasing tort lawyers that make up your chief contributors. You, sir, are a disgrace. You are a disgrace to patriotism, you are a disgrace to this country, you are a disgrace to the Senate, and you ought to be a disgrace to the Democratic Party but sadly you're probably a hero among some of them today . . .

—*Rush Limbaugh*, 11-15-03. DailyHowler.com, 11-22-03.

Another president began a war promising a "chance to test our weapons, to try our energy and ideas and imagination for the many battles yet to come." He said that as conditions change, "we will be prepared to modify our strategy." The heralded modifications never came, nor did an end to the war. President Lyndon Johnson's war on poverty turned out to be a bigger quagmire than Vietnam. Would that the Democrats would give the war in Iraq as much time to succeed as they are willing to give the "War on Poverty," now entering its 40th year. . . . Or how about an "exit strategy" for New York City's war on high rents? . . . Bush should promise the Democrats that there will be peace and democracy in Iraq long before the Democrats conceive of an exit strategy to the war on poverty, the war on high rents, and the war on white kids applying to Michigan Law School. The party of diversity is in lockstep in supporting all those idiotic programs. They're working just great. But our servicemen come under attack while clearing out a swamp of mur-

derous fanatics who seek the death of all Americans and the Democrats have had enough.
> —*Ann Coulter,* "No quagmire here!" Universal Press Syndicate, 9-4-03.

Why are they such supporters of Saddam Hussein?
> —*Talk Show Host Stacey Taylor* asking a caller about anti-war demonstrators. WLW-AM Cincinnati, Clear Channel News Network, 3-21-03.

Melanie Morgan: Anybody who has a son or daughter in the military, maybe you can get together with other people in the community, put their pictures together, display them publicly, and that would send such a larger message I think to the rest of the Bay area, so that these punk, liberal children, snot-nosed little brats will understand that there is a consequence for what they do which is basically anarchy.

Lee Rodgers: Yeah, and let's hope that at every opportunity that anyone who has the chance to do so will, oh shall we say, treat them rudely.
> —*"Lee Rodgers and Melanie Morgan Show,"* KSFO-AM 560, 3-21-03.

—Level a $10,000 fine on them—or if they're all a bunch of poor church mice as we suspect they are because they don't have real jobs, why don't you go after the organizers like Answer or Start who are getting hundreds of thousands of dollars from liberal organizations like the MacArthur Foundation, or Ford—or communist organizations like Workers of the World blah, blah. blah . . . some of these people have been arrested two or three times, where the hell is the three strikes and you're out law . . . They have got to do something seriously here, they have got to put these people in jail for a year.
> —*Ibid.* This was directed at the anti-war protesters who disrupted traffic in San Francisco after the war with Iraq began.

Mr. Speaker, I have no confidence in the ability of liberals to wage war. That is the truth that most of us believe and cannot deny . . . The liberal mentality simply is not equipped to deal with the harsh realities of war. They do not understand the first thing about using military force, about protecting America's national interest or about what is required to defeat a determined enemy. Vietnam, Iran hostages and now Bill Clinton's war in Kosovo. The liberals voted against using military force in the Persian Gulf when U.S. interests were clearly at stake, but where U.S. interests are not at stake, such as Haiti or Kosovo, then they are for military force. This is liberalism in the full glory of its contradictions and wrong-headedness.

—*Rep. Joe Pitts (R-PA). Congressional Record*, H1976, 4-14-99.

In the House, Democrats misread the electoral tea leaves and elected 62-year-old Nancy Pelosi. Pelosi hails from San Francisco where the Pledge of Allegiance is opposed, "alternative lifestyles" are promoted and American Talibans are spawned.

—*Oliver North*, "Pelosi's Party," TownHall.com, 11-15-02.

. . . And by the way a lot of these are the same left-wing Hollywood stars who are eager to go down to Cuba to hang out with Fidel Castro who is a similar dictator in the same tradition as Saddam who in fact tortures people, has prisons, and runs a totalitarian state like Saddam. I just find it fascinating that the Hollywood left can always find another excuse for dictators and finds it very hard to defend and explain democracy and freedom and the rule of law.

—*Newt Gingrich* on Fox News Channel's "Hannity & Colmes," excerpt aired the following day on "Don Wade and Roma," WLS-AM 890, Chicago, 4-16-03.

Free Republic has been rallying in support of our President and the war effort since shortly after the terrorist attack on America on September 11, 2001. Last year, as the inevitable war against

Iraq drew closer, more and more of the "useful idiots" of the left began crawling out of the woodwork, organizing so-called "anti-war" protests. FREEpers are working to ensure that these communist organized demonstrations do not go unanswered. Patriotic Americans are countering these misguided terrorist supporting leftists wherever and whenever they show up. Form a group, grab your signs, unfurl the flag, and prepare to support your country!
—*Freerepublic.com*, 4-19-03.

Linda Thompson: We have two million US troops, half of them are out of the country. . . . All of the troops they could muster would be 500,000 people. They would be outnumbered five to one, if only 1 percent of the country went up against them.
Chuck Baker: [Soldiers] would come over to our side.
—*Linda Thompson* of the Unorganized Militia of the United States, talking on the air with Baker as he broadcast from a gun shop in August, 1994. Later that day, a caller accused Baker of advocating "armed rebellion." The talk host corrected her: "An armed revolution." Jeff Cohen and Norman Solomon, "Guns, Ammo, and Talk Radio," *Seattle Times*, 2-21-95.

. . . **Caller:** The problem we have right now is who do we shoot. Other than Kennedy, Foley and Mitchell, the others are borderline traitors. They're the kingpins right now, besides the Slick One [Clinton]. . . . You've got to get your ammo.
Chuck Baker: Am I advocating the overthrow of this government? . . . I'm advocating the cleansing . . . Why are we sitting here?
—*Chuck Baker*, whose show, "On the Carpet" was broadcast on KVOR radio in Colorado Springs following the Rush Limbaugh show. *Ibid.*

Anti-War Republicans, Clinton Era

People in the Balkans have fought and have committed atrocities against one another for at least 500 years. Now we allow our Nation to be dragged into a quagmire for which there will be no exit.
> —*Rep. Charlie Norwood (R-GA). Congressional Record*, H2390, 4-28-99.

Victory means exit strategy, and it's important for the president to explain to us what the exit strategy is.
> —*George W. Bush* on Kosovo. R.G. Ratcliffe, "Bush toughens his stance on NATO bombing," *Houston Chronicle*, 4-9-99.

President Clinton is leading our nation down the path of "mission creep" that will suck our military into a quagmire that resembles Vietnam—a situation that America has vowed never to repeat.
> —*Rep. Terry Everett (R-AL). Congressional Record*, H2412, 4-28-99.

Who in America would willingly send their son or daughter to die in the Balkans based upon the President's explanation of the events? President Clinton has put our troops in precarious positions over and over again. We should say today that not one service man or woman should be placed in harm's way based upon the President's empty threats or hollow promises.
> —*Rep. Cliff Stearns (R-FL). Congressional Record*, H2413, 4-28-99.

The first rule of diplomacy is not to make the situation worse. Yet, the Administration's lack of foresight and planning for the refugee crisis has compounded the humanitarian tragedy unfolding in the Balkans . . . The military campaign also has suffered from deficiencies in political management and planning. The American military deserves better political leadership than this.

> —*Sen. John Ashcroft.* "Senator Ashcroft Faults Administration on Kosovo," Armed Forces Newswire Service, 4-7-99.

. . . My biggest fear is going to be is going to the funeral of some young Iowa man or woman who dies in this conflict and having their mother and father come up to me and ask whether or not their son or daughter died for America or died to save Bill Clinton's presidency. I don't know what I would say to those grieving parents. For that reason I believe the president must resign immediately . . .

> —*Jim Nussle (R-IA)* during the impeachment debate in the U.S. House. The "conflict" he refers to is a strike on Iraq ordered by President Clinton. *Congressional Record*, H11963, 12-18-98.

War Is Hell

I cannot tell you how proud watching that war coverage makes me. I know a lot of people are saying that they think that it's, that you know what we're doing is imperialistic. I watch the way we handle ourselves over there and I've never felt more patriotic in my life.
—*Dennis Miller.* "Tonight Show," NBC, 4-3-03.

. . . And finally, and most importantly, the next time we go to war, don't give a specific reason for the war that the Left can seize upon and later flog us with it ad nauseam, just do it. Remember, the first rule of Fight Club is that you don't talk about Fight Club.
—*Ibid.* "Hannity & Colmes," Fox News Channel, 6-27-03.

Throughout the Iraq conflict my analysis was mostly correct, but I did make a few mistakes. I bought the weapons of mass destruction argument too quickly and failed to predict how politicized the war would be. I should have known the Bush administration would have to fight with one hand tied behind its back in consideration of public opinion. For that reason, the U.S. military did not utilize most of its vast power.
—*Bill O'Reilly, Who's Looking Out For You?,* NY: Broadway Books, 2003, 153.

New Bridge Strategies, LLC is a unique company that was created specifically with the aim of assisting clients to evaluate and take advantage of business opportunities in the Middle East following the conclusion of the U.S.-led war in Iraq. Its activities will seek to expedite the creation of free and fair markets and new economic growth in Iraq, consistent with the policies of the Bush Administration. The opportunities evolving in Iraq today are of such an unprecedented nature and scope that no other existing firm has the necessary skills and experience to be effective both in Washington, D.C. and on the ground in Iraq. It is for this reason that we have created New Bridge Strategies and brought together the knowledge of American business professionals with over 25 years of experience in Iraq and throughout the Middle East and the political experience of some of the most successful governmental and political professionals in Washington, D.C., and London to provide a complete package of business services offering:

—Assistance to companies engaging the U.S. Government process to develop post war opportunities

—Identification of market opportunities and potential partners

—On-the-ground support in Iraq

—Legal, technical, cultural and potentially financial support for ventures

—New Bridge Strategies maintains a physical presence with staff on the ground in Beirut, Damascus, Geneva, Houston and Washington, D.C., and it has plans to expand into Iraq as soon as is possible.

New Bridge Strategies principals have years of public policy experience, have held positions in the Reagan Administration and both Bush Administrations and are particularly well suited to working with international agencies in the Executive Branch, Department of Defense and the U.S. Agency for International Development, the American rebuilding apparatus and establishing early links to Congress. Also, because of their long history of work in the Middle East and Iraq, they possess Arabic-language skills and business expertise in fields such as: telecommunications; real estate; food and beverages; energy; oil and gas; manufacturing; high-technology and distribution.

In addition to this core mission, New Bridge Strategies also will be able to provide risk-management and financial services in Iraq through its affiliates Diligence, LLC a premier global risk-consulting, corporate intelligence, due diligence and investigative research company staffed by former Central Intelligence Agency (CIA) and other intelligence agency personnel which is based in Miami, London and Washington, D.C., and Milestone Merchant Partners, a merchant bank with offices in Washington, D.C., Miami, and New Jersey.

The events unfolding in Iraq and the rest of the Middle East following the fall of the Hussein regime are giving rise to unprecedented opportunities for government and private enterprise to partner in the massive undertaking of rebuilding Iraq. The U.S. Government in Washington, D.C., as well as the postwar government in Iraq will need to rely on the economic strength and willingness of large, international companies and companies in neighboring countries to participate in the new Iraqi economy. New Bridge Strategies is providing the flexible and complete solutions as well as entrepreneurial ability necessary for companies seeking to open a path to these unique opportunities and engage in both long and short-term Iraqi business projects.

—*From the website of New Bridge Strategies*, a firm headed by Joe M. Allbaugh, who was George W. Bush's campaign manager in 2000. The firm was founded in May 2003. Newbridgestrategies.com.

The loss of innocent life is a tragedy for anyone involved in it, but the numbers are really very low.
   —*Paul Bremer*, the top U.S. administrator in Iraq, responding to questions about the deaths of innocent civilians. Gary Marx, "As Iraqis die, hate for U.S. spreads," *Chicago Tribune*, 8-17-03.

Reporter: What if the United States had allowed Vietnam to go communist after World War II?
Henry Kissinger: Wouldn't have mattered very much if the Vietnam domino had fallen then, no great loss.
   —*Stephen Talbot,* "The day Henry Kissinger cried," Salon.com, 12-5-02.

Boohoo, boohoo he's still beating his breast, right? Still feeling guilty.

> —*Henry Kissinger*, commenting on Robert MacNamara's re-
> grets about the Vietnam War. He spoke in a "mocking, sing-
> song voice" and patted his heart for emphasis. *Ibid.*

Talking Points has studied the Afghan situation. And there should be little wiggle room for the Taliban government. They should be given a short deadline in which to hand over bin Laden. If they don't, the U.S. should bomb the Afghan infrastructure to rubble—the airport, the power plants, their water facilities, and the roads.

This is a very primitive country. And taking out their ability to exist day to day will not be hard. Remember, the people of any country are ultimately responsible for the government they have. The Germans were responsible for Hitler. The Afghans are responsible for the Taliban.

We should not target civilians. But if they don't rise up against this criminal government, they starve, period.

> —*Bill O'Reilly*, "Talking Points: America Prepares for War,"
> FOXNews.com, 9-19-01.

Reporter: The foreign fighters you're most concerned about, how will you—just . . .

Donald Rumsfeld: You may have to impound them.

Reporter: How would the U.S. do that, though, with the limited force you have there?

Rumsfeld: Well, you'd probably use the opposition forces and encourage them to do it and provide a proper place for them to imprison them and hold them for appropriate periods and . . .

Reporter: Encourage them, but you can't direct them . . .

Rumsfeld: No. I mean, this is an unusual situation. People are looking for us—you know, it's the old glass box at the—at the gas station, where you're using those little things trying to pick up the prize, and you can't find it. (Laughter.) It's—and it's all these arms are going down in there, and so you keep dropping it and picking it up again and moving it, but—some of you are probably too young to remember those—those glass boxes, but . . . (laughter) . . . but they used to have them at all the gas stations when I was a kid. (Laughter)

> —*Secretary of Defense Donald Rumsfeld* during a Department of Defense news briefing on the war in Afghanistan. DoD transcript, 12-6-01.

I think preemption might have to be the way of the future if we're going to protect this country.

> —*Dennis Miller*. "Hardball," MSNBC, 1-31-03.

This group that engaged the US Army's 3rd Infantry Division, um, got killed! 500 of 'em got slaughtered! Give me a break, folks. If that's the best they can do, then they're all done. So, there's only 3500 of 'em left, well actually probably less than that folks, um, you know, I mean, who cares? We'll just kill off 4000 of 'em. Get rid of 'em. Not a big deal.

> —*Joe LaFlower*, analyzing the apparent success of Operation Iraqi Freedom during the conservative internet radio program, "Talk Show America," 4-19-03.

Last night was unbelievable! You know? I gotta, the ability of these guys to just on the fly in a short period of time they think they've got a location they've been able to confirm it three different ways between surveillance of people on the ground and it is, they call it in real quick their monitoring it to see that somebody's not leaving the location where they think Saddam is and his sons, and they go in there and they blow this thing up to smithereens with pin point accuracy . . .

. . . I find the ability of our military now to change on a dime—from all the different reports that I have been able to read here today we were able to pin-point this location because of intelligence that we had on the ground, some eavesdropping capability we have, special ops monitoring exactly where they thought the location was where he was and within just a very short period of time less than an hour, you know to not only target this location but to nail it with all these bunker-busting bombs it's pretty spectacular. . . . I'll tell ya, you gotta be proud of these guys with this story, these bunker bombs targeting Saddam, it's just, it couldn't be done any better!

> —*Sean Hannity* discussing the air attack on what the *New York Times* (4-9-03) described as "several upscale homes in the Mansur district of west Baghdad," 4-8-03. American commanders believed Saddam Hussein was in one of the buildings. An ABC news update on WLS during Hannity's show reported that a young woman and a baby had been pulled from the rubble. The *Times* quoted rescue workers as saying that as many as 14 people may have been killed by the attack which left "a huge smoking hole," according to an American official. Saddam was not in any of the buildings.

Gen. Richard B. Myers: The second video is of an AV-8B Harrier dropping a precision-guided weapon on a tank in the open, south of al-Amarah.
Rush Limbaugh: I love watching this stuff.
Gen. Myers: And the last video is of a Predator firing a Hellfire missile at an Iraqi communication dish outside the Ministry of Information yesterday in Baghdad.
Limbaugh: Blew up a dish!

> —*Rush Limbaugh* commenting on a Pentagon press briefing, 3-28-03.

It's just really amusing to watch Iraqis reaching for their white underwear so they can surrender, I mean they can't get there fast enough . . .

> —*Melanie Morgan.* "Lee Rodgers and Melanie Morgan Show," KSFO-AM 560, 3-21-03.

Shock and Awe, the massive, massive strikes scheduled for Baghdad is ostensibly under way. Shock and Awe, you may have

heard, is a two day attack that will in those two days drop more ordinance, more fire power on Baghdad then six weeks of the air war in the Gulf War. We're going to do in two days what we did in six weeks, unless of course they surrender before we actually get this going. I um—(laughter)—I know that some of you's, "No! Don't surrender! I want to see this!" (Laughter)
—*Rush Limbaugh, 3-21-03.*

This is a report from skynews.com "American forces say they have encountered tenacious resistance from the Iraqi army and Saddam Hussein's loyalist militia around the town of Najaf or Najef which is fifty miles south of Baghdad. The fighting said to have developed into the biggest battle of the war so far, and up to 1000 Iraqi troops have been killed." The main point about this story to me is, in addition to however else we decide to report on this war and I'm talking about the military itself, I don't think we need to hold back on the number of Iraqi casualties. Now I know the thinking, the thinking is that if we go overboard here or if we tell the truth, that the American people will go "Wait a minute! We didn't bargain for killing this many Iraqis." Screw that! This is war. This is how you define victory, folks. This is all about Victory. And I'll tell you, this, the, the, the American people want to keep score here, they want to know how this is going and if we killed 1000 Iraqis at Najaf, well, then say so. If we killed 2000, say so! Whatever the count is, say so! This is how many Iraqis have been killed to date, this is how many—this is war!
—*Rush Limbaugh, 3-26-03.*

BBI proudly introduces the latest issue in its Elite Force series of authentic military 12-inch figures, President George W. Bush in naval aviator flight suit. Exacting in detail and fully equipped with authentic gear, this limited-edition action figure is a meticulous 1:6 scale recreation of the Commander-in-Chief's appearance during his historic Aircraft Carrier landing. On May

1, 2003, President Bush landed on the USS Abraham Lincoln (CVN-72) in the Pacific Ocean, and officially declared the end to major combat in Iraq. While at the controls of an S-3B Viking aircraft from the "Blue Sea Wolves" of Sea Control Squadron Three Five (VS-35), designated "Navy 1," he overflew the carrier before handing it over to the pilot for landing. Attired in full naval aviator flight equipment, the President then took the salute on the deck of the carrier. This fully poseable figure features a realistic head sculpt, fully detailed cloth flight suit, helmet with oxygen mask, survival vest, g-pants, parachute harness and much more. The realism and exacting attention to detail demanded by today's 12-inch action figure enthusiast are met and exceeded with this action figure. This incredibly detailed figure is a fitting addition to the collection of those interested in U.S. history, military memorabilia and toy action figures. Actual figure may vary slightly from item shown.

   —*Ad copy from the website of KBtoys.com.* The George W.
   Bush action figure was released on 9-15-03.

And there is, I am certain, among the Iraqi people a respect for the care and the precision that went into that bombing campaign. It was not a long air campaign. It didn't last for weeks. And there was minimal collateral damage—unintended damage.

   —*Donald H. Rumsfeld*, Defenselink.mil, 4-9-03.

WMD—Weapons of Mass Destruction

Reporter: In regard to Iraq weapons of mass destruction and terrorists, is there any evidence to indicate that Iraq has attempted to or is willing to supply terrorists with weapons of mass destruction? Because there are reports that there is no evidence of a direct link between Baghdad and some of these terrorist organizations.

Donald Rumsfeld: Reports that say that something hasn't happened are always interesting to me, because as we know, there are known knowns; there are things we know we know. We also know there are known unknowns; that is to say we know there are some things we do not know. But there are also unknown unknowns—the ones we don't know we don't know. And if one looks throughout the history of our country and other free countries, it is the latter category that tend to be the difficult ones. And so people who have the omniscience that they can say with high certainty that something has not happened or is not being tried, have capabilities that are—what was the word you used, Pam, earlier?

Reporter: Free associate? (Laughs)

Rumsfeld: Yeah. They can—(chuckles)—they can do things I can't do. (Laughter)

—*Secretary of Defense Donald Rumsfeld* during a Department of Defense news briefing. Defenselink.mil, 2-12-02.

I believe they are continuing to manufacture weapons of mass destruction at many sites. A lot of them we don't know about, some of them we are suspicious of. Every month, every week,

Saddam Hussein will have more weapons of mass destruction to use against us. Why put it off?

—*Sen. Richard Shelby (R-AL)*, ranking member of the Intelligence Committee, speaking in support of preemptive war with Iraq. "Shelby: Beware 911," NewsMax.com, 8-5-02.

The Iraqi regime has in fact been very busy enhancing its capabilities in the field of chemical and biological agents. And they continue to pursue the nuclear program they began so many years ago. These are not weapons for the purpose of defending Iraq; these are offensive weapons for the purpose of inflicting death on a massive scale, developed so that Saddam can hold the threat over the head of anyone he chooses, in his own region or beyond . . . Simply stated, there is no doubt that Saddam Hussein now has weapons of mass destruction. There is no doubt he is amassing them to use against our friends, against our allies, and against us. And there is no doubt that his aggressive regional ambitions will lead him into future confrontations with his neighbors—confrontations that will involve both the weapons he has today, and the ones he will continue to develop with his oil wealth.

—*Vice-President Dick Cheney* speaking to the VFW National Convention, 8-26-02. Whitehouse.gov.

The Iraqi regime possesses biological and chemical weapons. The Iraqi regime is building the facilities necessary to make more biological and chemical weapons.

—*George W. Bush* in the Rose Garden, 9-26-02. Dana Priest and Walter Pincus, "Bush Certainty on Iraq Arms Went Beyond Analysts' Views," *Washington Post*, 6-7-03.

. . . And surveillance photos reveal that the regime is rebuilding facilities that it had used to produce chemical and biological weapons. Every chemical and biological weapon that Iraq has or makes is a direct violation of the truce that ended the Persian Gulf War in 1991. Yet, Saddam Hussein has chosen to build and keep these weapons despite international sanctions, U.N. demands, and isolation from the civilized world.

Iraq possesses ballistic missiles with a likely range of hundreds of miles—far enough to strike Saudi Arabia, Israel, Turkey, and other nations—in a region where more than 135,000 American civilians and service members live and work. We've also discovered through intelligence that Iraq has a growing fleet of manned and unmanned aerial vehicles that could be used to disperse chemical or biological weapons across broad areas. We're concerned that Iraq is exploring ways of using these UAVS for missions targeting the United States. And, of course, sophisticated delivery systems aren't required for a chemical or biological attack; all that might be required are a small container and one terrorist or Iraqi intelligence operative to deliver it . . .

. . . The evidence indicates that Iraq is reconstituting its nuclear weapons program. Saddam Hussein has held numerous meetings with Iraqi nuclear scientists, a group he calls his "nuclear mujahideen"—his nuclear holy warriors. Satellite photographs reveal that Iraq is rebuilding facilities at sites that have been part of its nuclear program in the past. Iraq has attempted to purchase high-strength aluminum tubes and other equipment needed for gas centrifuges, which are used to enrich uranium for nuclear weapons.

If the Iraqi regime is able to produce, buy, or steal an amount of highly enriched uranium a little larger than a single softball, it could have a nuclear weapon in less than a year. And if we allow that to happen, a terrible line would be crossed. Saddam Hussein would be in a position to blackmail anyone who opposes his aggression. He would be in a position to dominate the Middle East. He would be in a position to threaten America. And Saddam Hussein would be in a position to pass nuclear technology to terrorists.

Some citizens wonder, after 11 years of living with this problem, why do we need to confront it now? And there's a reason. We've experienced the horror of September the 11th. We have seen that those who hate America are willing to crash airplanes into buildings full of innocent people. Our enemies would be no less willing, in fact, they would be eager, to use biological or chemical, or a nuclear weapon.

Knowing these realities, America must not ignore the threat gathering against us. Facing clear evidence of peril, we cannot wait for the final proof—the smoking gun—that could come in the form of a mushroom cloud . . .
—*President Bush Outlines Iraqi Threat*; Remarks by the President on Iraq, Cincinnati, 10-7-02. Whitehouse.gov.

. . . And instead of full cooperation and transparency, Iraq has filed a false declaration to the United Nations that amounts to a 12,200-page lie. For example, the declaration fails to account for or explain Iraq's efforts to get uranium from abroad, its manufacture of specific fuel for ballistic missiles it claims not to have, and the gaps previously identified by the United Nations in Iraq's accounting for more than two tons of the raw materials needed to produce thousands of gallons of anthrax and other biological weapons.
—*Condoleezza Rice*, "Why We Know Iraq is Lying," *New York Times*, 1-23-03.

The British government has learned that Saddam Hussein recently sought significant quantities of uranium from Africa.
—*George W. Bush* during his 1-28-03, State of the Union address. Whitehouse.gov.

With nuclear arms or a full arsenal of chemical and biological weapons, Saddam Hussein could resume his ambitions of conquest in the Middle East and create deadly havoc in that region. And this Congress and the American people must recognize another threat. Evidence from intelligence sources, secret communications, and statements by people now in custody reveal that Saddam Hussein aids and protects terrorists, including members of al Qaeda. Secretly, and without fingerprints, he could

provide one of his hidden weapons to terrorists, or help them
develop their own.
—*George W. Bush*, 1-28-03 State of the Union Address.
Whitehouse.gov.

. . . Before September the 11th, many in the world believed that
Saddam Hussein could be contained. But chemical agents, le-
thal viruses and shadowy terrorist networks are not easily contained. Imagine those 19 hijackers with other weapons and other
plans—this time armed by Saddam Hussein. It would take one
vial, one canister, one crate slipped into this country to bring a
day of horror like none we have ever known. We will do everything in our power to make sure that that day never comes.
—*Ibid.*

The United States believes that time is running out. We will not
shrink from war if that is the only way to rid Iraq of its weapons of mass destruction.
—*Secretary of State Colin Powell.* "Hardball," MSNBC,
1-31-03.

We know that Iraq has embedded key portions of its illicit chemical
weapons infrastructure within its legitimate civilian industry.
—*Ibid.* Addressing the U.N. 2-5-03. Charles J. Hanley,
"Powell's case hasn't held up very well," *Wisconsin State
Journal*, 8-11-03.

. . . And we are opposing the greatest danger in the war on
terror: outlaw regimes arming with weapons of mass destruction. In Iraq, a dictator is building and hiding weapons that
could enable him to dominate the Middle East and intimidate
the civilized world—and we will not allow it. This same tyrant
has close ties to terrorist organizations, and could supply them
with the terrible means to strike this country—and America will
not permit it. The danger posed by Saddam Hussein and his
weapons cannot be ignored or wished away. The danger must

be confronted. We hope that the Iraqi regime will meet the demands of the United Nations and disarm, fully and peacefully. If it does not, we are prepared to disarm Iraq by force. Either way, this danger will be removed. The safety of the American people depends on ending this direct and growing threat. Acting against the danger will also contribute greatly to the long-term safety and stability of our world . . . We will also lead in carrying out the urgent and dangerous work of destroying chemical and biological weapons.

> —*George W. Bush*, speaking at the Washington Hilton to
> supporters of the American Enterprise Institute, 2-26-03.
> Whitehouse.gov.

. . . and I said on my program, if, if the Americans go in and overthrow Saddam Hussein and it's clean, he has nothing, I will apologize to the nation, and I will not trust the Bush administration again.

> —*Bill O'Reilly* on "Good Morning America," ABC, 3-18-03.

I've just met with our leaders here at the Pentagon, who are monitoring the course of our battle to free Iraq and rid that country of weapons of mass destruction.

> —*George W. Bush.* "President To Submit Wartime Budget;
> Remarks by the President on the Wartime Supplemental,"
> The Pentagon, 3-25-03. USembassy.state.gov.

. . . We have put together because of the strength and wisdom and insight and understanding of what it is we're dealing against [*sic*] and we have been proven right by the way it appears on every level that we found the chemical weapons we were discussing yesterday.

> —*Sean Hannity*, 4-8-03. Hannity made this assertion after
> interviewing Navy Lt. Commander Charles Owens, who
> Hannity said "works directly with General Tommy Franks."
> When Hannity asked him whether weapons of mass de-

struction had been found. Owens replied, "It's currently under investigation."

I voted for the president, I've supported him . . . I support him going to war and I think he's done a brave, very, very courageous thing here in tackling the Iraq situation even if they don't find the weapons of mass destruction, even if they only find one Petri dish that has basically a cold virus in it.
    —*Roe Conn.* "Roe and Gary Show," WLS-AM 890, 4-23-03.

Perhaps he destroyed some, perhaps he dispersed some.
    —*George W. Bush,* on Saddam's weapons of mass destruction. *Newsweek,* "Perspectives," 5-5-03.

U.S. Officials never expected that we were going to open garages and find weapons of mass destruction.
    —*National Security Advisor Condoleezza Rice,* 5-12-03.
    Molly Ivins, "Utter nonsense: Open Mouth, insert foot," *Chicago Tribune,* 9-4-03.

If he destroyed them we're gonna reconstruct what he had.
    —*Sen. Richard Shelby (R-AL),* on Iraq's weapons of mass destruction. "The Capitol Report," CNBC, 5-13-03.

The truth is that for reasons that have a lot to do with the U.S. government bureaucracy we settled on the one issue that everyone could agree on which was weapons of mass destruction as the core reason, but . . . there have always been three fundamental concerns. One is weapons of mass destruction, the second is support for terrorism, the third is the criminal treatment of the Iraqi people. Actually I guess you could say a fourth overriding one—which is the connection between the first two.
    —*Paul Wolfowitz,* quoted by Tim Russert. "Meet The Press," NBC, 6-1-03.

Iraq had a weapons program. Intelligence throughout the decade [of the 90s] showed they had weapons program. I am absolutely convinced with time we'll find out they did have a weapons program.
> —*George W. Bush* after a meeting of his cabinet on 6-9-03.
> "Bush Defends Iraq Intelligence, says "'time' will tell,"
> *Chicago Tribune*, 6-10-03.

We have confidence we're going to find them. They're still there.
> —*Ari Fleischer. Ibid.*

I think this remains an issue about did Iraq seek uranium in Africa, an issue that very well may be true. We don't know if it's true—but nobody, but nobody, can say it is wrong.
> —*Ari Fleischer.* Richard Benedetto, "Fleischer Spars with Press
> on Last Day," *USA Today*, 7-13-03.

The intelligent [*sic*] I get is darn good intelligence. And the speeches I have given, were backed by good intelligence.
> —*President George W. Bush*, defending his claim that Iraq
> tried to attain uranium from Africa for the purpose of creating weapons of mass destruction, 7-14-03. An Associated Press audio file of the press conference.

To focus on what was said in advance of the war here, and suggest he [Bush] wasn't being straight, is unfair . . . I do think there is one legitimate issue here, some of our intelligence has been very shaky. The fact that the CIA still doesn't know where Hussein is, the fact that the CIA never really had a handle on where Osama bin Laden was or to this point, is now. There is a problem in the CIA, and those are things that we don't have to run away from and we can look at. Those are reasonable public policy discussions that we could be having. Is our intelligence not that good? And if so, do we need to spend more money on it? Do we need to shake up the CIA? Do we need to encourage more covert operations? But the reason the Left hasn't raised any of those things, is that that's actually responsibly dealing with a problem. All they want to do is muddy up the President, which is why they're focused on silly, little things like the uranium statement.

—*Mark Belling*, substitute host on the "Rush Limbaugh Show," 7-15-03.

The president of the United States is not a fact-checker.

—*A "senior administration official"* referring to George W. Bush's use of false intelligence in his State of the Union speech. Greg Miller, "New Iraq Weapons Evidence Revealed," *Los Angeles Times*, 7-29-03.

In order to placate critics and the cynics about [the] intentions of the United States, we need to produce evidence. And I fully understand that. And I'm confident that our search will yield that which I strongly believe, that Saddam Hussein had a weapons program.

—*George W. Bush* in his 7-30-03 press conference. Bob Kemper, "Bush: Nuclear claim my fault," *Chicago Tribune*, 7-31-03.

Tammy Lytle: But you do believe that they [WMD] will be found at some point?
Rumsfeld: I do. I think that the U.S. intelligence and the intelligence services of the other countries were never perfect, and it was a closed society, but sufficiently good that we'll find the kind of evidence of programs that Secretary Powell presented to the United Nations.

—*Donald Rumsfeld.* "Secretary Rumsfeld Remarks at National Press Club Luncheon," Defenselink.mil, 9-10-03.

Condoleezza Rice: First of all, the CIA did clear the [State of the Union] speech in its entirety and George Tenet has said that. He's also said that he believes that it should not have been cleared. And we apparently, with the—in October for the Cin-

cinnati speech, not for the State of the Union, but the Cincinnati speech, George Tenet asked that this be taken out of the
Cincinnati speech, the reference to yellow cake [uranium]. It
was taken out of the Cincinnati speech because whenever the
director of Central Intelligence wants something out, it's gone.
Tim Russert: How'd it get back in?
Rice: It's not a matter of getting back in. It's a matter, Tim, that
three-plus months later, people didn't remember that George
Tenet had asked that it be taken out of the Cincinnati speech
and then it was cleared by the agency. I didn't remember. Steve
Hadley didn't remember. We are trying to put now in place
methods so you don't have to be dependent on people's memo-
ries for something like that.
    —*National Security Advisor Condoleezza Rice.* "Meet the
       Press," NBC, 9-28-03.

Diane Sawyer: Again, I'm just trying to ask, these are supporters,
people who believed in the war who have asked the question
[about exaggerated evidence of weapons of mass destruction].
President Bush: Well, you can keep asking the question and my
answer's gonna be the same. Saddam was a danger and the world
is better off 'cause we got rid of him.
Sawyer: But stated as a hard fact, that there were weapons of
mass destruction as opposed to the possibility that he could
move to acquire those weapons still—
Bush: So what's the difference?
Sawyer: Well—
Bush: The possibility that he could acquire weapons. If he were
to acquire weapons, he would be the danger. That's, that's what
I'm trying to explain to you. A gathering threat, after 9/11, is a
threat that needed to be de—dealt with, and it was done after
12 long years of the world saying the man's a danger. And so
we got rid of him and there's no doubt the world is a safer, freer
place as a result of Saddam being gone.
    —*ABC-TV News interview*, 12-16-03.

PART III

THE BEST YEARS OF OUR LIVES

"I really don't think that I'm going to be able to cause anybody to take out Bill Clinton. But if I can, I hope their aim is good and I hope that bullet passes through Al Gore first. And if you want a trifecta, take Hillary, too."

—TALK SHOW HOST ROLLYE JAMES

BASHING THE CLINTONS

Hitler was more moral than Clinton. He had fewer girlfriends.
—*Richard Mack*, at a right-wing "Patriot" gathering in Belle-
vue, WA., 1994. David Neiwert, "Rush, Newspeak and
Fascism: An Exegesis; VII The Transmission Belt,"
Cursor.org, 8-30-03.

To put it plainly, Bill Clinton is a sociopath, a liar, a sexual
predator, a man with recklessly bad judgment and a scofflaw.
Clinton has the classic symptoms of the sociopath. That is a
defective human being unable to relate to or feel genuine empa-
thy for another human being. Though often skilled at manipu-
lating people, the true sociopath is 100 percent self-centered.
Other human beings are just objects to be manipulated to achieve
the sociopath's goals.
—*Charley Reese,* "Clinton exhibits all the classic symptoms
of the sociopath he is," *Orlando Sentinel,* 8-23-98.

While this scandal no longer dominates newspaper headlines,
there continue to be aftershocks. The President's squalid affair
and his subsequent criminal acts have done palpable damage to
the nation. For the better part of a year Mr. Clinton engaged in
a full-scale assault on the Presidency, the Constitution, The Rule
of Law, Truth, Marriage Vows, Solemn Promises, the integrity
of words, the reputations of truth-tellers. It is an affectation to
say we can simply "move on" in the wake of all this. We will
keep returning to it, because many Americans understand, at a
deep level, that justice has not been done. Bill Clinton's year of
scandal will continue to reverberate, gnaw at our conscience,

rattle around in our minds. For we know things, deeply troubling things, that we did not know before.
—*William Bennett, The Death Of Outrage, Bill Clinton and the Assault on American Ideals*, NY: Simon & Schuster, 1999, p. 138.

I really don't think that I'm going to be able to cause anybody to take out Bill Clinton. But if I can, I hope their aim is good and I hope that bullet passes through Al Gore first. And if you want a trifecta, take Hillary, too.
—*Talk Show Host Rollye James*, KLBJ Radio, Austin, Texas, 10-15-96. When a caller to the show praised a bumper-sticker reading, "Where is Lee Harvey Oswald now that we need him?" Rollye James enthusiastically agreed and another caller complained, prompting James's response above. Gore, James added, is "more dangerous" than Clinton, because he "really believes in all these socialistic programs." As a result of this, KLBJ Radio fired James, who now has a syndicated show. Michael King, "It Was No Joking Matter," *Austin American-Statesman* editorial, 10-26-96.

HIRE ROLLYE JAMES

The recent elimination of the Rollye James program from KLBJ-AM radio was actually a political assassination of sorts. The LBJ family media dynasty has been and continues to be built upon a liberal Democrat base, notwithstanding their profitable dabbling in conservative talk show programs (and hosts).

Rollye James had become a problem, not because of her flippantly satirical discussion of an extremely anti-Clinton bumper sticker, but because of her thinly-veiled on-air support of Republican candidates; husband, John Doggett (who testified against Anita Hill during the Clarence Thomas hearings), had been getting national television coverage as a reporter and local radio exposure guest-hosting shows on a competing Austin station.

I heard the offending program segment, which I found quite humorous in a sharply satirical vein, but perfectly understandable and acceptable. And nobody in the LBJ hierarchy has pulled the plug on the First Amendment until now, because the financial profits have outweighed the political costs.

Hopefully, some other local station will have the good sense and good fortune to hire Rollye James—and keep her. After all, sharp intellect, good humor and the courage to not genuflect to the status quo are rare in radio discourse these days. If Austin radio permanently loses such a talent as Rollye James, the community at large will likely suffer a "dumbing-down" of media quality.

—*Cliff Sparks*, Travis County Republican Party Executive Committeeman. Letters, *Austin American-Statesman*, 11-1-96.

* Clinton didn't grow the economy: his own economic record depends on lies.
* Clinton sold out U.S. national security to campaign contributors.
* Clinton stood in the way of real welfare reform before being forced by the Republicans to sign a reform bill.
* Attorney General Janet Reno was AWOL on domestic security.
* Clinton's scandals were very real and he deserved impeachment.
* Clinton made sexual liberation the only cause for which he took career-endangering risks.
* Clinton's unwillingness to use force emboldened America's enemies.
* Clinton left the country vulnerable to the September 11th terrorist attacks.

—*Jacket copy, Rich Lowry, Legacy: Paying the Price for the Clinton Years*. Washington, D.C.: Regnery, 2003.

. . . We may have our faults; we may have our serious concerns about the role of the government. But, at least now, we are not laboring under a regime of corruption and lust for power and sex in which the conservatives are investigated for being the "enemy" of the left and terrorists are allowed into the open borders to build nests and breed. We live in a world of danger made more so by the Clintons; on the global scene, nuclear, chemical and biological weapons capable of destruction on a horrific scale (in the millions) proliferation and strengthening of the enemy while on the home scene, those who would kill us have taken root and spread out. Thank you so very much, Mr. and Mrs. William Jefferson Blythe Clinton. Not only are you white trash but deadly lowlifes.

We face, now, today, the result of eight years of letting the terrorists into our country.
> —*Barbara Stanley*, "American Jihadist Terrorism: Conversion And Recruitment," Bluestarbase.org, 10-28-02.

"First Lincoln, then Kennedy, now Clinton?" and "Where is Lee Harvey Oswald when his country needs him?"
> —*Bumper stickers sold at gun shows*. Nicolaus Mills, *The Triumph of Meanness: America's War Against Its Better Self*. Boston/NY: Houghton Mifflin, 1997, p.15.

If I could prove 10 percent of what I believe happened, he'd be gone. This guy's a scumbag. That's why I'm after him.
> —*Rep. Dan Burton (R-IN)*, Chairman of the Government Reform and Oversight Committee investigating Clinton/ Gore campaign financing. Andrea Neal, "Burton's Pursuit of President," *Indianapolis Star*, 4-16-98.

Mr. Clinton better watch it if he comes down here. He'd better have a body guard.
> —*Chairman of the Senate Foreign Relations Committee Jesse Helms (R-NC)*, on the 31st anniversary of the Kennedy assassination. "Helms' Gibe at Clinton Draws Fire, Panetta says Senator May Be Unsuitable," *Boston Globe*, 11-23-94.

Mr. Speaker, high taxes and low morals, that seems to be the winning formula these days for the leader of the free world.
> —*Former Rep. Bob Schaffer (R-CO)* on Bill Clinton. *Congressional Record*, H543, 2-10-99.

Wouldn't that be incredible if he were HIV positive . . . wouldn't that be delicious, though.
> —*Bob Grant,* former radio host for WABC-NY, on Bill Clinton. Alan Dershowitz, "Bob Grant finally gets his due," *Buffalo News*, 4-22-96.

I don't know if we'll ever get him on all the crimes he has committed, but the key thing is that we get him . . . It may be decades before history reveals the vastness of President Clinton's abuse of power or the extent of the damage it has wrought.
> —*Rep. Bob Barr (R-GA).* "Rep. Barr Comes Closer To Impeachment Goal He's Worked For Two Years Toward Ouster," *New Orleans Times-Picayune*, 12-12-98.

Barr: I didn't hear the "I" word out there did I? Impeach?
Crowd: Yes sir! Yes sir!
> —*Rep. Bob Barr (R-GA)* at the Iowa Republican Convention, 6-13-98. Dan Balz, "Republicans Talk Character, Values in Iowa," *Washington Post,* 6-14-98.

We're all painfully aware that Bill Clinton is still with us. From the unseemly—but not unexpected—criticisms of his successor in office, to the regular "Clinton sightings" at public and private events around the country, Americans have come to understand that unlike MacArthur's reminder that "old soldiers never die, they just fade away," old presidents—particularly bad ones—never die, nor do they fade away.

Things are actually much worse than they appear at first blush, however. It is not Clinton the mortal man that haunts and harms our society; it is the damnable ghost of Bill Clinton, his ethereal legacy, which continues to do great damage to the

very fiber of our country. Recent events across America's heartland, from school boards to corporate boardrooms to court-
rooms, have showed us that the bitter legacy of William Jefferson Clinton—"Boy Clinton" as R. Emmett Tyrrell so aptly
coined him—visits far deadlier consequences on us than did those
spirits who so briefly haunted Ebenezer Scrooge's London a century and a half ago.
>   —*Bob Barr,* "The Ghost That Just Won't Die," Bobbarr.org,
>   5-1-03.

For his own security, Bill Clinton has Pennsylvania Avenue bar-
ricaded, making the heart of our nation's capital resemble the
bunker of a Third World ruler living in fear.
>   —*George Will.* Tom Teepen, "Squabbling for Squabbling's
>   sake," *Atlanta Journal-Constitution,* 8-6-96.

Bill O'Reilly: No question, the most powerful Democrat in the
United States of America is Hillary Clinton . . . I tell you, I think
Hillary Clinton's a dangerous woman.
Tim Russert: What? Dangerous?! Why dangerous?
O'Reilly: I think she is, uh, unlike her husband, a true believer
in quasi-socialism, income redistribution, um, I think she will
pander to her base and deliver for that base, uh, at the expense
of working Americans. Um, I don't see the world the way she
sees it. I don't think she's a particularly honest woman. I think
she's ruthless, I think you know that she's ruthless. I think you,
Russert, know she's ruthless because all from the press have to
deal with her machine. She's unaccountable, she doesn't have
to answer questions, she's an elitist. Did I leave anything out?
>   —*Bill O'Reilly* on Hillary Clinton's possible run for Presi-
>   dent in 2008. "Tim Russert Show," CNBC, 4-26-03.

Madam Speaker, last Sunday, the Nation celebrated George
Washington's birthday. Washington was known for his honesty.
We all remember that story of how he admitted to chopping
down the cherry tree. Now, if that were Bill Clinton, he would

have blamed Ken Starr and the vast right-wing conspiracy for chopping down that poor cherry tree.
  —*Rep. Tom DeLay (R-TX)*. *Congressional Record*, H583, 2-28-98.

Sick of the media's puffery of Hillary Clinton and her new book in an obvious effort to help her presidential chances? Now NewsMax.com has the perfect antidote to the liberal media's Hillary love fest: the Deck of Hillary. That's right—the Deck of Hillary is a set of playing cards that will not only make you laugh out loud—it also blows the lid off her lies and her new book. In the Deck of Hillary, NewsMax.com reveals the real Hillary—by using her own quotes. These quotations are even sourced to some of the most respected writers and media sources. As the Pentagon proved with its deck of Most Wanted Iraqis, there's no better way to "out" the enemy than to depict it on a deck of cards. NewsMax was among the first to offer the Iraqi Most Wanted cards. Then we came out with the Deck of Weasels, which exposed the 54 worst celebrities and politicians who blame America first. Our Deck of Weasels became a national best seller.

  Now the Deck of Hillary is set to rock America.

  In fact, NewsMax has a goal—we want to sell more Decks of Hillary than Hillary sells of her own book. It's a big goal—but with your help we can do it and tell the big media about our success.

  Hillary thinks she can get away from her record by rewriting her history and that of her husband's sordid administration.

  We're calling her bluff with the Deck of Hillary, which raises the ante by spilling everything that her highness doesn't want you to know.

  You'll find out all about her:
* Outrageous racist and anti-Semitic rantings.
* Hilariously half-hearted defenses of her corrupt hubby and her never-before-revealed accusations about his philandering.
* Comical explanations for why men hate her so much.
* Bizarre claim that Christians can't be Republicans.

* Lies that she wouldn't run for the Senate and won't run for president.
* Vicious attacks on Secret Service agents, state troopers, presidential mistresses and other working stiffs.
* Deep-seated paranoid theories on why the Republicans are opposed to her.
* Knee-slapping comment about Bill's relative in the KKK.
* Foul-mouthed reference to the American flag.
* Shocking response as to why so many women are becoming lesbians.
* Don't worry, the cards are suitable for all audiences, because we've bleeped out Hillary's frequent use of profanity.
* In four suits of the deck, we tell Hillary's unvarnished story:

> The Aces reveal "The *real* Hillary"—including her phony claims she was a duck hunter and a Marine recruit.
>
> The Hearts tenderly and not so tenderly describe "Bill & Me"—her decades-long business and political partnership with her husband, the impeached former president.
>
> The Diamonds recount her money-grubbing and diamond-hard reign as "The First Lady." Learn what she really thought of the Secret Service—and about the special Secret Service Free Zone she created around herself!
>
> The Clubs, appropriately, offer Hillary "The Feminist." And yes, girls like baseball, too. Hillary was a Yankees fan. How do we know? Because she said so.
>
> And as for the Jokers, they expose Hillary's two biggest concoctions in recent memory—you'll just have to see them for yourself . . .

—*NewsMaxStore.com*, 8-10-03.

You see, we must make sure these Executive Orders are overturned. Only then will you be protected from the very real possibility of surviving martial law with Clinton in office! . . . My

friend, Bill Clinton is a power-hungry demagogue who will stop at NOTHING to keep his grip on power. After he seizes power and declares Martial Law—or any other "temporary" measure that keeps him in power—it will be too late to stop him! . . . From all newspaper and media reports the Y2K problem is real and would be just the emergency Clinton needs to seize power. Trying to have the necessities to sustain you and your family at that point would be impossible. Recent reports tell us 60% of the Y2K PROBLEM WILL HAPPEN IN 1999. We have found companies that can provide you with dehydrated food, water purification and a generator for electricty. I have enclosed information on them. PLEASE ACT ON THIS NOW FOR YOUR FAMILY'S SAKE!!
  —*Charles Phillips*, Coalition of Politically Active Christians (COPAC) affiliated with the American Center for Legislative Reform (ACLR). Smirknet.com, no date.

Get rid of the guy. Impeach him, censure him . . . assassinate him.
  —*Rep. James Hansen (R-UT)*, talking about President Clinton at an award dinner in Cedar City. Steve Miner, a reporter for radio station KSUB heard him. Hansen insisted he was quoting calls he received from constituents. Paul Rolly, "Jim Hansen Plays to Extreme Right With Recent Assassination Joke," *Salt Lake Tribune*, 11-1-98.

America: It's time to wake up to President Clinton and his—
  * High-Taxing,
  * Free-Spending,
  * Promise-Breaking,
  * Social Security-taxing,
  * Health care-socializing,
  * Drug-Coddling,
  * Power-Grabbing,
  * Business-Busting,
  * Lawsuit-Loving,
  * U.N.-Following,
  * F.B.I.-Abusing,

* I.R.S.-Increasing,
* 200-Dollar Hair-Cutting,
* Gas-Taxing,
* Over-Regulating,
* Bureaucracy-Trusting,
* Class-Baiting,
* Privacy-Violating,
* Values-Crushing,
* Truth-Dodging,
* Medicare-Forsaking,
* Property-Rights-Taking,
* Job-Destroying friends.

—*Sen. Kay Bailey Hutchison* addressing the 1996 Republican National Convention, 8-13-96. PBS.org.

. . . a triple-draft-dodging, cocaine snorting, sleazy, financially corrupt person . . .
—*Rep. Bob Dornan (R-CA).* "Hannity & Colmes," Fox News Channel, 9-17-99.

In this recurring nightmare of a presidency, we have a national debate about whether he "did it," even though all sentient people know he did. Otherwise there would be debates only about whether to impeach or assassinate.
—*Ann Coulter, High Crimes and Misdemeanors,* Washington, D.C.: Regnery, 1998, p. 107.

I can sum up the Clinton Administration's foreign policy in one sentence: Bill Clinton has done for foreign policy what Hillary did for health care. Over the last four years, the Clinton Administration has made over 25 trips to Damascus to pay court to Syria's dictator, and come up with exactly zero. So, when they write the history of Bill Clinton's foreign policy, they're going to call it "Gullible's Travels." We have also seen a representative of the IRA hosted in the White House just prior to its resumption of terrorist bombings in London. The result has been the worst relationship with our closest ally, Britain, since the Boston tea-party. So when people say Bill Clinton has been around and is wise in the ways of the world, they're sure not talking about his foreign policy.

—*Secretary of State James A. Baker*, Republican National Convention, 8-14-96.

If you liked "Schindler's List" then you've just got to love the Clinton-Gore-Reno Administration. Remember how it went in the movie? First, the central government gets a court order so that everything is nice and legal. Then the authorities dispatch heavily armed men in the dead of night to batter down doors and drag fearful people out of their homes and into the street where they are whisked away to "government facilities." Now look again at the defining photos of the Clinton-Gore-Reno years in Washington. In seven short years, from Waco to Miami, the incumbent administration has changed the way the world views America—and the pictures are not good.

—*Oliver North*, syndicated columnist. "It Takes a Swat Team," Townhall.com, 4-28-00.

How could we have a Commander in Chief of the U.S. Armed Forces who holds the military in contempt, who is anti-patriotic, who long ago embraced the dream of world socialism, and who, if he were not President, could not receive a security clearance?

—*Lt. Col. Tom McKenney (Ret.)*. Pat Matrisciance, ed., "Bill Clinton—The Unthinkable Commander in Chief," *The Clinton Chronicles Book*. Hermit, CA: Jeremiah Books, 1994. Quoted by Chip Berlet, Political Research Associates.

Interviewing Hillary Clinton last Sunday night about her book *Living History*, ABC's Barbara Walters . . . also astutely observed that "in addition to being first lady, you're a mother." Will Hillary's mind-boggling feats never end? Usually such phony liberal amazement at the staggering heroism of women ends with the woman drowning all her children.

—*Ann Coulter*, "True Grit," Anncoulter.org, 6-11-03.

I tell you one thing, when this Hillary gets to the Senate—if she does, maybe lightning will strike and she won't—she will be one of 100 and we won't let her forget it.

> —*Sen. Majority Leader Trent Lott (R-MS)*. CBSnews.com, 11-8-00.

I know something about Bill and Hillary Clinton right now. I know how their stomachs churn, their anxiety mounts, how their worry over the defenseless child increases. I know their inability to sleep at night and their reluctance to rise in the morning. I know every new incursion of doubt, every heartbreak over bailing out friends . . . every jaw-clenching look at front pages. I know all this, and the thought of it makes me happy.

> —*Rachel Abrams,* wife of Elliott Abrams, former Assistant Secretary of State in the Reagan Administration. "When a Special Prosecutor Comes into Your Life," *Washington Times* op-ed piece, 3-10-94. Elliott Abrams pled guilty in 1991 to two counts of withholding information from Congress in the Iran-Contra investigation, was put on probation for two years and pardoned in 1992 by George H.W. Bush. Abrams is now head of Middle East policy at the National Security Council.

I've come to believe that he [Pres. Clinton] needs a certain level of violence in this country. He's willing to accept a certain level of killing to further his political agenda and his vice president, too.

> —*NRA Executive Vice-President Wayne LaPierre,* accusing the Clinton administration of lax enforcement of existing gun laws. Calvin Woodward, "Clinton, NRA put on show of mutual hostility," Associated Press, 3-12-00.

What can I say about Hillary Clinton that I haven't already said over and over again? I mean, I have pounded this woman into pudding because she is definitely not looking out for you unless you are a member of one of her voting blocs.

> —*Bill O'Reilly, Who's Looking Out For You?* NY: Broadway Books, 2003, p. 65.

Demonizing Democrats
or Don't Kill All the Liberals

We have uncovered 132 scandals. And we're not proud of the fact that we uncovered scandals; and we're not proud of the fact that we have 80 lawsuits against this Clinton-Gore administration; and we're not proud of the fact that this Clinton-Gore administration is not gone—it has simply moved from the White House to the Democratic National Committee.

> —*Larry Klayman*, Chairman of Judicial Watch. Alicia Montgomery, "Where Clinton hating never dies; At a conference of conservatives, a new Republican president is no reason to forget about the last one," Salon.com, 2-20-01.

The majority of the voters in the state of Texas support President George W. Bush and his policies. The majority of our congressional delegation does not, and that's just not fair.

> —*Lt. Gov. David Dewhurst (R-TX)*. April Castro, "Texas lawmakers settle redistricting feud," Associated Press, 10-10-03.

The left are the ones that proposed abolishing the CIA in the 1990's. They rendered it impotent under the Clinton years. They're the ones that, while Ronald Reagan was deploying missiles in Europe, pursuing SDI, building up our nation's defenses and calling the Soviet Union an "evil empire," Al Gore, Tom Daschle, and Dick Gephardt were voting for a nuclear freeze. Based on that track record, I don't think they're the people to lead this country into the future, because they don't seem to have a fundamental understanding of good versus evil in the world and the need to destroy those that would otherwise destroy innocent human life.

> —*Sean Hannity*. "700 Club," CBN, 8-21-02.

By the way, it's probably a good thing Vice President Gore wasn't at Independence Hall in 1776! I bet he would have tried to talk Jefferson out of that risky independence scheme!
—*Gov. Tom Ridge (R-PA)* addressing the Republican National Convention. PBS.org, 8-3-00.

To be very blunt and God watch over Paul's soul, I am a 99 percent improvement over Paul Wellstone. Just about on every issue.
—*Sen. Norm Coleman (R-MN)* to *Roll Call,* 4-7-03. Rob Hotakainen, "Coleman apologizes for Wellstone remark," *Minneapolis Star-Tribune,* 4-9-03.

Democrats [who support President Clinton are] the enemy of normal Americans.
—*House Speaker Newt Gingrich (R-GA).* "Sayings of a Revolutionary," Newsweek, 11-21-94.

Today's Democrat leaders do not understand leadership. They reduce principles to tactics. They talk endlessly and confront nothing. They offer, not convictions, but alibis. They are paralyzed by indecision, weakened by scandal, and guided only by the perpetuation of their own power.
. . . Republicans do not duplicate or fabricate or counterfeit a vision for the land we love. With our fellow citizens, we assert the present power of timeless truths.
—*Preamble to the Republican Party Platform,* adopted 8-12-96.

All the Democrats have to offer is a lot of fearmongering, and scaremongering and lies about what the Republicans are doing.
—*Rush Limbaugh,* 8-19-96.

In his most famous admonition, Kennedy said, "And so, my fellow Americans: Ask not what your country can do for you— ask what you can do for your country. My fellow citizens of the world: Ask not what America can do for you, but what together we can do for the freedom of man." Modern Democrats, who seem to have made Faust-like bargains with every special interest devil in America, would never nominate a person who said such things today. They have disconnected from such ideals and now label as "intolerant" and "fundamentalists" and "bigots" those who presume a higher authority, a higher purpose to life than the supremacy of the state.

—*Cal Thomas, The Things That Matter Most.* NY: HarperCollins, 1994, p. 113.

How many different versions of Satan, the devil, have you seen in your life? I mean, the comic book devil with the red face and the horns, seen that one. We've seen the Satanic devil of the horror films. We've seen the devil portrayed as just an average man, a human being, in the movie "Rosemary's Baby." We've seen the comic devil of TV shows. We've even seen the smooth, tempting devil in Hollywood movies. Is Tom Daschle simply another way to portray a devil? Just yesterday, as Bush winged his way to Europe on a crucial mission to lead our allies into the 21st century, with Europe's flagging economy, talking about mutual defense in the 21st century, realistic environmental solutions, solutions for world poverty, not this stupid Kyoto stuff and not allowing the United States to be robbed blind by the UN and the poor nations of the world, up pops "El Diablo," Tom Daschle, and his devilish deviltry, claiming that George Bush is incompetent, criticizing Bush at the very moment he is engaging in these efforts to improve our relationship with these world leaders.

—*Rush Limbaugh*, 7-20-01. Spinsanity.org, 7-21-03.

Now he's decided to roll the dice and align himself with Iran, North Korea and Hussein. In essence, Daschle has chosen to align himself with the axis of evil.

—*Ibid.*, 2-11-02. Spinsanity.org, 2-15-02.

Democrats will be made happy if Gingrich really SUFFERS [*sic*]. Not just gets punished, but destroyed . . . His haters—who usu-

ally fancy themselves as the custodians of compassion, but who now have come up a little short in that department—will be happy when the family is driven into bankruptcy and eternal darkness.
> —*Dennis Byrne, Chicago Sun-Times* editorial board, "The Man Who Can't Do anything Right," 4-20-97.

If you're a proud Democrat you're an extreme leftist.
> —*Rush Limbaugh* to a Democratic Caller, 3-27-03.

It's just political fodder [the controversy over Bush's State of the Union falsehoods about Iraq]. To our estimation, the No.1 mission of the nine dwarfs [the nine Democratic presidential candidates] is to bring down the president and try to hang him on something.
> —*Houston Republican donor Phil Moss*. Deb Riechmann, "Bush's Two-Day Texas Trip pushes campaign war chest over $40 million," Associated Press, 7-20-03.

Democrats and liberals have sought to enslave black people with economic dependence . . . salvation is in God and the Church . . . We are sick of homosexuals piggybacking on the backs of blacks to exploit them for their own sick purposes.
> —*Bishop Earl Jackson*, head of the Samaritan Project and former National Director for Community Development for the Christian Coalition, speaking at the January meeting of the conservative Political Action Committee. "Right Wing Watch Online," PFAW.org, 2-21-99.

He's grown too cold and cynical after 50 years in Washington to realize that the affection this commander in chief has for his troops is genuine. It's a welcome change from a previous occupant of the Oval Office, who "loathed'" the dedicated young men and women of the armed forces.
> —*Oliver North*, "Byrd Droppings," TownHall.com, 5-9-03. North uses Sen. Robert Byrd's (D-WV) criticism of Bush's aircraft carrier landing to attack Bill Clinton. Byrd said: "To

me, it is an affront to the Americans killed or injured in Iraq for the president to exploit the trappings of war for the momentary spectacle of a speech." Byrd.senate.gov, 5-2-03.

Even fanatical Muslim terrorists don't hate America like liberals do.
—*Ann Coulter* at the Conservative Political Action Conference 2002, Crystal City, VA. PFAW.org, 2-26-02.

I just want to say, when the Republicans took over the Congress in 1995 and became the majority party, they started working on our budgets. Probably since then almost every single Democrat has voted against every single budget, it is fair to say. It is always because of the seniors, it is because of veterans, it is because of the children, it is because of the teachers, because of education, because save the whales, killing baby seals. It does not matter. If they want to vote no, they find good reasons to vote no.
—*Rep. Jack Kingston (R-GA)*. *Congressional Record*, H2165, 3-20-03.

I spent a better part of my weekend in Iowa wandering about, and had several meetings there in different parts of the state. Good crowds that we drew. And what was fascinating, I spent part of the time in my talks addressing the vote that had taken place on Friday, and making the point that in truth the Senate did not exonerate Bill Clinton, 'cause we all know he's guilty. They perjured themselves.
—*Alan Keyes*, discussing Clinton's impeachment trial on his radio show, "America's Wake-Up Call," 2-16-99.

It appears that Mr. Gore's motto is that when the good guy is down, let us pick his pocket. There is always a dollar or two left somewhere.
—*Rep. Jim Gibbons (R-NV)* referring to proposed legislation by Al Gore which would have required hard-rock mining companies to pay new fees for what they mine from federal land. *Congressional Record*, H12002, 11-16-99.

Most of what they have said is that they are trying to continue the policies so that they can continue to support their philosophy of government that has failed. We have tried their way for well over 50 years, and most of the problems that they describe, the problems with our public school system, with our government, with health care, most of that came from when they controlled this Congress. They have controlled most of the local governments, the state governments, this Congress, for the last 30 to 40 years, and the result are the problems that they have described.

—*Rep. Tom DeLay (R-TX). Congressional Record*, H10540, 10-11-98.

And we learned a lot, of course, about the Democrats in the course of all of this—a party without a heart or principle or respect for law or anything else, which, because of that lack of a sense of principle, now I think poses a deep threat to our future as a free people. The Democrat Party has announced itself as the potential instrument of anybody who would want to serve their political agenda at the expense of law and Constitution. A party that is willing to throw aside respect for the Constitution and the constraints of law in order to pursue their policy agenda is a party that has adopted the kind of "ends justifies the means" approach that characterized the communist parties in Eastern Europe and the Soviet Union—and such a party is potentially an instrument of deep repression.

And we need to, I think, be wary of that. They have allowed themselves to be complicit in the campaign of political thuggery, intimidation, blackmail and character assassination that has characterized the last several months. They have now kowtowed to the criminal element in their party, though openly acknowledging its criminality, and have entertained the arguments made by Dershowitz and others, "the President's above the law." Some of them even argue that if he committed murder, he wouldn't be impeachable. All of this making it clear that we now have a Democrat Party that has done more than just over the years surrender to moral relativism, it has surrendered to that total abdication of moral concern which then says that so long as you succeed at doing what we want done, we don't care how you do it. And in a nation that's supposed to be based on Constitutionalism and the rule of law, that is a party that is a danger, indeed . . .

> —*Alan Keyes* on his radio show, "America's Wake-Up Call," 2-16-99.

I tell people don't kill all the liberals. Leave enough around so we can have two on every campus—living fossils—so we will never forget what these people stood for.

> —*Rush Limbaugh*. Bill Tammeus, "The Year of Talking Dangerously: Next time, folks, consider silence," *Denver Post*, 12-29-95.

The myth of "McCarthyism" is the greatest Orwellian fraud of our times. Liberals are fanatical liars, then as now. The portrayal of Sen. Joe McCarthy as a wild-eyed demagogue destroying innocent lives is sheer liberal hobgoblinism. Liberals weren't hiding under the bed during the McCarthy era. They were systematically undermining the nation's ability to defend itself, while waging a bellicose campaign of lies to blacken McCarthy's name. Liberals denounced McCarthy because they were afraid of getting caught, so they fought back like animals to hide their own collaboration with a regime as evil as the Nazis.

> —*Ann Coulter*, "I dare call it treason," Anncoulter.org, 6-25-03.

Tragically, it seems Barbara Boxer is more concerned with saving dolphins from Mexican fishermen than with saving our children from drug cartels,

> —*Rep. Darrell Issa,* running for the GOP Senate nomination in California. Tony Perry, "GOP's Issa Refers to Clinton as a 'Slut'," *Los Angeles Times*, 4-8-98.

What Democrats are doing to Mr. Bush's judges goes far beyond partisan tit-for-tat or anything the Founders meant by the Senate's "advise and consent" power. Democrats are trying to turn themselves into judicial co-nominators, as if they'd won the Presidential election, and using a committee cabal of 10 liberals to do it. The White House and Senate Republicans had better wake up and smell the cordite.
—"The Pickering Precedent, Denying him a vote defies the constitutional order," *Wall Street Journal* editorial, 3-12-02.

Civility is just an excuse for hiding things that liberals don't want exposed. If Hispanics here knew what Barney Frank and Loretta Sanchez stood for, they'd throw up.
—*Steve Sheldon,* Orange County Republican and Dornan backer. Christopher Georges, "Liars, Gays, Aliens, Hispanics, Women: It's All Their Fault," *Wall Street Journal,* 11-20-96.

In their world, government regulates and dominates every walk of life, it replaces the family, the church and the neighborhood.
—*Rep. David Funderbuck (R-NC)* on the "liberal left" and welfare reform. *Congressional Record,* H3377, 3-21-95.

They haven't been right about one thing. That's one of the most amazing aspects of this, the Left hasn't been right about one aspect of this whole Iraq situation . . . they've not been right about what would happen in Iraq, they haven't been right about anything. And this is not pointed out by the mainstream press. The more wrong these people are, the greater their stature is. It's amazing.
—*Rush Limbaugh,* 4-21-03.

From now on, if official Washington promises benefits, official Washington must pay for them. We will apply that same principle to the ill-conceived Motor-Voter Act, the Democrats' costly invitation to ballot fraud.
—*Republican Party Platform,* adopted 8-12-96.

Our country's most experienced and dedicated prosecutors were replaced with Clintonite liberals, some of whom have refused to prosecute major drug dealers, foreign narcotics smugglers, and child pornographers.
> —*Ibid.*, "Solving the Drug Crisis," adopted 8-12-96, p. 20.

You have convicted drug peddlers working in the White House, many of them using hard drugs today. . . . CNN is the Clinton News Network, CBS is the Clinton Broadcasting Service, NBC stands for National Broadcasting for Clinton, and ABC is America Broadcasts for Clinton.
> —*Bill Cunningham*, WLW 700-AM, Cincinnati, on Veterans Day 11-11-96, declaring that the media won't touch negative stories about Clinton, but love to carry them about military personnel.

Somehow, somewhere along the line the Democrats have decided or believe that somehow they can make, by telling the same lie over and over and over, that they can somehow get a wedge with the American people . . . Republicans are still under the impression that politics is about ideas and ideals. But this is about the politics of deceit and the politics of the big lie.
> —*Rep. Martin Hoke (R-OH)*, defending Republican cuts in school nutrition programs. *Congressional Record*, H3532, 3-22-95.

The Democrats' iron-handed, one-party rule of the House of Representatives over the last four decades led to arcane, arbitrary and often secretive procedures that disenfranchised millions of Americans from representation in Congress. This autocratic rule was a direct attack on the free democratic principles upon which our nation was founded.
> —*Contract With America, etc.*, NY: Times Books, 1994. p. 13.

In the coming days, liberal icons like U.N. Secretary General Kofi Annan will be given the commencement stage at Duke

University; the dancing diva of the Clinton administration, Maddy Albright, will perform an encore at Washington University in St. Louis; and one-time Democratic vice presidential candidate Geraldine Ferraro will be trotted out at Case Western University. The monopoly of leftist commencement speakers this spring, from famous to obscure, provides an unseemly reminder that higher education's love for diversity extends only from liberal to extremely liberal.

> —*Oliver North.* "Campus Critics," Townhall.com, 5-23-03.

[The Senate is a] giant sinkhole on the other side of the Capitol.

> —*Rep. Jack Kingston (R-GA),* complaining about the Senate's failure to approve several bills, including Homeland Security. "Temporary spending OK'd as budget bill bogs down," [Fort Wayne, IN] *Journal Gazette,* 9-27-02.

We're going to keep on building the party [the Texas G.O.P.] until we're hunting Democrats with dogs.

> —*Phil Gramm (R-TX)* after winning his race for the United States Senate. "Slick Philly," *Mother Jones,* 8-95, p. 68.

What these members have done represents politics at its worst. This walkout is an absolutely shameful display of partisanship that ought not be tolerated by the public. We fully support the efforts of the Texas Department of Public Safety (DPS) and Texas Rangers to take all necessary steps to apprehend and arrest these fugitives, but it is outrageous that these legislators have forced officers to devote time to this that could otherwise be spent on homeland security and criminal investigations.

> —*Press release, Young Texas Conservatives,* 5-14-03, on the occasion of the Democrats in the state legislature leaving the state to prevent the Republicans from passing a Congressional redistricting plan.

We're just not going to negotiate with them. If we negotiate on this we'll be negotiating on every calendar, every bill, every day.
—*Tom Craddick,* Republican Speaker of the Texas House. "Comments about walkout by House Democrats," Austin-AmericanStatesman.com, 5-13-03.

I heard a dear friend of mine, a great Republican, say, "I trust Hamas more than I trust my own government." Those words hurt.
—*Rep. Henry Hyde (R-IL).* John McCaslin, "Regrettable Remarks," *Washington Times,* 4-23-96.

There have been more people tortured, more people murdered in the name of this socialist, utopia, communism that he [Ed Asner] still wants to try . . . America is not about a cradle to grave society. It's not about socialism, although we're developing into it, a mini version of it, certainly. America's always been about freedom, and liberty, and human choices, and about your own morality. And that's what freedom of religion is all about . . . We punish all the right behavior, we take 40 percent of the income from people that wake up at 7:00, shovel coffee down their throat, take their kids off to school, pack their lunches for 'em, race through traffic in any big city, get aggravated on their way to work, they put in their 10, 12, 14 hours a day, every day, serving the rest of society in some capacity. And after they pay their 40 percent, they're lectured by liberal socialists like Ed Asner, that they're not doing enough!
—*Sean Hannity,* 8-25-03.

Don't do it because the Republicans represent a great alternative—because they don't. Do it because the Democrats—far too many of them—are evil, pure and simple. They have no redeeming social value. They are outright traitors themselves or apologists for treasonous behavior. They are enemies of the American people and the American way of life.
—*Joseph Farah,* "Baghdad Bonior," WorldNetDaily, 10-8-02.

THE INQUISITION

Perhaps the best thing we can hope for is that remorse and regret set in among the public and even among Clinton apologists ... If this does happen it will be one of the very few good things to emerge from Bill Clinton's Year of Lies.
>   —*William Bennett, The Death of Outrage, Bill Clinton and the Assault on American Ideals*, NY: Simon & Schuster, 1999, p. 156.

I must say, I don't mind reliving the greatest night of my life over and over and over again. I was dancing a jig. I was bouncing off the walls.
>   —*Ann Coulter*, describing the night Jim Moody, Linda Tripp's attorney, and Coulter's friend George Conway brought the Monica Lewinsky–Tripp tape recordings to Coulter's apartment in Washington. David Daley, "Spin on the Right, Ann Coulter: Light's All Shining on Her," *Hartford Courant*, 6-25-99.

Physical evidence conclusively establishes that the President and Ms. Lewinsky had a sexual relationship ... Ms. Lewinsky turned over a navy blue dress that she said she had worn during a sexual encounter with the President on February 28, 1997. According to Ms. Lewinsky, she noticed stains on the garment the next time she took it from her closet. From their location, she surmised that the stains were the President's semen.

Initial tests revealed that the stains are in fact semen. Based on that result, the OIC [Office of the Independent Counsel] asked the President for a blood sample. After requesting and being given assurances that the OIC had an evidentiary basis for making the request, the President agreed. In the White House Map Room on August 3, 1998, the White House Physician drew a vial of blood from the President in the presence of an FBI agent and an OIC attorney.

By conducting the two standard DNA comparison tests, the FBI Laboratory concluded that the President was the source of the DNA obtained from the dress. According to the more sensitive RFLP test, the genetic markers on the semen, which match the President's DNA, are characteristic of one out of 7.87 trillion Caucasians.

—From *The Starr Report*, "Narrative" section I.B.1., "Physical Evidence," 9-9-98.

Tony Snow: Let me ask you, if you're a member of the United States Senate and you're reading the Constitution, would a strict constructionist have ruled that Bill Clinton should have been voted out of, left office?
George W. Bush: Yeah, I mean, he broke the law. He lied under oath. Although I don't think that's got anything to do with, necessarily, strict constructionism. I think that's got everything to do with upholding the law.

—*Fox News Sunday.* "Bush: Clinton Should Have Been Convicted and Removed From Office," NewsMax.com, 1-30-00.

Mr. Sensenbrenner: Judge Starr, folks back home have come up to me and said, why don't you drop this whole impeachment thing because everybody lies about sex, and the President ought to have the opportunity to lie about sex just like everybody else. I am concerned about the impact of that attitude if it ends up being adopted around the country, on a lot of essential protections that the law provides, particularly for women. For example, every sexual harassment suit is about sex. That is of its very nature. And much of our litigation, both civil and criminal, of domestic violence has at least some element of sex involved in it. If people can perjure themselves in court about sex, don't you think that that makes our sexual harassment laws and our domestic violence laws less meaningful and in many cases unenforceable? **Mr. Starr:** Yes. It certainly makes them, I agree fully that it would make them less meaningful, and it would certainly make it much more difficult to enforce if we did not take acts of perjury or obstruction seriously in this particular category of case.

—*Rep. James F. Sensenbrenner* (R-WI), impeachment trial manager, questioning Independent Counsel Kenneth Starr during Bill Clinton's impeachment hearing, 11-19-98. From the hearing transcript before the Committee on the Judiciary, House of Representatives, 105th Congress, 2nd Session, Appearance of Independent Counsel.

OK, folks, I think I got enough information here to tell you about the contents of this fax that I got. Brace yourselves. This fax contains information that I have just been told will appear in a newsletter to Morgan Stanley sales personnel this afternoon. . . . What it is is a bit of news which says . . . there's a Washington consulting firm that has scheduled the release of a report that will appear, it will be published, that claims that Vince Foster was murdered in an apartment owned by Hillary Clinton, and the body was then taken to Fort Marcy Park.

—*Rush Limbaugh,* 3-10-94. *EXTRA,* the magazine published by FAIR [Fairness and Accuracy in Reporting], July–August 1994.

I don't think there's any question that Bill Clinton will go down in history as the most accomplished and polished liar that we have ever had serving in the White House.

—*Sen. Robert F. Bennett (R-UT).* Richard A. Serrano, Art Pine, and Edwin Chen, "Senators to Vote Today as Margins for Acquittal Grow; Impeachment: Fifth Republican rejects perjury charge. Both counts against Clinton may not even win majorities, much less two-thirds threshold needed to oust president," *Los Angeles Times,* 2-12-99.

Mr. Speaker, my colleagues of the People's House, I wish to talk about the rule of law. After months of argument, hours of debate, there is no need for further complexity. The question before this House is rather simple. It is not a question of sex. Sexual misconduct and adultery are private acts and are none of Congress's business. It is not even a question of lying about sex. The matter before the House is a question of lying under oath. This is a public act, not a private act. This is called perjury. The matter before the House is a question of the willful, premeditated, deliberate corruption of the Nation's system of justice. Perjury and obstruction of justice cannot be reconciled with the Office of the President of the United States.

    —*Rep. Henry Hyde (R-IL). Congressional Record*, 12-18-
      98, H11776.

The truth is still the truth, and a lie is still a lie, and the rule of law should apply to everyone, no matter what excuses are made by the president's defenders. The news media characterizes the managers as 13 angry men. They are right in that we are angry, but they are dead wrong about what we are angry about. We have not spent long hours poring through the evidence, sacrificed time with our families, and subjected ourselves to intense political criticism to further a political vendetta. We have done so because of our love for this country and respect for the office of the presidency, regardless of who may hold it. We have done so because of our devotion to the rule of law and our fear that if the president does not suffer the legal and constitutional consequences of his actions, the impact of allowing the president to stand above the law will be felt for generations to come.

    —*Rep. James Sensenbrenner (R-WI).* "Senate Impeachment
      Trial of President Bill Clinton, Day 17," CNN.com, 2-9-99.

So I am standing there and out comes that battered wife, George Stephanopoulos. . . . Look, here comes the President . . . I was going to remind him that Paula Corbin Jones had her day in court and he will have his day in court because I am filing impeachment papers. I have got lawyers working on them and have been for about 5 or 6 months, and this may be the crowning issue, this may be the straw on the camel's back, telegraphing pardon messages to people. It is unbelievable.

—*Rep. Bob Dornan (R-CA)*, on the floor of the House. *Congressional Record*, H11389, 9-26-96.

COUP D'ETAT 2000

This morning brings news from Florida that the final vote count there shows that Secretary Cheney and I have carried the state of Florida . . . And if that result is confirmed by an automatic recount as we expect it to be, then we have won the election. . . . We have to make sure the outcome is finalized as quickly as possible.

> —*George W. Bush* as the first recounts in Florida began. Lynn Sweet, "Confident Bush predicts he'll win Florida recount," *Chicago Sun-Times*, 11-8-00. At the time of this first recount, Bush led Gore by 1,700 votes.

I believe Secretary Cheney and I won the vote in Florida. And I believe some are determined to keep counting in an effort to change the legitimate result.

> —*George W. Bush*, on the hand recounts requested by Al Gore in some Florida counties. Ron Fournier, "County stops recount in blow to Gore: Presidential race reaches new levels of unpredictability," *Charleston* (WV) *Gazette*, 11-23-00. The GOP Bush team strongly opposed hand recounts in Florida counties typically considered Democratic. However, the GOP requested and was granted a hand recount in some Republican counties in New Mexico for the same reasons cited by Al Gore in Florida. Wayne Barrett, "The five worst Republican outrages," *Village Voice*, 12-26-00.

If we were not witnessing, in effect, the stealing of a presidential election it would be laughable.

> —*Rep. Lincoln Diaz-Balart (R-FL)*, on Al Gore's request for additional hand recounts because of the ever-changing margin between Bush's and Gore's vote totals. Ron Fournier, *Charleston* (WV) *Gazette*, 11-23-00.

Cheaters! Let us in!
> —*A mob of GOP-organized demonstrators*—many of them
> lawyers and staff assistants to Republican legislators and
> campaign people—screaming in the hall outside the Mi-
> ami-Dade vote-counting center while hand recounts were
> taking place inside. Ron Fournier, *Ibid*. On national televi-
> sion, these demonstrators were seen forcing their way into
> the office building and banging on the locked doors of the
> counting center. Theodore Olson, former assistant to Ken
> Starr and now Solicitor General, later admitted that the
> demonstrations were organized by the GOP to pressure the
> local canvassing boards. Jonathan Alter, "Far from the
> madding crowd," *Newsweek*, 12-4-00.

He [Gore] is going to concede. Otherwise, we're going to take
the country. Get out of Cheney's house!
> —*Philip Niedermair* leading the chant of a Republican mob
> outside Vice-President Gore's house. CNN.com, 12-13-00.

The vice president's people are trying to undo that election.
Really, what they're trying to do is steal the election.
> —*Rep. Christopher Shays (R-CT)* on the 2000 presidential
> election and the Florida recounts requested by the Demo-
> crats. "The Capital Gang," CNN, 11-18-00.

For the first time in history, the party currently in control of the
White House is refusing to cooperate with the transition to a
new administration. Vice President Gore should concede, end
his legal challenges, and allow the President-elect to prepare to
take on the awesome responsibilities of the office.
> —*Rep. Cliff Stearns (R-FL)*. *Congressional Record*, H11930,
> 12-4-00.

This may be the worst thing I've ever seen . . . I praise Democrats when I think they do the right thing, criticize Republicans
[when] they do the wrong thing. Al Gore is trying to steal this

election . . . If you don't call the kind of thuggish tactics that the Gore campaign is doing right now for what they are, I think the notion of objectivity in the media is gone.

> —*William Bennett*, author and Secretary of Education under Reagan. "The Capital Gang," CNN, 11-18-00.

All the rest of this, dragging people in from Chicago, Reverend Jackson from wherever he comes from, and all these other folks, is just in fact a sham, and it sort of insults the process. I am sorry to see that so many people have ganged in here. We need to follow the law and the procedures, and we will elect a president.

> —*Rep. John L. Mica (R-FL)* on the 2000 Presidental election, as the recounts continued and national attention focused intently on Florida. *Congressional Record*, H11870, 11-13-00. At the time, there were allegations of racially biased voter intimidation at polling places. As a result, leaders in the African-American community, like Jesse Jackson, came to Florida demanding answers.

[Impeachment] taught the Democrats that they can get away with anything.

> —*Weekly Standard* editorial on the 2000 Presidential election. Thomas B. Edsall, "Rage Sharpens Conservative Rhetoric; Gore Accused of Trying to Mount Coup," *Washington Post*, 11-22-00.

Gore and Clinton have lost the democratic branches of government. They know that in a fair fight, they will lose their presidency and they are retreating to their redoubt of trial lawyers and politicized judges.

> —*Grover Norquist* of Americans for Tax Reform. *Ibid.*

[T]here would have been a conservative ascendancy had not it been for the venality of the Clinton-Gore team. From the 1994 election to the government shutdown, through impeachment, to this point, it has been a seamless web, tied back to the 1992

Clinton campaign and Gennifer Flowers and draft-dodging—
and Gore is viewed as the person spinning that web.

—*Marshall Wittmann*, an analyst at the Hudson Institute,
describing the views of his fellow right-wingers, but not
himself. *Ibid.*

There's a movie opening this weekend called "The Grinch Who
Stole Christmas," and some of my listeners are wondering if
there are some grinches afoot that might steal an election.

—*Talk Show Host Janet Parshall. Ibid.*

Al Gore's attempted coup has exactly tracked the trajectory of
the Monica Lewinsky episode, his mentor's own triumph over
ancient taboos of American public life . . . Gore has pursued his
goal with a speed and cynical genius that Bill Clinton never
dreamed of . . . Why are the peasants not in the streets with
torches? I would leave that to a sociologist.

—*David Tell* in the *Weekly Standard* and in an interview with
Thomas B. Edsall. *Ibid.*

The Gore-Clinton Democratic Party is trying to steal the election. . . . This crew we have now, Messrs. Gore and Clinton and
their operatives, they seem, to my astonishment as an American, to be men who would never put their country's needs before their own if there were even the mildest of conflicts between the two. America is the platform of their ambitions, not
the driving purpose of them.

—*Peggy Noonan. Ibid.*

[Al Gore suffers from] an unquenchable thirst for power.

—*Rush Limbaugh. Ibid.*

In his campaign to follow in the presidency a man defined by
moral turpitude, Al Gore promised, "You ain't seen nothing yet."
Now we know what he meant. Credit him with a promise kept.

—*George Will*, "Slow-Motion Larceny," *Washington Post*,
11-14-00.

So the Clinton-Gore era culminates with an election as stained as the blue dress, a Democratic chorus complaining that the Constitution should not be the controlling legal authority, and Clinton's understudy dispatching lawyers to litigate this: "It depends on what the meaning of 'vote' is" . . . His [Gore's] serial mendacity should be remembered during his seamless post-election transition to desperately seeking lawyering strategies and a friendly court to hand him the presidential election. Gore is the distilled essence of contemporary liberalism, which enjoys imposing its will—about abortion, racial preferences, capital punishment, tobacco, firearms, etc.—through litigation rather than legislation. Liberalism's fondness for judicial fiat rather than democratic decision-making explains the entwinement of the Democratic Party and trial lawyers.

> —*George Will,* "Gore, Hungry for Power," *Washington Post,*
>   11-12-00.

The holdup of transition assistance due to a technicality in the law is unacceptable. The election was a month ago and Gov. Bush has been certified the winner. Every day that goes by without a smooth transition of power damages the next administration's ability to deal with the problems facing America . . . Presidential transitions are of vital importance to our country and crucial to a successful presidency. This delay will likely mean that a new administration will not be fully in place until 2002 . . . The election is over and the winner is more than apparent—George W. Bush has been certified the winner . . . The Governor must be given full access to these transition funds to get his administration going. My bill makes it clear this assistance must be given immediately.

> —*Rep. Spencer Bachus (R-AL),* on H.R. 5643, intended to
>   revise the Presidential Transition Act, under which funds and
>   office space designated for the president could not be re-
>   leased to a candidate while an election was being contested.
>   Bachus's bill sought to change the law so that transition funds
>   in the amount of $5.3 million could be given to George W.

Bush, even though the election was still being contested by
Al Gore; that the U.S. government would reimburse Bush
for any funds he spent renting office space while awaiting
the transition, and that the keys to 90,000 square feet of
office space in downtown Washington D.C. be turned over
to Bush immediately. Bachus.house.gov, 12-6-00.

Gore's concession made the Bill unneccesary, but it is still
with the House Committee on Government Reform.
Frwebgate6.access.gpo.gov.

The D.C. Chapter of Free Republic [Freep] invites all Freepers
and lurkers in good standing to join us on Saturday, December
7 from 2 p.m. until at least 4 p.m. as we freep former Vice
Perpetraitor Al Gore and his wife and co-author, Tipper, at a
promotional appearance in Arlington, Virginia for their new
not-so-best-selling books.

We'll be there to remind the Gore's [sic] just who it was that
was outside the Naval Observatory demanding they "Get Out
of Cheney's House!" two years ago this month—and why. Details from the Olssons Books website: Saturday, December 7 at
3:00 PM

—*Posting from Free Republic*, an Online Gathering Place for
Independent Grass-Roots Conservatism, 11-29-02.
Freerepublic.com.

PART IV

HAIL TO THE CHIEF

"I'm the commander—see, I don't need to explain—I do not need to explain why I say things."

—GEORGE W. BUSH

ALL HAIL KING GEORGE

A dictatorship would be a heck of a lot easier, there's no question about it.
> —*George W. Bush*. Richard S. Dunham, Washington Watch,
> "A Gentleman's 'C' for W," *BusinessWeek* online, 7-30-01.

I told all four [congressional leaders] that there were going to be some times where we don't agree with each other. But that's OK. If this were a dictatorship, it'd be a heck of a lot easier, just so long as I'm the dictator.
> —*George W. Bush*. *Newsday*, 12-18-00.

Even the president is not omnipotent. Would that he were. He often says that life would be a lot easier if it were a dictatorship. But it's not, and he's glad it's a democracy.
> —*Joshua B. Bolten*, White House Budget Director. Elisabeth
> Bumiller, "Bush 'Compassion' Agenda: An '04 Liability?"
> *New York Times*, 8-26-03.

. . . I'm the commander—see, I don't need to explain—I do not need to explain why I say things. That's the interesting thing about being the president. Maybe somebody needs to explain to me why they say something, but I don't feel like I owe anybody an explanation.
> —*George W. Bush*. Bob Woodward, "A Course of 'Confident
> Action'; Bush Says Other Countries Will Follow Assertive
> U.S. in Combating Terror," *Washington Post*, 11-19-02.

When I say I'm not answering questions, it means I'm not going to answer questions. But thank you for asking . . . I'd hate to stick this Titleist between your eyes.
>   —*George W. Bush*, brandishing "a golf club like a sword at a reporter" and warning a photographer to get out of his way during a golf game. Elisabeth Bumiller, "The President Goes Off Duty, With a Vengeance," *New York Times*, 5-12-03.

It means that—first of all, I'm proud to be an American, and they [war protesters] should be, too. They've got all the right in the world to express their opinion. If they tried to do that in Iraq they'd have their tongues cut out.
>   —*George W. Bush*. Alison Bethel, "Bush Tries to Sell War Beyond D.C.," *Dertroit News*, 3-4-03.

. . . Make no mistake of it, the president may not carry the aura of FDR or speak with the command of Churchill. Yet he has exactly what the American people need in a leader to carry this great nation to victory in our war on terror. Whether the critics like it or not, the American people know in their gut that George W. Bush is the real deal.
>   —*Joe Scarborough*. "The Real Deal on Pres. Bush," MSNBC.com, 7-30-03,

BEAT THE PRESS

If Thomas Edison invented the electric light today, it would be reported on the evening news that the candle-making industry was threatened. Ralph Nader would announce a lawsuit on behalf of poor people who might get electrocuted. And the candle workers union would have at least two Senators introduce a bill to block electricity on behalf of their industry.

> —*House Speaker Newt Gingrich* during a luncheon sponsored by the Georgia Chamber of Commerce. Kevin Sack, "Gingrich Attacks Media as Out of Touch," *New York Times*, 4-23-97.

I had been suffering under the delusion that the Fourth Estate, the people of "The Press," were supposed to jot down what was happening where I wasn't, print it up and make it available to me. At least that's how it used to be.

But ever since George Bush came into office, the role of the press, for the most part, is to challenge the president, to mock him and make him explain himself for all the things they think he says and does. Every press conference, every appearance by the Prez in front of the libmedia is a gotcha session, a challenge, a scold . . . almost as if they were the folks who voted for him. Oddly, they did not take any of this responsibility into action when the man they really voted for, er, the "blue plate special co-presidents two-fer" and I do mean "fer" when it comes to listening to Hillary speak. Notice how folksy and down-home she gets in her patter when she's running for something and how it changes when she already was elected.

I watched in awe as the Clinton press conferences and appearances became a major laugh fest, all of the libmedia sucking up like sucking up was going out of style in the morning. All softball questions and yucking it up was not only not at all informative but also nauseating in its saccharinesque tones. After all, the libmedia were "hanging out" with their guy. They were partying like it was 1999 on the lawn at the White House, drinking and dancing and b-b-q-ing to their delight. I wonder if some (or more) of the reporterettes weren't hoping for a groping, to be touched by their idol. Softball questions and propagandizing as though they were a wing of the Goebbels annex inside the beltway.

> —*Barbara Stanley*, "The President And The Press: Watchdogs Or Just Dogs?" Bluestarbase.org, 11-2-03.

Seymour Hersh is a liar.

> —*George W. Bush* at a press conference with Gen. Pervez Musharraf of Pakistan. Mike Allen, "CIA's Cash Toppled Taliban," *Washington Post*, 11-16-02.

[Seymour Hersh is] the closest thing American journalism has to a terrorist.

> —*Richard Perle* to Wolf Blitzer on CNN. Stanley I. Kutler, "There Will Absolutely Be No Dissension," *Chicago Tribune*, 3-18-03. Perle disliked Hersh's article about him: "Lunch With the Chairman," *The New Yorker*, 3-17-03.

George W. Bush: There's Adam Clymer, major-league asshole from the *New York Times*.
Dick Cheney: Oh, yeah, he is, big-time.

> —*Exchange overheard during a Labor Day campaign rally at a high school in Naperville, IL.* R.G. Ratcliffe, "Campaign 2000/Remark aimed at reporter might end up biting Bush," *Houston Chronicle*, 9-5-00.

I regret that it ["asshole" remark] made it to the public airwaves. I was making a comment to Vice-President Cheney, I

didn't obviously realize the mikes were gonna pick it up. I regret that everybody heard what I said.
     —*George W. Bush.* Adamclymerfanclub.com.

It is amazing to me as I look out at the worldwide press, I do not think by the way the worldwide population, but as I look at the worldwide press, their media is slanted towards building up the good character of Saddam Hussein and destroying the good character of George W. Bush and America.
     —*Rep. Scott McInnis (R-CO). Congressional Record, H1719, 3-11-03.*

Most of the people in the U.S. media loathe the military, anything that has to do with guns and the military, they hate it.
     —*Don Wade.* "Don Wade and Roma," WLS-AM 890, Chicago, 4-16-03.

Looking for Saddam maybe in one of the rooms that CNN has in the Palestine Hotel? Well, can we surmise that maybe some key Iraqi leaders are being protected by CNN under the guise of journalists in their rooms at the Palestine Hotel? Let me tell you something, when these Marines hit the Palestine Hotel they didn't hit every room, they knew where they were going, they knew who was staying where and hit some rooms occupied by CNN journalists.
     —*Rush Limbaugh*, 4-15-03.

Remember on our TV screens—I'm not suggesting which network did this—but it said "March to War" every day from last summer till the spring. March to war, march to war, that's not a very conducive environment for people to take risks when they hear march to war all the time.
     —*George W. Bush* speaking about the sluggish economy. "In Bush's Words: 'Taking the fight to the Enemy' in Iraq," *New York Times*, 7-31-03.

TAKE THEM AT THEIR WORDS

An unbending rule of Washington life is that the one thing critics can never forgive you for is being right. This is worth keeping in mind amid the obloquy now being heaped on Donald Rumsfeld. Judging by all the blind-quote vituperation the Secretary of Defense is receiving, a casual reader might be surprised to learn that we haven't yet lost the Iraq war. U.S. troops are within 50 miles of Baghdad, probing Republican Guard lines that are being shredded from the air. The surrounded enemy has suicide bombers, guerrilla harassment and Peter Arnett left as an offensive strategy. We can hit the enemy, he can't much hit us . . .
   —*Wall Street Journal* editorial, 4-1-03.

A sight-unseen campaign against "The Passion" began after the scandal ridden, fiction-publishing *New York Times* ran an article about the controversial traditionalist beliefs of Gibson's elderly father, Hutton Gibson.
   —*NewsMax.com,* "Mel Gibson defends 'The Passion,'"
   6-13-03.

Question: What more can be done to turn around the media's overwhelming negative coverage of the war?
Donald Rumsfeld: But I think there's not anything you can do—with our Constitution, which is a good one that allows for free speech and free press—about it, except to, you know, penalize the papers and the television and the newspapers that don't give good advice, and reward those people that do give good advice. That's about all we can do, and that's probably enough.
Gen. Richard B. Myers: The only thing I would add to that—and I would agree; I mean, that's—that's—it's untidy at times, but we have a great Constitution.
   —Pentagon Town Hall Meeting, 4-17-03. Defenselink.mil.

My only regret with Timothy McVeigh is he did not go to the New York Times Building.
   —*Ann Coulter* in an interview with George Gurley,
   "Coultergeist," *New York Observer*, 8-26-02.

I think, on the basis of the recent Supreme Court ruling that we can't execute the retarded, American journalists commit mass murder without facing the ultimate penalty. I think they are retarded. I'm trying to communicate to the American people and I have to work through a retarded person!

—*Ann Coulter. Ibid.*

I picked up a newspaper today and I couldn't believe it. I read eight headlines that talked about chaos, violence, unrest. And it just was Henny Penny—"The sky is falling." I've never seen anything like it! And here is a country that's being liberated, here are people who are going from being repressed and held under the thumb of a vicious dictator, and they're free. And all this newspaper could do, with eight or 10 headlines, they showed a man bleeding, a civilian, who they claimed we had shot—one thing after another. It's just unbelievable how people can take that away from what is happening in that country!

—*Donald H. Rumsfeld*, U.S. Department of Defense website, Defenselink.mil, 4-11-03.

NBC White House Correspondent David Gregory: I wonder why it is you think there are such strong sentiments in Europe against you [Bush] and against this administration? *Et vous Monsieur le President Chirac, qu'en pensez-vous?*
President Bush: Very good. The guy memorizes four words, and he plays like he's intercontinental.
David Gregory: I can go on.
President Bush: I'm impressed—*que bueno*. Now I'm literate in two languages.

—*George W. Bush* in Paris at a joint press conference with the French President. Matt Born, "Bush snarls as White House pack closes in," *Daily Telegraph*, 5-31-02.

Do As I Say, Not As I Do

Bill Janklow speeds when he drives. Shouldn't, but he does. When he gets the ticket, he pays it.
—*Rep. William Janklow (R-SD)* during a 1999 speech to the Legislature. Rep. Janklow killed a motorcyclist when he drove his Cadillac through a stop sign at 71 m.p.h. Steve Kraske, "Fatal wreck could bring down Dakota politician," *Kansas City Star*, 8-27-03.

I'm appalled at people who simply want to look at all this abhorrent behavior and say people are going to do drugs anyway, let's legalize it. It's a dumb idea. It's a rotten idea and those who are for it are purely 100 percent selfish.
—*Rush Limbaugh,* 12-9-93. Scott Loughrey, "Limbaugh Demagoguery on Drugs," Baltimore Independent Media Center, 10-10-03.

If [Surgeon General Jocelyn Elders] wants to legalize drugs, send the people who want to do drugs to London and Zurich, and let's be rid of them.
—*Rush Limbaugh. Ibid.*

Kurt Cobain died of a drug-induced suicide, I just—he was a worthless shred of human debris.
—*Rush Limbaugh,* 4-8-94. Lumberjackonline.com.

When you strip it all away, Jerry Garcia destroyed his life on drugs. And yet he's being honored, like some godlike figure. Our priorities are out of whack, folks.
—*Rush Limbaugh* on Jerry Garcia's death, 8-20-95. Robert P. Laurence, "Now Limbaugh asks for a rush to change judgment of drug use," *San Diego Union-Tribune*, 10-15-03.

What this says to me is that too many whites are getting away with drug use. Too many whites are getting away with drug sales. Too many whites are getting away with trafficking in this stuff. The answer to this disparity is not to start letting people out of jail because we're not putting others in jail who are breaking the law. The answer is to go out and find the ones who are getting away with it, convict them and send them up the river, too.
> —*Rush Limbaugh*, 10-5-95. Scott Loughrey, "Limbaugh Demagoguery on Drugs," Baltimore Independent Media Center, 10-10-03.

There's nothing good about drug use. We know it. It destroys individuals. It destroys families. Drug use destroys societies. Drug use, some might say, is destroying this country. And we have laws against selling drugs, pushing drugs, using drugs, importing drugs. And the laws are good because we know what happens to people in societies and neighborhoods which become consumed by them. And so if people are violating the law by doing drugs, they ought to be accused and they ought to be convicted and they ought to be sent up.
> —*Rush Limbaugh*, 10-5-95. Robert P. Laurence, "Now Limbaugh asks for a rush to change judgment of drug use," *San Diego Union-Tribune*, 10-15-03.

You know I have always tried to be honest with you and open about my life, so I need to tell you today that part of what you have heard and read is correct. I am addicted to prescription pain medication. Immediately following this broadcast, I am checking myself into a treatment center for the next 30 days to once and for all break the hold this highly addictive medication has on me.
> —*Rush Limbaugh*, 10-10-03.

Rush, I think, has proven today that he always is honest and levels with people. That's what people love about him. He's

honest, straightforward and genuine, and, yes, he's a human
being who also has faults like we all do.
  —*Greg Mueller,* president of a conservative public relations
  firm. Lisa Anderson and Raoul Mowatt, "Limbaugh confesses drug habit to listeners, will enter rehab," *Chicago
  Tribune,* 10-11-03.

It's a minor, minor offense.
  —*Fred Barnes,* editor of the *Weekly Standard,* on Rush
  Limbaugh's illegal drug purchases. "Special Report with
  Brit Hume," Fox News Channel, 10-2-03.

His [Rush Limbaugh's] career will be invigorated by this color-
ful episode, which makes him a more interesting person.
  —*Michael Harrison,* editor of *Talkers* magazine, on
  Limbaugh's drug addiction. John Cook and Raoul Mowatt,
  "Limbaugh back on air after drug treatment," *Chicago
  Tribune,* 11-17-03.

. . . But the question of correct order of the soul is not simply
the domain of sublime philosophy and drama. It lies at the heart
of the task of successful everyday behavior, whether it is controlling our tempers, or our appetites, or our inclinations to sit
all day in front of the television. As Aristotle pointed out, here
our habits make all the difference. We learn to order our souls
the same way we learn to do math problems or play baseball
well—through practice.
  Practice, of course, is the medicine so many people find hard
to swallow. If it were easy, we wouldn't have such modern-day
phenomena as multimillion-dollar diet and exercise industries.
We can enlist the aid of trainers, therapists, support groups,
step programs, and other strategies, but in the end, it's practice
that brings self-control.
  —*William J. Bennett,* "Self-Discipline," from *The Book of
  Virtues,* NY: Simon & Schuster, 1993, pp. 19–20.

Over ten years, I'd say I've come out pretty close to even. You may cycle several hundred thousand dollars in an evening and net out only a few thousand . . . I play fairly high stakes. I adhere to the law. I don't play the "milk money." I don't put my family at risk, and I don't owe anyone anything . . . You don't see what I walk away with. They [the casinos] don't want you to see it . . . I view it as drinking. If you can't handle it, don't do it.

> —*William J. Bennett,* Republican moralist, responding to questions about his gambling addiction. According to *Newsweek,* he lost $8 million in a ten-year period, $340,000 on July 12, 2002, and $500,000 on April 5–6, 2003. Jonathan Alter and Joshua Green, "Bennett: Virtue Is as Virtue Does?" *Newsweek,* 5-12-03.

I've gambled all my life and it's never been a moral issue with me. I liked church bingo when I was growing up. I've been a poker player.

> —*Bill Bennett.* Joshua Green, "The Bookie of Virtue," *Washington Monthly,* 6-03.

Not an addiction, not a problem, no therapy, gambling too much, stopped it.

> —*William Bennett* on his gambling problem. Jacques Steinberg, "Limbaugh is back on the air, with fans and foes all ears," *New York Times,* 11-17-03.

The preoccupation with Bill Bennett's gambling has reaffirmed something I long ago realized: Only conservatives can be hypocrites. Can you think of one prominent liberal ever labeled a hypocrite in the mainstream press? President Bill Clinton was labeled many things for his extramarital affairs and his lying, but never a hypocrite. But when the press discovers flawed behavior in the personal life of a prominent conservative, he is discredited as a hypocrite . . . What matters is that he is a conservative, advocates virtue, judged President Clinton guilty and

gambled too much. It is surely much easier to be a liberal in our times. You aren't judged.
>   —*Dennis Prager*. "Bill Bennett and the charge of hypocrisy," Creators Syndicate, 7-8-03.

Newt's willingness to acknowledge an unintentional mistake is refreshing.
>   —*Rep. John Boehner (R-OH)*, Chairman of the Republican caucus, defending Speaker Newt Gingrich against the findings of the House ethics subcommittee, that the Speaker had used tax-exempt foundations for political purposes, and that he had given the House Ethics Committee, "inaccurate, incomplete, and unreliable information." Adam Clymer, "Panel Concludes Gingrich Violated Rules On Ethics," *New York Times*, 12-22-96.

This committee has not found this Speaker has intentionally lied or intentionally misled the committee . . . What he is being charged with today is during the process he happened to screw up. That is what is going on here. I just find that really sad that we have abused the process like this . . . Let us stop using the ethics process for political vendettas . . . Let us stop this madness. Let us stop the cannibalism. Let us not fall victim to unrealistic expectations that do not forgive the common flaws of normal Americans.
>   —*House Majority Whip Tom DeLay (R-TX)*, on the House floor. *Congressional Record*, H195, 1-21-97.

The statute of limitations has long since passed on my youthful indiscretions. Suffice it to say Cherie Snodgrass and I were good friends a long time ago. After Mr. Snodgrass confronted my wife, the friendship ended and my marriage remained intact. The only purpose for this being dredged up now is an obvious attempt to intimidate me and it won't work. I intend to fulfill

my constitutional duty and deal with the serious felony allegations presented to Congress on the Starr report

> —*Rep. Henry Hyde (R-IL)*, leader of the Managers of
> Clinton's impeachment trial. Hyde was in his 40s when he
> carried on the adulterous years-long affair with Mrs
> Snodgrass. Howard Kurtz, "Report of Hyde Affair Stirs
> Anger," *Washington Post*, 9-17-98.

It appears that the lawsuit will be dismissed as a result of nego-
tiations among parties other than myself. I have not agreed, nor
will I agree to make any payment in settlement of this case.

> —*Rep. Henry J. Hyde (R-IL)*, Chairman of the House Judi-
> ciary Committee, stating his position on the settlement of a
> lawsuit filed against him and 11 others by the Resolution
> Trust Corporation. Rep. Hyde was one of the directors of
> the Clyde Federal Savings and Loan Association from 1981–
> 1984. Bank regulators took over Clyde in 1990, and its
> collapse cost taxpayers $67 million. The lawsuit was settled
> for $850,000 but Rep. Hyde refused to pay anything, while
> the other defendants split the cost of the settlement. Michael
> Gillis, "Hyde Avoids Any Payment in Settlement for failed
> S & L," *Chicago Sun-Times*, 11-20-96.

It's not illegal, anything I've done. But my wife and I—and I
hate to tell you this—but my wife and I were separated three
times in our 38-year marriage. [But] if something comes out
that you read about, that you think Danny shouldn't have done,
I will own up to it. I won't lie about it. I will tell the truth.

> —*Rep. Dan Burton (R-IN)*. John Strauss, Mary Beth
> Schneider, "Burton Forsees Report On His Sex Life," *Se-
> attle Times*, 9-1-98.

There was a relationship many years ago from which a child
was born. I am the father. With my wife's knowledge, I have
fulfilled my responsibilities as the father. In an effort to protect

the privacy of those involved, it was decided years ago among all parties that this matter would remain private. The intense speculation about this matter has caused a lot of pain for some innocent people. The woman in question is now married. After talking with her and her husband, as well as my wife and family, we have decided that it would be best for everyone involved that I make this matter public.

> —*Rep. Dan Burton (R-IN).* Bill Sammon, "Burton reveals fathering child from '80s affair," *Washington Times,* 9-5-98.

Rowland Evans: In the Senate the investigation [into fundraising] will cover Republican violations, alleged violations. In the House, Dan Burton wants to pretty much limit that to Democrats. Which one is correct?

Jim Nicholson, Republican Party Chairman: Well, what's important to me and I think to the party and to the people that I represent, which is Republicans, you know, all over the country out there, in the countryside, the worker, the farmer and the plumber, is that we get at and brought [*sic*] into the light of day, how the unions raised this money. They need to be subpoenaed.

> —*"Evans & Novak Show,"* CNN, 4-26-97.

FREE SPEECH FOR ME
(BUT NOT FOR THEE)

October 31, 2003
Mr. Leslie Moonves
President, CBS Television
524 W. 57th Street
New York, NY 10019

Dear Mr. Moonves:

I have recently seen reports about the upcoming CBS miniseries "The Reagans" and am concerned that its portrayal of our 40th President and Mrs. Reagan and the Reagan Presidency may not be historically accurate.

A CBS statement describes the series as "programming that informs, entertains and hopefully, stirs meaningful discourse." But if your series contains omissions, exaggerations, distortions or scenes that are fiction masquerading as fact, the American people may come away with a misunderstanding of the Reagans and the Reagan Administrations. Those graduating from college this year were only about five years old when President Reagan left office, and this broadcast will have a significant impact on their understanding of his legacy.

One producer, Neil Meron, said, "This is not a vendetta, this is not revenge. It is about telling a good story in our honest sort of way." I'm not sure "honest sort of way" meets a proper standard for historical accuracy . . .

To avoid any confusion as to what constitutes treating the President, Mrs. Reagan and the Reagan Administrations in an honest sort of way, I respectfully request that you allow a team of historians to review the program for historical accuracy, and a panel of people who actually know the Reagans personally to review it for accuracy in its portrayal of them as individuals before it is aired.

If you're unwilling to do so, I respectfully request that you inform your viewers via a crawl every ten minutes that the program is a fictional portrayal of the Reagans and the Reagan Presidency, and they should not consider it to be historically accurate.

Public exposure of an improper implication caused you to delete from the program itself a scene that was included in the very limited promotional release. It would be reassuring to know that the program in its entirety, rather than only the ten-minute promotional video, had been subject to review for accuracy.

I feel confident the American people would appreciate your clarity and it would go a long way towards the meaningful discourse you desire.

Sincerely,

Ed Gillespie, Sent Via Fax and Email

—*This letter was written by the Republican National Committee Chairman, and posted on the RNC website. RNC.org.*

Statement of RNC Chairman Ed Gillespie on CBS Decision to Move Reagan Series to Showtime:

Washington, DC—The CBS decision to air "The Reagans" miniseries on Showtime does not address the central concern over historical accuracy, nor does it correct the fact that the program does not present, in their own words, a balanced portrayal of the Reagans.

The only proper thing to do is to correct the imbalance and have the program reviewed for historical accuracy or inform viewers that it is a fictionalized portrayal and not intended to be historically accurate.

Misleading a smaller audience of viewers is not a noble response to the legitimate concerns raised about this program. I respectfully request Showtime to allow a panel of historians and people who know the Reagans to review the program for accuracy before it airs.

    If they are unwilling to correct the imbalance they themselves acknowledge and review the program for historical accuracy, Showtime should inform its viewers through a crawl every ten minutes that the program is a fictional portrayal of the Reagans and the Reagan Presidency, and is not intended to be historically accurate.

    —*RNC press release,* 11-4-03. It should be noted that when these objections were raised, no one had yet seen this film, which aired for the first time on Showtime on 12-7-03.

I'll say this about the war protesters: At least most of them are only putting duct tape across their mouths so I can still tell the rest of them to blow it out their ass.

    —*Dennis Miller.* "Tonight Show," 4-3-03.

I don't mind people trying to pick apart my policies, and that's fine and that's fair game but, you know, I don't think we're serving our nation well by allowing the discourse to become so uncivil that people say, use words that they shouldn't be using.

    —*George W. Bush* in an interview with Brit Hume on Fox News, "Bush responds to Kennedy's criticism of Iraq policies," Associated Press, 9-22-03.

Kennedy's brand of hate speech has become mainstream in the Democratic Party. Senator Kennedy owes the president and the country an apology, but we all know no apology will come.

    —*House Majority Leader Tom DeLay (R-TX)* referring to Kennedy's comments that the Iraq war was "a fraud." "Iraq Remarks Set Off Furor; Kennedy Fires Back at Critics," *Richmond Times-Dispatch,* 9-24-03.

Given the choice, it's better to be viewed as a foot soldier for Bush than a spokeswoman for al Qaeda.

    —*Irena Briganti* of Fox News, in response to CNN's Chistiane Amanpour, who said that broadcasters were intimidated by "the administration and its foot soldiers at Fox News." Peter Johnson, "CNN reporter blasts White House 'disinformation' on Iraq," *Chicago Sun-Times,* 9-17-03.

The *New York Times* is either in a constant state of denial, or they have thrown off all attempts to remain truthful and objective in favor of an ideological purpose. Just exactly what that purpose is remains locked in their cold hearts, but it has nothing to do with the love for President Bush or our Traditional American Values. On the contrary, it has much to do with their illogical and irrational love of the Left—the Hard-Left—and I haven't met a single person who can explain why people like those at the *Times* hate this country so much that they would try to undermine it. But for some reason they do. Make no mistake, *The New York Times* is willing to print a daily lie to perform maintenance on a fiction that promotes their political agenda—salvaging some positive aspect of Clinton's eight years in office.

    —*Gary Aldrich*, "Clinton Bashing Book Burning," Townhall.com, 10-1-03.

To those who pit Americans against immigrants and citizens against non-citizens, to those who scare peace-loving people with phantoms of lost liberty, my message is this: Your tactics only aid terrorists, for they erode our national unity and diminish our resolve. They give ammunition to America's enemies, and pause to America's friends.

    —*Attorney General John Ashcroft* attacking critics of the Bush Administration during testimony before the Senate on 12-6-01. "Justice defends Ashcroft's congressional testimony," CNN, 12-7-01.

I'm not here to be grilled. I'm here to conduct a hearing. I'm not going to continue answering questions that people pull from thin air.

    —*Rep. Dan Burton (R-IN)* refusing to answer questions posed by several Democratic Congressmen, including Rep. Henry A. Waxman, about whether he intended, as Chairman of the House Government Reform and Oversight Committee, to investigate fund-raising practices of members of Con-

gress from both political parties. Democrats accused Burton, who himself was under investigation for questionable
fund-raising activities, of using the process to launch a partisan attack against the Clinton White House. Eric Schmitt,
"House Republicans Back Away From Wide Fund-Raising
Inquiry," *New York Times*, 4-11-97.

The liberals who control our colleges and universities don't hesitate to silence students they spot as conservative . . . *liberals
enjoy a near stranglehold on American college campuses.* They
often overwhelm students with a flood of leftist propaganda.
Liberals usually control the textbooks, the course selection, the
"official" student newspaper, the student government and, of
course, what's taught in the classes. They aggressively promote
their failed socialist economic policies, work to undermine traditional moral values and mask their "blame America first"
agenda with "politically-correct" multi-culturalism. *Liberals
want impressionable young people to believe their radical viewpoint is the new, true "intellectual" viewpoint.* Campus leftists
know the culture of our nation depends largely on the young
people of today. *And it seems they'll stop at nothing to end
conservative challenges to their control.*
    —*A mailing by House Majority Leader Dick Armey (R-TX).*
    "Right Wing Watch Online," PFAW.org, 11-12-99.

The Townhallathon:

SUPPORT YOUR LOCAL ~~PBS STATION~~ TOWNHALL.COM

Individual donations from ~~viewers~~ readers like you represent
the single largest source of support for ~~public television stations around the country~~ Townhall.com, and help your ~~PBS
station~~ favorite website to bring you outstanding ~~programs~~
columnists like ~~Now with Bill Moyers~~, Ann Coulter, ~~Master-
piece Theatre~~, David Limbaugh, ~~Frontline~~, Cal Thomas and
~~Antiques Roadshow~~ William F. Buckley Jr. Thank you! ~~PBS~~
Townhall.com wouldn't be the same without you. Give to-

day! Will you ensure that Townhall continues to spread the conservative message across the nation and join our Pledge Campaign?

—*A portion of a fundraising e-mail from the conservative website Townhall.com, 9-14-03.*

Fox News [Network], the owner and operator of the world famous Fox News Channel ("FNC"), is the owner of a federal trademark registration in the mark "Fair & Balanced." Fox News has used the mark "Fair & Balanced," sometimes depicted as "Fair and Balanced," (the "Trademark") to distinguish and brand FNC's distinctive method of newsgathering and reporting since its well-publicized launch in October 1996 . . .

Fox News employs a variety of on-air news personalities to give FNC its distinctive, number-one rated position in the national cable news marketplace. Prominent among those news personalities is Bill O'Reilly ("O'Reilly"), who is the host of cable television news's number-one rated program "The O'Reilly Factor." Penguin, through its imprint, EP Dutton ("Dutton"), plans to publish "Lies and the Lying Liars Who Tell Them: A Fair and Balanced Look at the Right," written by Franken (the "Book"), on September 22, 2003 . . . The preliminary cover of the Book (the "Preliminary Cover"), which is on display, among other places, in advertisements for the Internet sale of advance copies of the Book and on defendant Franken's official web site, prominently features Fox News' trademark "Fair and Balanced" as well as a photograph of O'Reilly in what appears to be the FNC television studio . . .

Defendants' intent in using the Trademark in this unauthorized fashion is clear—they seek to exploit Fox News' trademark, confuse the public as to the origin of the book, and accordingly, boost sales of the Book. This behavior constitutes willful trademark infringement . . . Moreover, since Franken's reputation as a political commentator is not of the same caliber as the stellar reputations of FNC's on-air talent, any association between Franken and Fox News is likely to blur or tarnish Fox News' distinctive mark . . . FNC was launched in October 1996. From the time of its launch until the present, FNC has been dedicated to presenting news in what it believes to be an unbiased fashion, eschewing ideological or political affiliation and allowing the viewer to reach his or her own conclusions about the news. FNC was created as a specific alternative to what its founders perceived as a liberal bias in the American media . . .

Defendants' use of the Trademark in the Book is likely to cause confusion among the public about whether Fox News has authorized or endorsed the Book . . .

Franken has recently been described as a "C-level political commentator" who is "increasingly unfunny." Franken has physically accosted Fox News personalities in the past, and was reported to have appeared either intoxicated or deranged as he flew into a rage near a table of Fox News personalities at a press correspondents' dinner in April 2003. Franken is neither a journalist nor a television news personality. He is not a well-respected voice in American politics; rather, he appears to be shrill and unstable. His views lack any serious depth or insight. Franken is commonly perceived as having to trade off of the name recognition of others in order to make money. One commentator has referred to Franken as a "parasite" for attempting to trade off of Fox News' brand and O'Reilly's fame in the Preliminary Cover of his Book . . .

As a result of Defendants' actions, Fox News is irreparably harmed . . .

—*From the legal complaint filed against Al Franken by Fox News.* Al Franken replied, ". . . I'd like to thank Fox for all the publicity. As far as the personal attacks go, when I read "intoxicated or deranged" and "shrill and unstable" in their complaint, I thought for a moment I was a Fox commentator. And by the way, a few months ago, I trademarked the word "funny." So when Fox calls me "unfunny," they're violating my trademark. I am seriously considering a countersuit. Mark Follman, "Fox Vs. Franken," Salon.com, 8-14-03.

If the conservative movement is to survive, we must neutralize the national liberal media. The national press has become the most powerful arm of the Left. And they are bent on destroying our movement through deceit, lies and character assassination. I've seen firsthand how the liberal biased media operate. For years, I've been one of their primary targets of ridicule and scorn. Why? Because I'm a conservative! Quite frankly, I'm fed up. I'm tired of watching conservatives getting bullied and threatened by the Left. I'm tired of watching principled men and women getting ridiculed and disparaged by liberal hypocrites . . . I believe the leaders of our country owe it to America's children to set a strong moral example that says character still counts!

> —*Former Speaker of the House Newt Gingrich.* "Right Wing Watch Online," PFAW.org, 11-12-99.

. . . but on a whole I think most people would agree that the media has a very liberal bent to it; that the media favors Al Gore as the next President of the United States. I think it has been clearly demonstrated in the last few days. I guess a couple of weeks ago, an advertiser hired by George W. Bush put an ad out that had rats or something on the ad. You could not believe it. Many of you saw it. That became the headlines and the starting news story on the newscasts in the evening. They have played this story over and over and over and over. That word did not come out of George W. Bush's mouth, but they tagged him with it; and they have been tagging him day after day after day.

> —*Rep. Scott McInnis (R-CO). Congressional Record,* H7859, 9-19-00. The TV ad was run by the Republican National Committee, starting in 9-00, 4400 times in 33 cities over two weeks. The word "rats" in huge letters flashed for 1/30th of a second before the word "bureaucrats." Some Democrats complained it was a subliminal message. "Newshour," PBS, 9-12-00.

Tom DeLay: Frankly, what irritates me the most are these blow-dried Napoleons that come on television and, in some cases, have their own agendas. They're not involved in daily briefings. They're not involved in the Command Center. They're not on the ground.

Judy Woodruff: Who are you referring to?

DeLay: Well, General Clark is one of them that is running for president, yet, he's paid to be an expert on your network. And he's questioning the plan and raising doubts as he becomes this expert. I think they would serve the nation better if they just comment on what they see and what they know, rather than putting their own agenda forward as an expert.

> —*House Majority Leader Tom DeLay (R-TX).* "Inside Politics," CNN, 4-3-03. General Clark did not announce his candidacy until 9-17-03.

They're reminders to all Americans that they need to watch what they say. Watch what they do. This is not a time for remarks like that; there never is.

> —*Former White House Press Secretary Ari Fleischer* criticizing remarks made by Bill Maher on "Politically Incorrect." Fleischer's comments were made on 9-26-01. Elisabeth Bumiller, "Bush's Spokesman is Stepping Down for Now," *New York Times,* 5-20-03.

We believe your very public criticism of President Bush at this important—and sensitive—time in our nation's history helps undermine the U.S. position, which ultimately could put our troops in even more danger.

> —*Baseball Hall of Fame President Dale Petroskey,* from a letter he wrote to Tim Robbins and Susan Sarandon cancelling a 15th-anniversary celebration of the film *Bull Durham* because of the actors' anti-Iraq-war stance. Petroskey is a former White House assistant press secretary to Ronald Reagan. Mark Naegele, "Who Brought Up Politics?" *Columbus Dispatch,* 4-11-03.

Recently a newspaper in my district in Michigan ran an editorial saying that people have the right to protest against the war; and they do, certainly. But now that we are in the war, I think we should encourage everybody to rethink what protesting does ... Imagine an analogy where a mom did not want her son to go out for boxing because it is too dangerous, or football; but once the decision was made, does she not cheer him and go to the game and cheer him on? Or a mom and dad that did not want their daughter to go out for basketball because, after all, that was sort of wrong for a young lady to do. That was a boy's sport. But once that young lady goes out for the team, the parents cheer her on and say, good game, do your best.

—Rep. Nick Smith (R-MI). *Congressional Record,* H2281,
   3-25-03.

PART V

This Land Was Made for You and Me

"150 parks . . . need to be dropped."
—REP. JAMES V. HANSEN (R-UT)

COMPASSIONATE CONSERVATISM

I believe that the homeless people should essentially be put to sleep. They should. I don't see any reason for them to exist. They are more of a burden than anything else. And, as a matter of fact, those who can survive, are the only ones worth surviving. These homeless people, for some reason, cannot survive anymore. . . . Not only they're a burden, but it's a waste of space. It's a waste of a human life, and I just don't see any other solution that's out there that works. They should just be, the homeless should just be put out of their misery. It's as simple as that . . .

    —*Emiliano Limon,* talk radio host, KFI-AM, Los Angeles, 11-17-94.

Part of the reason he [Minnesota Republican Gov. Arne Carlson] hasn't gone is that he doesn't want to get in the way. It may be a good place to get media attention, but it's not helpful to be parading around on the sandbags.

    —*Brian Dietz,* Carlson's press secretary, offering an explanation for why the governor had not visited the flooded towns on the Minnesota side of the Red River. Dane Smith, "Where's Arne? Some Victims Are Asking," *Minneapolis Star-Tribune,* 4-21-97.

Unfortunately, the children are very often just the victims of poverty. Unfortunately, a few more children will suffer for the conduct of their parents. But they suffer far more now. What

we're trying to do is solve the problems of poverty so there will
be fewer poor children.

> —*Rep. E. Clay Shaw (R-FL),* Chairman of the House Ways
> and Means subcommittee on human resources, admitting
> that the so-called "welfare reform" law will cause poor
> children to suffer deprivation. Peter T. Kilborn, "Shrinking
> Safety Net Cradles Hearts and Hopes of Poor Children,"
> *New York Times,* 11-30-96.

One of the major accomplishments of the last Congress was the
end to the Federal entitlement to welfare. And I recognize that
there are many skeptics, many doomsayers who wail and la-
ment and beat their chests and say that society, specifically those
poor and needy in our communities, that they are doomed . . .
Of course, we recognize how tough it is. There are single parents. There are two-income families that are struggling to juggle
family and jobs. There are businesses that are swimming might-
ily against the tide of regulation and bureaucracy which often
dissuades them from getting involved in community outreach.

> —*Rep. Kenny Hulshof (R-MD), Congressional Record,* H883,
> 3-11-97.

There are a few killers who want to stop the peace process that
we have started, and we must not let them. I call upon all nations to do everything they can to stop these terrorist killers.
Thank you. Now watch this drive.

> —*George W. Bush,* on a golf course in Kennebunkport, Maine,
> reacting to a suicide bombing in Israel that killed nine
> people. Mike Allen, "Before Golf, Bush Decries Latest
> Deaths in Mideast," *Washington Post,* 8-5-02.

If a helicopter were hit an hour later, after he came out and
spoke, should he come out again?

> —*White House Communications Director Dan Bartlett* after
> the downing of a Chinook helicopter, discussing the need
> for the president to express sympathy for the bereaved fami-

lies of soldiers and at the same time keep his eye on "the big picture." Elisabeth Bumiller, "Issue for Bush: How to Speak of Casualties?" *New York Times*, 11-5-03.

Should I feel guilty because I'm glad he's [Paul Wellstone] dead? If I feel like liberal democrats are American traitors, isn't that a logical response?
—*Posted on Lucianne.com*, 10-29-02. TheRant.info.

Before they lost interest in human rights, the radicals were all over animal rights and went around claiming McDonalds was exploiting the world's bovine population. And whatever happened to all those red anti-AIDS red ribbons the fashionistas used to wear? All that boring stuff's been forgotten in the rush to condemn President Bush as the "new Hitler" and volunteering to do Saddam's bidding by acting as human shields. It's as if they have Issue Deficit disorder—every year or two they lose interest and move on to something Newer! Trendier! More tear-inducing!
—*Laura Ingraham, Shut Up And Sing*, NY: Regnery, 2003, p. 156.

Pete: You probably weren't even born when Kennedy was killed, right?
Wayne: Ted Kennedy was killed?
Pete: Yeah, there'll be a party at my place later. (Laughter.)
—*Pete Davis and Wayne Kitchens* filling in for talk radio host Kim Peterson on Atlanta Newsradio WGST 640 AM, 9-11-03.

We will establish no-frills prisons where prisoners are required to work productively and make the threat of jail a real deterrent to crime.
—*Republican Party Platform*, adopted 8-12-96, p.18. This is consistent with Republican Sen. Phil Gramm's speech to the National Rifle Association during the '96 presidential

campaign. He said he aimed to "decriminalize prison labor," and that he found it amusing whenever the Congress passed a resolution condemning the use of prison labor in other countries.

One of the most common, and surely the most persuasive, arguments against capital punishment is that the state may execute an innocent person. One reason for its effectiveness is that proponents of capital punishment often do not know how to respond to it. That's a shame. For while the argument is emotionally compelling, it is morally and intellectually shallow. First of all, there is almost no major social good that does not lead to the death of innocent individuals. Over a million innocent people have been killed and maimed in car accidents. Would this argue for the banning of automobiles? To those whose criterion for acceptable social policy is that not one innocent die, it should. If it were proven that a strictly enforced 40-miles-per-hour speed limit on our nation's highways would save innocent lives, should we reduce highway limits to 40 miles per hour? Should all roller coasters be shut down because some innocents get killed riding on them? Anyone whose criterion for abolishing capital punishment is saving innocent lives should be for a 40-mile-per-hour speed limit and for abolishing roller coasters.

—*Dennis Prager.* "More innocents die when we don't have capital punishment," Townhall.com, 6-17-03.

Mr. Speaker, in conclusion, this Unfunded Mandate hurts State and local governments; it hurts schools and hospitals; it hurts nursing homes; it hurts workers who lose their jobs; and it hurts the businesses who have to lay them off. Perhaps the only people it does not hurt are us here in Congress. But, most importantly, it hurts the trust we have developed with State Houses and city halls. It is a reversion to an old way of doing business.

—*Rep. Steve Largent (R-OK)*, speaking out strongly against H.R. 3846 a bill to raise the minimum wage by $1 over a 2-3 year period. *Congressional Record,* H879, 3-9-00.

I don't understand how poor people think.
> —*George W. Bush* confiding in the Rev. Jim Wallis. Elisabeth
> Bumiller, "Bush 'Compassion' Agenda: An '04 Liability?"
> *New York Times,* 8-26-03.

. . . First, let me make it very clear, poor people aren't necessarily killers. Just because you happen to be not rich doesn't mean
you're willing to kill.
> —*George W. Bush* during a press conference in the Philip-
> pines. He was asked if terrorism in that country was caused
> by poverty. "Text of Bush Arroyo Remarks," Associated
> Press, 5-19-03.

We're the only nation in the world where all our poor people
are fat.
> —*Sen. Phil Gramm.* Bill Tammeus, "The Year of Talking Dan-
> gerously: Next time, folks, consider silence," *Denver Post,*
> 12-29-95.

I think we're showing sensible compassion.
> —*Rep. Jim Kolbe (R-AZ),* Chairman of the House Appro-
> priations subcommittee on foreign assistance, endorsing the
> White House request for funding of the global AIDS fight,
> a request $1 billion short of what the president promised.
> Elizabeth Bumiller, "Bush 'Compassion' Agenda: An '04
> Liability?" *New York Times,* 8-26-03.

Hunger relief is in transition, but I think as the Federal Government, Mr. Speaker, steps out of the equation, then the solution
does shift to the faith-based and community-based charities to
reach out to those in need. And I think this transition actually
strengthens the resolve of those creative people, those ministers, lay ministers, and others within the communities, to reach
out to those in need.
> —*Rep. Kenny C. Hulshof (R-MO),* in praise of welfare re-
> form. *Congressional Record,* H884, 3-11-97.

Particularly curious is the phenomenon of some conservatives, who ordinarily decry the welfare state, defending Social Security, which after all is just another welfare program. And just like other welfare programs, it isn't family friendly: Social Security transfers some of the responsibility for the care of one's parents to the state.

> —*Doug Bandow*, Senior Fellow at the Cato Institute. "Can 'Unbridled Capitalism' Be Tamed?" *Wall Street Journal* op-ed piece, 3-19-97.

On September 11, we saw clearly that evil exists in this world, and that it does not value life. The terrible events of that fateful day have given us, as a Nation, a greater understanding about the value and wonder of life. Every innocent life taken that day was the most important person on earth to somebody; and every death extinguished a world. Now we are engaged in a fight against evil and tyranny to preserve and protect life. In so doing, we are standing again for those core principles upon which our Nation was founded.

NOW, THEREFORE, I, GEORGE W. BUSH, President of the United States of America, by virtue of the authority vested in me by the Constitution and the laws of the United States, do hereby proclaim Sunday, January 20, 2002, as National Sanctity of Human Life Day. I call upon all Americans to reflect upon the sanctity of human life. Let us recognize the day with appropriate ceremonies in our homes and places of worship, rededicate ourselves to compassionate service on behalf of the weak and defenseless, and reaffirm our commitment to respect the life and dignity of every human being.

IN WITNESS THEREOF, I have hereunto set my hand this eighteenth day of January, in the year of our Lord two thousand two, and of the Independence of the United States of America the two hundred and twenty-sixth.

> —*George W. Bush*. National Sanctity of Human Life Day, 2002. By the President of the United States of America: A

Proclamation. This proclamation was issued 4 days before the 29th anniversary of the Supreme Court decision in *Roe v. Wade*. Whitehouse.gov.

The three men who murdered James Byrd, guess what's going to happen to them? They're going to be put to death. A jury found them guilty. It's going to be hard to punish them any worse after they get put to death.
—*George W. Bush* during the second Gore/Bush 2000 Presidential Debate, 10-11-00. Debates.org.

Tucker Carlson: Did you meet with any of them [Bianca Jagger and others seeking clemency for double murderer Karla Faye Tucker]?
George W. Bush: No, I didn't meet with any of them. I didn't meet with Larry King either when he came down for it [the interview with Tucker]. I watched his interview with [her] though. He asked her real difficult questions, like "What would you say to Governor Bush?"
Carlson: What was her answer?
Bush: Please [whimpering, lips pressed in mock desperation], don't kill me.
—*Tucker Carlson*, "Devil May Care," *Talk* magazine, 9-99, p. 106. This Karla Tucker-Larry King exchange never took place. But Carlson comments that during her interview with King, Tucker implied that Bush was pandering to pro-death penalty voters and this may have angered Bush, who "has a long memory for slights."

"Corrections Day"
or Damn the Public, Full Speed Ahead

We commend House Speaker Newt Gingrich and congressional Republicans in their innovative efforts to rescind, overturn, and zero-out absurd bureaucratic red tape and rules through the process known as "Corrections Day."
—*Republican Party Platform*, 8-12-96, p.12.

I think if we have some gridlock on the regulatory agencies . . . the American people will stand up and say, "Yeah! Hallelujah!"
—*Rep. David M. McIntosh (R-IN)*, on the GOP drive to stall the enforcement of regulations protecting public health and safety. *Boston Globe*, 2-24-95.

As far as I am concerned, the shutdown of non-essential Federal agencies would constitute the fulfillment of my mission as a Member of Congress. However, in the past, the Government has, in fact, shut down temporarily as Congress and the President fought over the details of the funding for the Federal agencies. I suspect that, outside the Capital Beltway, no one noticed when it was shut down.
—*Rep. Philip M. Crane (R-IL)* defending the actions of his party which resulted in a partial shut-down of the government. *Congressional Record*, E1973, 10-18-95.

. . . Any restraint placed on broadcasters' free speech rights must be a reasonable means to further our public interest goals. The federal court opinions specifically tell me that any restrictions we place on ownership must be based on concrete evidence—not on fear and speculation about hypothetical media monopolies intent on exercising some type of Vulcan mind control.

—FCC Commissioner Kathleen Q. Abernathy (R), explaining her vote to remove long-established regulations on media ownership. "Excerpts from Statements Issued by the Commission Members After the Vote," *New York Times*, 6-3-03.

Mr. Speaker, as a lawyer, I am the last person to suggest that everybody in my profession is a money-grubbing, scum-sucking toad. The actual figure is only about 73 percent. Ha ha, I am of course just pulling the Speaker's honorable leg. The vast majority of lawyers are responsible professionals, as well as, in many ways, human beings. But we really do need to do something about all these frivolous lawsuits. We have reached the point where a simple product such as a stepladder has to be sold with big red warning labels all over it, telling you not to dance on it, hold parties on it, touch electrical wires with it, hit people with it, swallow it, and so forth, because some idiot somewhere, some time, actually did these things with a stepladder, got hurt, filed a lawsuit and won. My feeling, Mr. Speaker, is that anybody who swallows a stepladder deserves whatever he gets.

—Rep. Steven C. LaTourette (R-OH) speaking about plantiffs' attorneys and lawsuits. *Congressional Record*, H2899, 3-9-95.

OSHA [the Occupational Safety and Health Administration] is one agency that has turned a reasonable and an important mission into a bureaucratic nightmare for the American economy. Common sense was long ago shown the door over at OSHA. OSHA is one agency that needs to be restructured, reinvented, or just plain removed.

—Rep. Charles Norwood (R-GA). *Congressional Record*, H30893-14-95.

Most employers would describe OSHA as the Gestapo of the Federal Government.
   —*Rep. John A. Boehner (R-OH)*. *Washington Post National Weekly Edition*, 9-4-95.

I don't think we need any more legislation regulating tobacco.
   —*Rep. Thomas J. Bliley, Jr. (R-VA)*.*Washington Post*, 11-11-94.

[The Food and Drug Administration is] the leading job-killer in America [and FDA Commissioner David A. Kessler is] a bully and a thug.
   —*House Speaker Newt Gingrich (R-GA)*. "Don't Undermine the FDA; It's a Needed Protection, Speeding Drugs to Market Isn't the Only Concern," *Buffalo News* editorial, 2-5-95.

. . . I was going to take this hour to highlight the fact that I am introducing a bill establishing a moratorium on Federal regulations . . . Detailed safety data sheets are required for such dangerous material as Joy dishwashing liquid, chalk, and even air . . . OSHA has classified childrens' teeth as Hazardous Waste . . .
   —*Rep. Tom DeLay (R-TX)*, in support of the Republican effort to roll back federal environmental and work safety regulations. *Congressional Record*, H157 & H158, 1-9-95.

. . . We will enact the TEAM Act to empower employers and employees to act as a team, rather than as adversaries . . . another way to replace conflict with concerted action is to transform OSHA from an adversarial agency into a pioneering advocate of safer productivity.
   —*Republican Party Platform*, adopted 8-12-96, p. 7.

The Bill [The Job Creation and Wage Enhancement Act] requires federal agencies to issue an annual report projecting the cost to the private sector of compliance with all federal regulations. The cost of the regulations will then be capped below its current level forcing agencies to (1) find more cost-effective ways

to reach goals and (2) identify regulatory policies whose benefits exceed their cost to the private sector.
—*Contract With America, etc.* NY: Times Books, 1994. p. 132.

We will target resources on the most serious risks to health, safety, and the environment, rather than on politically inspired causes, and will require peer-reviewed risk assessments based on sound science. We will require agencies to conduct cost-benefit analyses of their regulations and pursue alternatives to the outdated Clinton command-and-control approach.
—*Republican Party Platform*, adopted 8-12-96, p.12.

. . . the one fact that must be kept in mind is that our government operates in such a way that the common good is no longer the goal. Regulation has become a goal in and of itself. Not only is that dangerous, it is unfair and extraordinarily expensive—almost $600 billion a year.
—*Sen. Bill Frist (R-TN). Congressional Record*, S9829, 7-13-95.

I don't want to abolish government. I simply want to reduce it to the size where I can drag it into the bathroom and drown it in the bathtub.
—*Grover Norquist*, President of Americans for Tax Reform, at a meeting of conservatives in the offices of his organization. NPR Morning Edition, 5-25-01. ATR.org.

PUBLIC ENEMY: PUBLIC SCHOOLS

*... You know if there was any piece of legislation I would pass
it would be to blow up colleges of education. I know that's not
politically correct ...*

—*Reid Lyon,* Chief, Child Development and Behavior Branch,
National Institute of Child Health and Human Development, and an advisor on child health and education research
to George W. Bush, 11-19-02. Excelgov.org.

Mr. Speaker, if we were a manufacturer that produced an inferior product, what would we think if we had to face real competition for the first time? My guess is that we would feel the
same as those government-owned schools which are absolutely
terrified by school choice. Mr. Speaker, they are terrified by
school choice because they know that kids whose parents do
not have the money to move or to send their kids to a private
school have no choice but to send their kids to another government school where they have to pass through metal detectors,
where there is no order in the classroom, and where the idea of
standards and accountability leave them lagging behind their
international peers. Government-owned schools have a complete monopoly, plain and simple, and all monopolies fear competition. I can 100 percent guarantee an inferior product of any
human endeavor if producers are shielded from competition, if
producers are not forced to innovate and improve. Mr. Speaker,
just look at the Communist legacy in every single case, especially education. The bureaucrats who just love their government-owned schools and want to protect their monopoly will
do so at just about any cost, regardless of whether kids have to
receive an inferior education and blighted futures. Mr. Speaker,

it is wrong and I have lost patience with those who refuse to do best for the kids. School choice is the answer.
    —*Rep. Bob Schaffer (R-CO)*. *Congressional Record*, H7124, 9-10-97.

Uncle Sam darkened our doorway and began to dictate to us how to raise our children. The public education system that was established by our founding fathers as a means for teaching every child the word of God became a vehicle for the federal government to turn our children from God and from his law. Our children are taught to tolerate homosexuality, but to frown upon Christianity. To trust teachers and government more than parents and God. Instead of affirming what is taught in the home, our schools have become the enemy of the family.
    —*Carmen Pate*, President of Concerned Women for America, 2-98. PFAW.org.

Madam Speaker, as a former schoolteacher myself, I would like to review the liberals' record on the issue of education in this country. In the 1960s, the liberals decided to "dumb down" the curriculum and now across the country academic rigor is absent from many of our public schools. The predictable result is that student achievement in many areas has plummeted. The liberals also decided that self-esteem was in and that actual knowledge was out. The liberals embraced bogus, faddish teaching methods and produced a generation of children who never learned to read. And now the liberals oppose legislation we recently passed here in Congress which would allow parents to put their own money in accounts and not to pay tax on the money in those accounts for educating their children, kindergarten through high school. They say it would somehow hurt the public schools. Baloney. Let us make it a little easier for parents, particularly middle-class parents, to provide a quality education for their children.
    —*Rep. Steve Chabot (R-OH)*. *Congressional Record*, H5300, 6-25-98.

Now, what passes for education consists of assimilating "information," not truths, taught by an army of propagandists who begin with certain assumptions about history (it was dominated by dead white males and so we must rewrite and reinterpret it through the prism of the contemporary political framework called "political correctness"); about science (the only truth we can discover is that taught to us by science, and Carl Sagan is right—the cosmos is all there is, was, or will be); about life ("your parents are dumb; listen to your teachers and counselors instead; we know what is best for you; here, have a condom").

> —*Cal Thomas, The Things That Matter Most*. NY: HarperCollins, 1994, p.162.

The system in Houston is still standing, it's vertical and it has been reviewed by some of the best. And the data can take it because it is earnest, it is open, it is objective and it is there . . . Because I have not been there since December 2000 I wasn't in a position to know the details.

> —*Education Secretary Rod Paige* on the previously under-reported high dropout rate among Houston public school students in 2000–2001. Dr. Paige was superintendent of Houston schools from 1994–2001, and was widely praised for the schools' performance. Diana Jean Schemo, "Education Secretary Defends School System He Once Led," *New York Times*, 7-26-03.

The federal antitrust lawsuit against Microsoft has illustrated the evil of monopolies and the tactics that monopolists use to maintain their power. But the biggest monopoly in our midst, the public school system guarded by the teachers unions, seems so far untouchable.

> —*Phyllis Schlafly*, "NEA fights to maintain school monopoly," Copley News Service, 7-26-00.

Todd Starnes: Given the choice between private and Christian—or private and public universities, what do you think—who do you think has the best deal?

Sec. Rod Paige: That's a judgment, too, that would vary because each of them have real strong points and some of them have some vulnerabilities. But, you know, all things being equal, I would prefer to have a child in a school where there's a strong appreciation for values, the kind of values that I think are associated with the Christian communities, and so that this child can be brought up in an environment that teaches them to have strong faith and to understand that there is a force greater than them personally.

Starnes: What do you think one of the chief benefits of a religious education is?

Paige: Because of the strong value system support. Values go right along with that. In some of our other schools, we don't have quite as strong a push for values as I think we would need. In a religious environment the value system is pretty well set and supported. In public schools there are so many different kids from different kinds of experiences that it's very hard to get consensus around some core values.

> —*Education Secretary Rod Paige*, during a 3-7-03 interview with Todd Starnes of the *Baptist Press*, published 4-7-03. Bpnews.net. This article caused a strong reaction from public school educators, who called for Paige's resignation. Paige said his remarks were taken out of context. The *Baptist Press* announced they would no longer use articles by Todd Starnes.

. . . We will abolish the Department of Education, end federal meddling in our schools, and promote family choice at all levels of learning.

We know what works in education, and it isn't the liberal fads of the last thirty years. It's discipline, parental involvement, emphasis on basics including computer technology, phonics instead of look-say reading, and dedicated teaching.

> —*Republican Party Platform*, adopted 8-12-96, p. 22. This point is apparently so important to the Republican Party that it is written twice in their Party Platform.

KILLING BIG BIRD

Mr. Speaker, we would not possibly kill Big Bird if we wanted to kill Big Bird. Nobody wants to kill Big Bird. The fact is that Big Bird generates hundreds and hundreds of millions of dollars of revenue every single year to the great benefit of the people who created it, and any suggestion that Big Bird is going anywhere is crazy.

> —*Rep. Martin Hoke (R-OH)*, responding to Rep. Eliot Engel's (D-NY) plea not to drastically cut funds for Public Broadcasting and thus "kill Big Bird." *Congressional Record*, H3161, 3-15-95.

The Soviet system tried to manage production based on the values of the central government and say how money ought to be spent, and it collapsed. And when it came down, it wasn't long before the Berlin wall fell, too. Thankfully, the people are free there, and they are rejoicing over their freedom, and the government that was at the center of things no longer tells them what to produce or what not to produce . . . Here we have the National Endowment for the Arts with the argument or suggestion that it is a good thing to have Government telling people from the center of the Nation what they should or should not reward with their own support.

> —*Sen. John Ashcroft (R-MO)*. *Congressional Record*, S9388, 9-16-97.

I don't understand why they call it public broadcasting. As far as I am concerned, there's nothing public about it; it's an elitist enterprise. Rush Limbaugh is public broadcasting.

> —*Newt Gingrich*, attacking the Corporation for Public Broadcasting. *Charlotte Observer*, 3-10-96.

I am honored to co-sponsor this amendment, which would eliminate funding for the National Endowment for the Arts. Other
Senators will voice their support, I believe, for the Ashcroft-
Helms amendment . . . the Senate has learned a very great deal
about the way the National Endowment for the Arts conducts
its affairs, and, thank the Lord, so have many millions of Americans found out about it across the land. They constitute loud
voices to echo exactly what the House of Representatives did
the month before last, I believe it was, in cutting off all funding,
zeroing the National Endowment for the Arts. For one thing, it
is self-evident that many of the beneficiaries of NEA grants are
contemptuous of—how to say it—traditional moral standards
. . . Following that vote in the House of Representatives, the
NEA's supporters did the usual thing. They trotted out their
customary absurdities in describing an America without art, an
America without culture unless the Senate restores full funding
to the NEA. And they did that with violins being played and
weeping voices. Baloney. Perhaps the Senate will default on its
responsibilities, but it will have to do it after a number of Senators have made clear why the House action with reference to
the NEA was entirely justified.
 —*Sen. Jesse Helms (R-NC). Congressional Record*, S9314,
  9-15-97. The Helms-Ashcroft amendment was defeated, 9-
  17-97, by a vote of 77 to 23.

The NEA [National Endowment for the Arts] is welfare for
artists.
 —*Wes Minter,* radio host, WCCO-AM, Minneapolis, 8-7-95.

As a first step in reforming government, we support elimination of the Departments of Commerce, Housing and Urban
Development, Education and Energy, and the elimination,
defunding or privatization of agencies which are obsolete, re-
dundant, of limited value, or too regional in focus. Examples of
agencies we seek to defund or to privatize are the National En-

dowment for the Arts, The National Endowment for the Humanities, the Corporation for Public Broadcasting, and the Legal Services Corporation.
        —*Republican Party Platform*, adopted 8-12-96, p.10.

Mr. Chairman, we face a lot of hard budget choices, but we have still got some pretty easy decisions to make as well, like ending the National Endowment for the Humanities, the NEH. My amendment would do just that.
        —*Rep. Steve Chabot (R-OH)*. *Congressional Record*, H7055, 7-17-95.

I don't know what all they [budget committee negotiators] have discussed. I believe we are going to zero out NEA [National Endowment for the Arts] and, in doing so, it will be good for art and freedom in the arts. It is long overdue to be done.
        —*House Majority Leader Richard K. Armey (R-TX)*. Eric Pianin, "Disagreements on Details of Budget Deal May Delay Congressional Action," *Washington Post*, 5-14-97.

CARING FOR OUR HEALTH

As incredible as this may seem to you and me, the Clintons' health care plan provides for just such penalties and imprisonment. But even worse, your child would suffer or die needlessly. You would be powerless. The government has stripped you of your God-given right to provide for your child's care as you see fit. Federal bureaucrats would have more say-so over your child's treatment than you, your spouse, or even your doctor. . . . We must stop the Clinton administration from destroying our rights as parents and our constitutional freedoms as citizens.

—*John W. Whitehead*, President of the Rutherford Institute, in a 3-94 fund-raising letter. AU.org.

If we're going to continue to mandate these things, ultimately, employers will just stop offering health care to their employees.

—*State Rep. Lee Daniels (R-IL)*, commenting on the HMO reform bill passed by the Illinois House, 73-37, to curb the anti-consumer excesses of HMO's. "New HMO rules OK'd by House," *Chicago Tribune*, 4-26-97.

I was blessed Wednesday by the birth of a grandson, Max Novak. His mother, Angie, left the hospital after one night. She was dying to bring her son home. A new law guaranteeing a 48-hour stay for new mothers was pushed by President Clinton as a campaign gimmick: A classic case of unneeded governmental meddling, further burdening the overburdened health care system.

—*Robert Novak*. "Capital Gang," CNN, 1-25-97.

Protection of Women's Health—Because of the personal and social pain caused by abortions, the Party calls for the protection of both women and their unborn children from pressure for unwanted abortions. We call for laws requiring abortion providers, prior to an abortion, to provide women full knowledge of the health, surgical and psychological risks to abortion, development of the unborn child, and abortion alternatives. We urge state and federal legislation to be enacted defining failure to obtain informed consent prior to abortion as medical malpractice with all attendant civil liability.
—*Texas State GOP Platform 2002*. TexasGOP.org.

Stem Cell Research—We commend the President for banning any further human embryo stem cell harvesting and call upon the US Congress to pass legislation supporting the President. The Party opposes any furtherance of this directive, by legislation or otherwise, that would result in the destruction of human embryos for medical research. The Republican Party encourages stem cell research using cells from umbilical cords, from adults, and from any other means which does not destroy human embryos and/or adults. The party opposes any state funds used to destroy human embryos for research.
—*Ibid*.

I knew when I voted against it [legalizing drug imports from Canada] that it would be an attack issue. But as a physician, I took a Hippocratic oath to do no harm, and some of these drugs are dangerous.
—*Rep. Ernie Fletcher (R-KY)*, non-practicing physician and candidate for governor, responding to criticism from his opponent Kentucky Attorney General Ben Chandler. During a televised debate, Chandler accused Fletcher of "being in the pocket of prescription drug manufacturers." Fletcher won the election. Gardiner Harris, "Cheap Drugs From Canada: Another Political Hot Potato," *New York Times*, 10-23-03.

I think your figure is around, I think, 40, 41, or 42 or 43 million people were, uh, do not have health insurance. That accordingly probably is not any higher than it was, say, in 1950.
There's always people that choose to spend their money somewhere else, or they're people like I—small businessmen—I in-
sured my employees, but I didn't insure myself, so I would be in
among the uninsured . . . If Medicare is driving the cost of medical care, then let's take a look at that and get the patient more
involved. We can't control the cost, and we can't continue to
try to push out and cover all the ills that happen to people along
the way in life. And I think it's just part of life, and we have to
kind of plan for it . . .
  —*Sen. Conrad Burns (R-MT).* "Washington Journal," C-
     SPAN, 10-1-03.

Universal coverage is a myth. It does not exist anywhere in the
world. The effort to get there becomes a code word for socialized medicine. I am opposed to socialized medicine.
  —*Rep. Bill Archer (R-TX),* Chairman of the Ways and Means
     Committee. Bennett Roth, "Election '94/Health care bill
     could re-emerge in total makeover," *Houston Chronicle,*
     11-13-94.

My friends, can I just tell you the way this is, two dollars, a co-
payment of two dollars means that these drugs are essentially
free! Two bucks! . . . In addition to Medicaid, the major drug
companies offer compassionate care programs for those who
can demonstrate they can't afford their medicines, and these
companies spend billions of dollars a year in dispersing free
drugs in hardship cases like this. So you come up with a law
that says "oh, if somebody says they can't afford a co-payment
you gotta give the medicine anyway" so, the co-pay goes up
from 50 cents to two bucks and all the patients have to do is say
they can't afford it . . .

This is how serious the entitlement mentality in this country has gotten. People can't—Two bucks co-payment, that's all it is! For prescrip—two dollars! But can you buy a can of dog food for two dollars? You can't even say that I am faced with the choice here of dog food or my prescription co-payment because dog food's more expensive than two bucks. And we don't have dog food co-pays yet, but I'll bet you to hell they're coming. Dog food co-pays just so Democrats will have some hardship cases to demonstrate how it is the country doesn't care anymore about the seasoned [sic] citizens of America! Two bucks!
—Rush Limbaugh, 3-17-03.

. . . There exists a surplus of tiny human embryos in cold storage, left there until the mothers and fathers can decide what to do with them. The surplus is a result of infertile couples resorting to in vitro fertilization of sperm and egg in an effort to induce a successful pregnancy—a test tube baby, if you will. Doctors, hoping for success, harvest and fertilize more eggs than necessary. Some want to use these as an endless source of stem cells for medical research. Others see them as valuable members of the human race awaiting a home of their own. The Snowflakes Embryo Adoption Program in Fullerton, Calif., has a solution: adopting the embryos. This releases them from their "frozen prison" in what Dr. James Dobson has referred to as "adoption at an earlier age." And now President George W. Bush is encouraging this with $1 million in the form of a grant to help publicize frozen embryo adoption . . .
—Tom Neven, "Seeing Them for What They Are," Focus on the Family magazine, 2-26-03.

Newt's ideas are influencing how we at AARP are thinking about our national role in health promotion and disease prevention and in our advocating for system change. He writes: "The healthcare debate is not about Democrats and Republicans. It's not about liberals and conservatives. The health debate is about your life and the lives of your family. The healthcare debate is about your money and your family's money." I would only add, it's also about your future . . . and America's.

—*William D. Novelli*, Executive Director and CEO of AARP, from his preface to Newt Gingrich, *Saving Lives and Saving Money*, Washington, DC: Gingrich Communications, 2003.

What do you think the health care financing administration [Medicare] is? It's a centralized command bureaucracy. It's everything we're telling Boris Yeltsin to get rid of. Now we don't get rid of it in round one because we don't think that's politically smart and we don't think that's the right way to go through a transition. But we believe it's going to wither on the vine because we think people are going to voluntarily leave it. Voluntarily.

—*Newt Gingrich* in a speech to Blue Cross, 10-24-95.

Whether they were upset about—about this [Mad Cow Disease] and would be less inclined to eat beef, and they say yes. And I think it is the pounding by the cable news networks, by the—by the media. But it's also I think we're turning into a—a country of wimps and whiners who think—people who think they're going to live forever. And I think it just—the chances of anybody having trouble with this is ridiculous, but the kind of country we're coming in, there could be an economic fallout. I can't believe there's a political fallout, although the Democratic candidates are claiming it's all George W. Bush's fault, . . . whining and wimping that you get about—people wringing their hands about, "My goodness, I might get sick eating beef!" It's just ridiculous!

—*Robert Novak*, "Capital Gang," CNN, 1-3-04.

Earth Day at the GOP

. . . When did nature get so whiney? We're not allowed to do anything to nature anymore, except look at it. It's like porn with leaves. And where's this delicate balance I always hear so much about? Every time I watch "Animal Planet," I see a rabid harp seal popping penguins down his gullet like they were maitre d'Tic Tacs. To me, nature always appears more unbalanced than Gary Busey with a clogged eustachian tube.

And then there's global warming. I didn't even know the details on global warming so I looked it up. There are a lot of vying statistics, but I think the crux of it is the temperature has gone up roughly 1.8 degrees over a hundred years. Am I the only one who finds that amazingly stable? Hey, I'm happy it's gone up. I'm always a little chilly anyway.

—Dennis Miller, FOXNews.com, 9-12-03.

We condemn the current [Clinton] administration's policy of resorting to confrontation first. Instead we should work cooperatively to ensure that our environmental policy meets the particular needs of geographic regions and localities.

—Republican Party Platform 2000. RNC.org.

Wherever is environmentally responsible to do so, we will promote market-based programs that are voluntary, flexible, comprehensive, and cost-effective. The Endangered Species Act (ESA), for example, is sometimes counter-productive toward its truly important goal of protecting rare species, 75 percent of which are located on private land. Its punitive approach actually encourages landowners to remove habitat to avoid federal intervention. This serves as a disincentive for private landowners to do more to restore habitat and become private stewards of wildlife. The legislation needs incentive-based cooperation among federal, state, local, and tribal governments, and private citizens. The result will be a more effective ESA that better protects wildlife diversity.

. . . research is needed to understand both the cause and the impact of global warming. That is why the Kyoto treaty was repudiated in a lopsided, bipartisan Senate vote. A Republican president will work with businesses and with other nations to reduce harmful emissions through new technologies without compromising America's sovereignty or competitiveness—and without forcing Americans to walk to work.
—*Ibid.*

God said, "Earth is yours. Take it. Rape it. It's yours."
—*Ann Coulter.* "Hannity & Colmes," Fox News Channel, 6-20-01.

Tapping Alaskan oil would help America become far less dependent on foreign oil and less vulnerable to disruptions in the flow of oil imports from the Persian Gulf and other OPEC countries. After September 11th and new and persisting rumors of oil wars and embargoes against the United States by Islamic countries in the Middle East, tapping ANWR makes real sense. There's just one problem: left-wing environmentalists hate the idea of drilling for oil in most places in the United States, onshore or off. But they say they are particularly exercised about drilling in ANWR because of their concern for this barren acreage and a certain species of animal inhabiting it—the Porcupine Caribou. A Porcupine Caribou? If you were in Congress, would you shape the economic and energy security of over 280 million Americans around the sexual migration patterns and birthing habits of a bunch of Porcupine Caribou?
—*Sean Hannity, Let Freedom Ring*, NY: Reganbooks, HarperCollins, 2002, p. 188.

In fact, if I had my choice, I believe that the existing law [Endangered Species Act] should be repealed and Congress should start over and develop a program that achieves national interests in the protection of endangered species without encroaching on private property and the prerogatives of states.

> —*Bennett W. Raley*, written testimony to the U.S. House of Representatives, Committee on Resources, Oversight Hearings on the Implementation of the Endangered Species Act, 7-24-99. Raley is now Assistant Secretary for Water and Science at the Department of the Interior. Resourcescommittee.house.gov.

The huge debate that's looming . . . is whether or not the purpose of the act is to protect water quality for use—whether human, agricultural or industrial—or whether it's a radically different goal of returning the streams to a pristine condition.

> —*Bennett W. Raley*, lobbying against a 1994 bill to reauthorize the Clean Water Act. Zachary Coile, "Bennett W. Raley/ Bush picks his man for water wars/ Lawyer would have big sway in California issues," *San Francisco Chronicle*, 4-19-01.

This [current environmental] legislation puts the rights of these Americans who do the work, pay the taxes, and pull the wagon on the same par as the blind cave spider and the fairy shrimp.

> —*Rep. Lamar S. Smith (R-TX)*, in support of the Private Property Protection Act of 1995. *Congressional Record*, H2233, 2-27-95.

Since [the 1970s], times have changed. People have changed. Go to any person you know and show him or her the "Wilderness Letter" that the late, great Western writer, Wallace Stegner, wrote in 1960, from which I quote:

"Something will have gone out of us as a people if we ever let the remaining wilderness be destroyed; if we permit the last virgin forests to be turned into comic books and plastic cigarette cases; if we drive the few remaining members of the wild species into zoos or to extinction; if we pollute the last clean air and dirty the last clean streams and push our paved roads through the last of the silence, so that never again will Americans be free in their country from the noise, the exhausts, the stinks of human and automotive waste."

Who today is not moved by such words? No one. But how relevant are they today? Not very.

. . . There are important differences between the actions of Teddy Roosevelt and Bill Clinton. Bill Clinton is trying to harness extremism in the environmental movement for broader political gain. Teddy Roosevelt founded a conservation club named after Daniel Boone and Davy Crockett.

—*Mark Rey*, now Undersecretary for Natural Resources and Environment (Dept. of Agriculture), then an aide to Sen. Larry Craig (R-ID). The S.J. Hall lecture, University of California, Center For Forestry, Berkeley, CA, 10-13-00. CNR.berkeley.edu.

. . . As with education, Social Security and so many other issues, the Democrats have been expert at constructing a narrative in which Republicans and conservatives are the bad guys. And if Americans swallow that story, then whatever comes later is mere detail.

Indeed, it can be helpful to think of environmental (and other) issues in terms of "story." *A compelling story, even if factually inaccurate, can be more emotionally compelling than a dry recitation of the truth . . . As with those other issues the first (and most important) step to neutralizing the problem and eventually bringing people around to your point of view on environmental issues is to convince them of your sincerity and concern . . .* (italics in original).

—*Republican pollster Frank Luntz*. From a 2002 briefing book for officials and candidates. A copy was obtained by the Environmental Working Group. "Winning the Global Warming Debate—an Overview," p. 132. EWG.org

... You cannot allow yourself to be labeled "anti-environment" simply because you are opposed to the current regulatory configuration (your opponents will almost certainly try to label you that way). The public does not approve of the current regulatory process, and Americans certainly don't want an increased regulatory burden, but they will put a higher priority on environmental protection and public health than on cutting regulations.

Even Republicans prioritize protecting the environment. That is why you must explain how it is possible to pursue a common sense or sensible environmental policy that preserves all the gains of the past two decades without going to extremes, and allows for new science and technologies to carry us even further. Give citizens the idea that progress is being frustrated by over-reaching government, and you will hit a very strong strain in the American psyche.
—*Ibid.*, p. 136.

... The "arsenic in the water" imbroglio of Spring 2001 was the biggest public relations misfire of President Bush's first year in office ... How do we avoid such debacles in the future? It's all about how you frame your argument, and the order in which you present your facts. Don't allow yourself to become bogged down in minutiae when you should be presenting the big picture. You should have the details at hand to back you up, to be sure, but don't be afraid to begin painting in broad strokes. A more effective, step-by-step approach to educating the public would have been:

THE "ARSENIC" COMMUNICATION LADDER

Every American has the right to clean, healthy and safe drinking water.

Republicans are dedicated to the continued improvement of our nation's water supply, and to ensuring that Americans have the best quality water available. We all drink water. We all want it safe and clean.

Today, there are minute, tiny amounts of arsenic in our drinking water. It has always been this way. It will always be this way.

Based on sound science, the government's standard is that there should be no more than 50 parts of arsenic per billion.

In the last weeks before Bill Clinton left office, he issued an executive order reducing the standard from 50 to 10 parts of arsenic per billion—but he did not act for eight years because it was neither a priority nor a health risk.

Before this new standard takes effect, we would like to make sure that it is necessary to make this change. The decision was reached quickly, without public debate, and without evidence that this change will make our water appreciably safer.

—*Ibid.*, p. 138.

. . . The most important principle in any discussion of global warming is your commitment to sound science. Americans unanimously believe all environmental rules and regulations should be based on sound science And common sense. Similarly, our confidence in the ability of science and technology to solve our nation's ills is second to none. Both perceptions will work in your favor if properly cultivated.

The scientific debate is closing [against us] but not yet closed. There is still a window of opportunity to challenge the science . . .

—*Ibid.*

I believe a responsible nation is one that protects the environment. Yet the government sometimes doesn't help. And that's what I'm here to discuss—(laughter)—those moments when the government doesn't help, when the government stands in the way. For example, power plants are discouraged from doing routine maintenance because of government regulations. And by routine maintenance, I mean replacing worn-out boiler tubes or boiler fans. And all that does is it makes the plant less reliable, less efficient and not as environmentally friendly as it should be. So I changed those regulations, my administration did . . . The old regulations, let me start off by telling you, undermined our goals for protecting the environment and growing the economy. The old regulations on the books made it difficult to either protect the economy or—protect the environment or grow the economy. Therefore, I wanted to get rid of them. I'm interested in job creation and clean air, and I believe we can do both . . . That's the reality. Regulations intended to enhance air quality made it really difficult for companies to do that which is necessary, to not only produce more energy, but to do it in a cleaner way.

    —*George W. Bush.* "President Visits Detroit Edison Monroe Power Plant in Monroe, Michigan Remarks by the President to Plant Employees and Local Community Leaders," Whitehouse.gov, 9-15-03.

I think the only good dove is a dead dove and that's what the people of Ohio said at the polls on Nov. 3.

    —*Talk Radio Host Bill Cunningham*, WLW, Cincinnati, on a statewide vote that defeated an effort to ban dove hunting. Greg Paeth, "WLW says dove blast is no joke," *Cincinnati Post*, 11-13-98.

150 parks of the some 368 [in the National Park System] need to be dropped . . . When a bureaucracy reaches a certain critical mass, its only goal is to ensure its own propagation. It begins to serve the monster rather than the people.

    —*Rep. James V. Hansen (R-UT).* "ESA Rewrite Dominated Western States Summit," *Elko Daily Free Press*, 7-31-95.

I'd like to get every environmentalist, put 'em up against a wall, and shoot 'em.

    —*Bob Grant. New York Magazine*, 10-24-94.

I consider the EPA to be a regulatory agency out of control.

    —*Rep. Jerry Lewis (R-CA). Congressional Record*, H7933, 7-28-95.

The EPA, the Gestapo of government, pure and simply has been one of the major claw-hooks that the government maintains on the backs of our constituents.
—*Rep. Tom DeLay (R-TX).* "House Rejects GOP Effort to Impede EPA's Work," Associated Press, 7-29-95.

[Environmentalists] are a socialist group of individuals that are the tool of the Democrat Party . . . I'm proud to say that they are my enemy. They are not Americans, never have been Americans, never will be Americans.
—*Rep. Don Young (R-AK),* member of the House Committee on Resources, speaking on Alaska Public Radio Network, 8-19-96

Much of the debate over global warming is predicated on fear rather than science. Global-warming alarmists see a future plagued by catastrophic flooding, war, terrorism, economic dislocations, drought, crop failures, mosquito-borne diseases, and harsh weather, all caused by man-made greenhouse gas emissions. Hans Blix, the guy who could not find anything with both hands, chief of the U.S. weapons inspectors [*sic*], sounded both ridiculous and alarmist when he said in March: I am more worried about global warming than I am of any major military conflict. It is no wonder he could not find any weapons of mass destruction . . .
. . . So I will just conclude by saying: Wake up, America. With all the hysteria, all the fear, all the phony science, could it be that man-made global warming is the greatest hoax ever perpetrated on the American people? I believe it is.
—*Sen. James Inhofe (R-OK),* Chairman of the Environment and Public Works Committee, *Congressional Record,* pp. S10012–S10013, 7-28-03.

This Nation has changed dramatically. When I was a child, a person went to turn the light switch on and the lights came on. When they went to fill their gas tank, it was reasonable to fill their gas tank. In those days, we swatted flies and we poisoned rats. Today we set aside habitat for flies and rats. And who pays for it? Private property owners have to pay the price of setting their property aside for some stupid endangered species that some wacko Democratic politician wants to preserve.

In the words of the gentleman from Ohio (Mr. Traficant), beam me up, too. Both of us need to be out of here. This is crazy. And we talk about big oil. If we had enough oil, we would not have enough energy to provide an argument for these people to complain about. So if we have less oil, they can complain more about Republicans not providing oil. Wake up, America. There is something seriously wrong and it is the Democratic Party, excluding the gentleman from Ohio (Mr. Traficant) who has finally learned what real world life is like. Buy America; provide energy; close our borders. It is realistic.

—*Rep. Gary Miller (R-CA). Congressional Record*, H2717, 5-25-01.

[The EPA is] the biggest job-killing agency in inner-city America.

—*House Speaker Newt Gingrich.* Gary Lee, "Gingrich Lashes Out at EPA; Browner Praises Its Efforts," *Washington Post*, 2-17-95.

What has happened over the last 10 to 20 years is the environmental extremists have had their way with regulators and with Congress and they've gone way beyond reasonableness and common sense. What we're trying to do is bring common sense, good science and reasonableness to environmental regulations. If you ask any questions at all, you are automatically labeled a polluter and . . . pillager of the environment,

. . . There is a question about the whole climatic change argument.

—*House Majority Whip Tom DeLay (R-TX).* Nancy Mathis, "EPA under House siege; DeLay plans to lead assault for changes in environmental policy, agency funding," *Houston Chronicle*, 10-8-95.

... DDT probably did cause some environmental harm when it was extensively used in agriculture in the 1950's and 1960's. Though that harm was shown to be reversible, it may have included things like thinner egg shells in certain birds of prey.

> —*Columnist Betsy Hart*, "Environmentalist hysteria should be banned—not DDT," *Chicago Sun-Times*, 6-29-03.

June 30, 1972 is a date that lives in junk science infamy. That's when the U.S. Environmental Protection Agency banned the insecticide DDT. The ban survives 30 years later, even as it has helped kill millions of people, mostly children.

> —*Steven Milloy* of the Cato Institute. "Rethinking DDT," FOXNews.com, 6-20-02.

Paradoxically, many of my colleagues give millions of dollars away to someone who can study the mating habits of fruit flies and yet at the same time vote for an amendment that would effectively take the food off the tables of thousands of hardworking families in Nevada and elsewhere. Mr. Speaker, what I would like to tell these families is, why would Congress do this? What will I tell them? Tell them that they and half of their community lost their jobs so that a small handful of hikers did not have to see a mine on their bird watching hike? I would like to remind my colleagues that a majority of mining States have a cleaner environmental bill of health than most non-mining States in this country. Also, the millions of dollars in tax dollars paid by mines across the country rule out the "free ride" argument that some of my colleagues would suggest. Mr. Speaker, sound science and common sense should rule this Congress, not the extremist environmental groups who prey on public emotion.

> —*Rep. Jim Gibbons (R-NV)* lamenting the passage of an amendment revising the Mining Law of 1872. *Congressional Record*, H5758, 7-19-99.

A sparrow does not a spring make, but in the Druid religion of environmentalism, every warm summer's breeze prompts apocalyptic demands for a ban on aerosol spray and paper bags. So where is global warming when we need it? . . . In 1995, the U.N. Intergovernmental Panel on Climate Change produced a computer model purportedly proving "a discernible human influence on global climate." According to the U.N., there was not enough evidence to determine if Saddam Hussein was a threat, but the evidence is in on global warming. The key to the U.N.'s global warming study was man's use of aerosol spray. You have to know the French were involved in a study concluding that Arrid Extra Dry is destroying the Earth. In a world in which everyone smelled, the French would be at no disadvantage. Aerosol spray. How convenient . . . Now environmentalists are in a panic that African nations will use DDT to save millions of lives. Last year, 80,000 people in Uganda alone died of malaria, half of them children. The United States and Europe have threatened to ban Ugandan imports if they use DDT to stop this scourge. Environmentalists would prefer that millions of Africans die so that white liberals may continue gazing upon rare birds. Liberals don't care about the environment. The core of environmentalism is a hatred for mankind. They want mass infanticide, zero population growth, reduced standards of living and vegetarianism. Most crucially, they want Americans to stop with their infernal deodorant use.
    —*Ann Coulter*, "Global Warming: The French Connection,"
    Townhall.com, 5-29-03.

. . . They also use the maximum tolerated dose for rats, which is when they stuff so much of the substance that they are studying into a rat, the rat is going to die from stress. For part of the Clean Air Act, they also observed the effects of emissions on asthma patients. But what they did was take away their medicine and force them to jog in 110 degrees heat, and nobody does this. This again is not realistic. The only realism you will find is in the minds of bureaucrats who do not live in the real world.

—*Sen. James Inhofe (R-OK)* on a purported Environmental Protection Agency study of asthmatics. *Congressional Record,* S9829, 7-13-95. More specific information about the study was requested on 8-12-96 and again on 8-13-96. An Inhofe staff member promised to provide this information, but never did.

Mr. Speaker, I just want to close my comments by stating just a few things that wood provides, including rayon, photographic film, alcohol, football helmets, piano keys, on and on and on. This Nation cannot do without wood.

—*Rep. Helen Chenoweth (R-ID),* speaking in support of the Taylor Amendment, which, according to the late Rep. Sidney R. Yates (D-IL), "almost doubles the cutting of timber from our national forests over the amount cut last year. At the same time it suspends all environmental laws protecting the preservation of our forests." *Congressional Record,* H3154 & H3230, 3-14-95.

. . . I can tell you, some of the most dynamic, intelligent engineers in the world have spent years finding out how to drill holes in Mother Earth . . . Let me just suggest, if oil is about 400 yards over there and you found it—about four football fields away— and you don't want to touch that ground, you can start here, where I am standing, and you can drill over there in what is called slant drilling . . . I have a little picture up here from *Science Times.* It was covered in the *Times.* It is called "Hunting For Oil: New Precision, Less Pollution" . . . Here is a giant reservoir underground. It is many yards from where you have set out to manage and control the destiny of the tundra. There you are with this dramatic picture of how, just like a curved straw, you put it underground and maneuver it, and the "milk shake" is way over there, and your little child wants the milk shake, and they sit over here in their bedroom where they are feeling ill, and they just gobble it up from way down in the kitchen, where you don't even have to move the Mix Master that made the ice cream for them. You don't have to take it up to the bedroom. This describes the actual drilling that is taking place . . .

> —Sen. *Pete Domenici (R-NM)*, defending the idea of drilling in the Arctic National Wildlife Refuge. The proposal to drill was defeated. *Congressional Record*, S3928–S3929, 3-19-03.

Christmas trees are causing all of this! Reagan was right!

> —*Rush Limbaugh* citing a new study published in the journal *Nature* which he claims shows that certain coniferous trees emit pollutants, 3-13-03.

And finally, the Federal Government needs to promote a better partnership between all levels of government, job-providers, environmental interest groups, and the taxpayers. With this in mind I believe that on this Earth Day we must collect the extremist rhetoric found on both sides of the environmental debate and flush it down the toilet—remember to flush twice, though, if it's a new, EPA-mandated low-flow toilet, or it might not be gone for good.

> —Sen. *Rod Grams (R-MN)* observing Earth Day 1998. *Congressional Record*, S3408, 4-22-98.

April 22nd, Earth Day, is also the birthday of Vladimir Ilyich Lenin. It's not a coincidence that these extremist environmentalist wackos celebrate their movement on the birthday of the Soviet Union's first communist dictator.

> —*Rush Limbaugh*. Rushlimbaugh.com, 4-24-03.

Why is Earth Day, today, also Lenin's birthday? Coincidence? Or does it signal the true intent of the national and worldwide environmental movement? . . . The list of green lies is endless. The forced requirement for "environmental education" in our schools is creating generations of misinformed students, ready to accept even more lies. They're even infiltrating our churches and synagogues with their ideology, substituting Earth worship. . . . If you think Lenin was one heck of a guy, celebrate Earth Day.

> —*Alan Caruba*, founder of the National Anxiety Center. "Is it just coincidence that Earth Day is Lenin's birthday?" *Fargo Forum* op-ed page, 4-22-97.

The states and communities are the laboratories of environmental innovation. Inflexible requirements hurt the environment. While we have made substantial environmental progress, we must reject failed approaches created by fear-mongering and centralized control, which will not serve our environment well in the century ahead. The Super-fund program to clean up abandoned toxic waste sites is a classic case in point . . . Without the opposition of Bill Clinton, we will fix the broken Superfund law.

. . . The current Endangered Species Act is seriously flawed and, indeed, is often counterproductive because of its reliance on Federal command-and-control measures.

. . . Republicans consider private property rights the cornerstone of environmental progress.

> —*Republican Party Platform*, adopted 8-12-96, pp. 26, 27, 28.

A species goes out of existence every 20 seconds. Surely a new species must come into existence every 20 seconds.

> —*Rep. Helen Chenoweth (R-ID)*. Timothy Egan, "Look Who's Hugging Trees Now," *New York Times Magazine*, 7-7-96.

. . . [U.S. Secretary of the Interior] Mr. Babbitt has made it clear that environmentalism—the religion—is driving this Nation's regulatory scheme. This is a violation of the establishment clause of the Constitution. It smothers our values and it threatens our liberties.

. . . Mr. Speaker, the very first clause of the very first amendment to our Constitution states that "Congress shall make no law respecting an establishment of religion," and yet there is increasing evidence of a government sponsored religion in America. This religion, a cloudy mixture of new age mysticism, Native American folk lore, and primitive Earth worship (Pantheism), is being promoted and enforced by the Clinton administration in violation of our rights and freedoms.

> —*Rep. Helen Chenoweth (R-ID). Congressional Record,*
> H1002–H1003, 1-31-96.

I am shocked, I am absolutely penetratively [*sic*] shocked . . . I look at the individuals that are offering this. Is there any shocking doubt, the same people that would vote to cut defense $177 billion, the same ones that would put homos in the military, the same ones that would not fund BRAC [Base Realignment and Closure], the same ones that would not clean up.

> —*Randy Cunningham (R-CA)*, arguing against Rep. Peter A.
> DeFazio's (D-OR) proposed amendment intended to make
> certain that naval facilities had to observe the Clean Water
> Act. *Congressional Record*, H4837, 5-11-95.

Frankly, we're just not satisfied with the level of reduction you get from the mercury MACT [maximum achievable control technology], so we're making the dual proposal. This all fits into the construct of aggressively making the next decade the most productive period in U.S. history in terms of air-quality improvement.

> —*EPA Administrator Mike Leavitt*, defending his agency's
> move to weaken mercury emission regulations governing
> coal and oil-fired power plants. This initiative was described
> in a draft EPA proposal of 11-26-03 leaked to reporters by
> environmental groups. Eric Pianin, "White House, EPA
> Move to Ease Mercury Rules," *Washington Post*, 12-3-03.

SUPPORTING OUR TROOPS
OR VETERANS' BENEFITS

Why am I running stores? Why am I in education?
>—*Defense Secretary Donald Rumsfeld*, talking about cutting
military-run commissaries and schools. Karen Jowers, "An
act of 'betrayal.' In the midst of war, key family benefits face
cuts," *Army Times*, 11-3-03.

I appreciate the difficulty of decisions to close commissary store
operations. [But] we can no longer justify marginal stores in
close proximity to another commissary.
>—*Charles Abell*, Principal Deputy Undersecretary of Defense
for Personnel and Readiness. *Ibid*.

The days of the "weekend warrior" are gone. It's a new world
and we need to transition.
>—*Thomas Hall*, Assistant Secretary of Defense for Reserve
Affairs. Gina Cavallaro, "Army makes deployment clarifi-
cation; Guard, Reserve units will pull 1-year tours in Iraq,"
Army Times, 9-22-03.

. . . what was left was sucked into the intake, trained for a
period of months, and then went out, adding no value, no advantage, really, to the United States armed services over any
sustained period of time, because the churning that took place,
it took enormous amount of effort in terms of training, and
then they were gone.
>—*Defense Secretary Donald H. Rumsfeld* on those who were
drafted into the Armed Services in the past. Pamela Hess,
"Veterans decry Rumsfeld's draft comments," *Washington
Times*, 1-10-03.

While we are sympathetic to the plaintiffs' position and acknowledge the likelihood that plaintiffs believed these promises and relied on them, the government is not legally bound to abide by them.

> —*U.S. Appeals Court Circuit Judge Paul R. Michel* in an 11-02 opinion in *William O. Schism and Robert L. Reinlie v. United States*. The plaintiffs are retired veterans each of whom have served over 20 years in the U.S. military. Both enlisted during WWII after being promised free lifetime health care for themselves and their families when they retired. David Stout, "Justices Reject Veterans' Suit Over Promises By Recruiters," *New York Times*, 6-3-03. For more about the case, see Law.emory.edu.

Two hundred and seventy-seven U.S. soldiers have now died in Iraq, which means that, statistically speaking, U.S. soldiers have less of a chance of dying from all causes in Iraq than citizens have of being murdered in California . . . which is roughly the same geographical size. The most recent statistics indicate California has more than 2,300 homicides each year, which means about 6.6 murders each day. Meanwhile, U.S. troops have been in Iraq for 160 days, which means they are incurring about 1.7, including illness and accidents, each day.

> —*Brit Hume*. "Grapevine," FOXNews.com, 8-27-03. Cited by Buzzflash.com.

We ought to keep the casualties in perspective. We do have violent deaths in this country.

> —*Rep. Jerry Lewis (R-CA)*. Rick Maze, "Put Iraq casualty count into perspective, lawmaker says," *Army Times*, 9-30-03.

The story of what we've done in the postwar period is remarkable. It is a better and more important story than losing a couple of soldiers every day.

> —*Rep. George Nethercutt (R-WA)* at the University of Washington's Daniel J. Evans School of Public Affairs. Wyatt Buchanan, "Nethercutt hails Iraq's recovery," *Seattle Post-Intelligencer*, 10-14-03.

Part VI

From Their Mouth
to God's Ear

*"I'm a firm believer in feeding people their own
words back to them, when it's appropriate."*
—TRENT LOTT (R-MS).

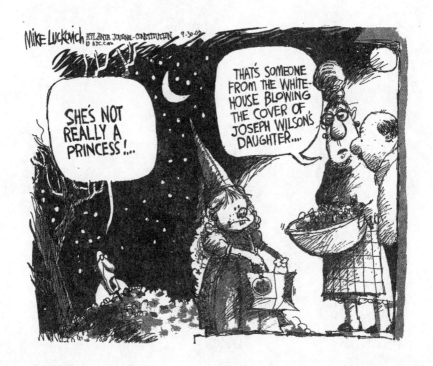

The Clouded Crystal Ball

Brit Hume: How do you get your news?
Pres. Bush: I get briefed by Andy Card and Condi in the morning. They come in and tell me. In all due respect, you've got a beautiful face and everything. I glance at the headlines just to kind of [*sic*] a flavor for what's moving. I rarely read the stories, and get briefed by people who are probably reading the news themselves. But like Condoleezza, in her case, the National Security Advisor is getting her news directly from the participants on the world stage.
Hume: Has that been your practice since day one, or is that a practice that you've . . .
Bush: Practice since day one.
Hume: Really?
Bush: Yes. You know, look, I have great respect for the media. I mean, our society is a good, solid democracy because of a good, solid media. But I also understand that a lot of times there's opinions mixed in with news. And I . . .
Hume: I won't disagree with that, sir.
Bush: I appreciate people's opinions, but I'm more interested in news. And the best way to get the news is from objective sources. And the most objective sources I have are people on my staff who tell me what's happening in the world.
　　—*"Raw Data: Text of Bush Interview,"* Fox News Channel,
　　　9-22-03, p. 15.

Knowing all the cards liberals will try to play is enormously helpful. But knowing how best to respond and to play the cards in our own hand is absolutely essential. For this we must look

to three modern conservative leaders who offer an extraordinary model of how to move our ideas from vision to victory in the twenty-first century: Ronald Reagan, Newt Gingrich, and George W. Bush. Each has been a strong leader. Each has been a man of ideas . . .
>   —*Sean Hannity, Let Freedom Ring*, NY: Reganbooks, HarperCollins, 2002, pp. 246–247

David Asman, Host: But, Rich, you don't want—you don't want to do these make-work programs, these phony government programs where they manufacture jobs.
Rich Karlgaard, *Forbes* Publisher: No. No. No. I'll tell you exactly what I would do. You know, when a white collar person loses his or her job, they become a consultant. So what I would do is give massive tax breaks to people who are establishing home offices and trying to become consultants. This is what we need to do . . .
>   —*"Forbes on Fox,"* Fox News Channel, 9-6-03.

Success in Iraq could also begin a new stage for Middle Eastern peace and set in motion progress towards a truly democratic Palestinian state.
>   —*George W. Bush*, speaking at the Washington Hilton to supporters of the American Enterprise Institute, 2-26-03. Whitehouse.gov.

Newt Gingrich is an incredible leader. He is a leader of our time, and he's going to lead us into the future. And we're going to accomplish the things that we've all dreamed of.
>   —*House Majority Whip Tom DeLay*. "Late Edition," CNN, 4-6-97.

I'm a firm believer in feeding people their own words back to them, when it's appropriate.
>   —*Senate Majority Leader Trent Lott (R-MS)*, commenting on his wish to use President Clinton's campaign speeches

against him in the '96 Presidential campaign. Paul Gigot, "The Price of Being Relevant," *Wall Street Journal* editorial, 11-8-96.

We are dealing with a country [Iraq] that can really finance its own reconstruction and relatively soon.
—*Deputy Defense Secretary Paul D. Wolfowitz* before a House Appropriations sub-committee, 3-27-03. Richard W. Stevenson, "War Budget Request More Realistic but Still Uncertain," *New York Times*, 9-10-03.

. . . At the end of this whole thing we're going to be safer and better off.
—*Talk Radio Host Sean Hannity* on the war with Iraq, 3-19-03.

Taiwan's elected legislature and the recent inauguration of the first popularly elected president in over 4,000 years of Chinese history provide a model not only for the People's Republic of China, but for the world.
—*Newt Gingrich*. "Gingrich Backs Taiwan During Visit," *Washington Post*, 4-3-97.

So why don't we put more troops in there? There is an answer, my friends, and it's this: when you are fighting terrorists and people who have adopted terrorist tactics, victory is not assured by the volume or number of troops. Victory over terrorism is really a function of your intelligence. If you know where to hit 'em, then we've got plenty of troops. We don't need any more troops than we have now if you know where they are, if you know how to wipe them out. If we don't know where they are, we'll never have enough troops to deal with it . . . but the firefights and the daily massive hand-to-hand combat of war is over, it's terrorist actions that are taking place now, intelligence is the answer.
—*Rush Limbaugh*, 8-22-03.

In the early days of the war, the plan was criticized by some retired military officers embedded in TV studios. But with every day and every advance by our coalition forces, the wisdom of that plan becomes more apparent.
> —*Vice-President Dick Cheney*, taking a special slap at General Wesley Clark (Ret.). "Inside Politics," CNN, 4-25-03.

The terrorist threat to America and the world will be diminished the moment that Saddam Hussein is disarmed.
> —*George W. Bush.* Michael Tackett, "Bush Taps America's New Fear," *Chicago Tribune*, 3-18-03.

. . . I tell you George W. Bush, I just, he's the right guy in the right place at the right time . . .
> —*Sean Hannity*, 3-19-03.

There's another story out there today that Bush is gonna turn over to private U.S. companies the rebuilding of Iraq and I hope that's true and screw the UN. Because if this is really not making them irrelevant the only way to make 'em irrelevant is to not involve them in anything and for us not to involve ourselves there. If we're gonna do that, they're gonna stay relevant, no other way around it.
> —*Rush Limbaugh*, 3-17-03.

They [foreign governments] don't care about the fate of the Iraqi people, you know why? Because if they did they would have supported our allies. What they want to do here and let's not be ignorant, they want to exploit business opportunities in Iraq, they're especially interested in profiting from Iraq's oil and, you know, contrary to left-wing propaganda in this country by the so-called anti-war nuts, we didn't spill blood for oil, and we sure as heck didn't spill our blood to enrich the French, the Germans, the Russians, or the Chinese oil companies. And there's

gonna be a coalition of countries that help to rebuild Iraq, and
it's gonna be led by us . . .
> —*Sean Hannity*, 4-8-03.

I sometimes say one of the few qualifications I have for the U.S.
Senate is I am not a lawyer. So that when I read the Constitution, I know what it says; when I read the oath of office, I know
what it says; when I read the law, I know what it says. I don't
have to clutter up my mind with what the definition of "is" is.
So it makes it a little easier for me.
> —*Sen. James Inhofe (R-OK)* in a preface to his speech urging
> the impeachment of Bill Clinton. *Congressional Record,*
> S1522, 2-12-99.

I am the federal government.
> —*House Majority Leader Tom DeLay (R-TX)*, to a govern-
> ment employee who tried to prevent him from smoking on
> Government property. Paul Krugman, "Some Crazy Guy,"
> *New York Times*, 6-13-03.

The world is becoming more free and, therefore, more peaceful.
> —*George W. Bush.* "President Visits Detroit Edison Monroe
> Power Plant in Monroe," 9-15-03. Whitehouse.gov.

Mr. Speaker, the tired, old drumbeat of bigger government, bigger taxes, and bigger spending goes on. Thankfully, the American people have stopped listening. They have started reading
the "Contract With America," soon to be No. 1 on the best
seller list and the No. 1 priority of this New Republican Congress.
> —*Rep. J.D. Hayworth (R-AZ)*, in a one-minute address to
> the House. *Congressional Record*, H1221, 2-6-95.

Martin Anderson: The economy is back and looks terrific.
Chris Matthews: You posed the questions. Marty Anderson,
will we have good jobs with high pay?

Anderson: Sure. We always have whenever the economy comes back. We not only get new jobs, we get better jobs. Look at the record on this . . .

    —*Former Bush Campaign Advisor Martin Anderson.*
    "Hardball," MSNBC, 10-31-03.

SAY WHAT?

This [the passage of a law in Florida preventing the death of Terri Schiavo, a woman in a 13-year vegetative state] was a huge victory for one innocent woman, and it was a small victory for the return to self-government.
  —*Randall Terry.* Abby Goodnough, "Victory in Florida Feeding Case Emboldens the Religious Right," *New York Times,* 10-24-03.

If we don't know for sure they're going to do something, or not, we need to make sure that we prevent anything they may be planning, whether or not we know or don't know about it.
  —*FBI agent.* Nicholas von Hoffman, "This Week's Question: Why Are We in Iraq?" *New York Observer,* 11-3-03.

Chris Matthews: When you go down the streets of any major city, there's an area called usually the DMZ where they sell adult books, they sell the adult videos. Are they illegal?
Sandy Rios: Well, many of them are. Absolutely.
Matthews: They are?
Rios: Oh, yes, because, Chris . . .
Matthews: Nobody ever shuts them down.
Rios: Well, I know that. You know what we have found, that law enforcement doesn't even know what's illegal anymore because it is—you know, during the Clinton years, eight years under Reno, obscenity was not prosecuted, and, Chris, what happened was law enforcement has forgotten that it's illegal.
  —*Sandy Rios,* Concerned Women For America. "Hardball," MSNBC, 10-31-03.

It [Rush's drug problem] is going to help his career because Rush is now humanized—people love when people show a human side. It may make some of his people scratch their heads and say: "Oh, my gosh. Rush is a human being and not a god."
  —*Michael Harrison*, publisher of trade magazine *Talkers*.
  James Barron, *New York Times*, "Limbaugh, telling of pill addiction, plans to be treated," 10-11-03.

Today I'm still a movie nut. I try to see a movie a week—and when I don't, because of work or other obligations, I feel weird and anxious.
  —*Laura Ingraham, Shut Up And Sing.* NY: Regnery, 2003, p. 75.

They think we're stupid. They think our patriotism is stupid. They think our church-going is stupid. They think our flag-waving is stupid. They think where we live—anywhere but near or in a few major cities—is stupid. They think our SUV's are stupid. They think owning a gun is stupid. They think our abiding belief in the goodness of America and its founding principles are stupid. They think the choices we make at the ballot box are stupid. They think George W. Bush is stupid. And, without a doubt, they will think this book is stupid. Meet the elites. Who are they? Essentially, elites are defined not so much by class or wealth or position as they are by general outlook.
  —*Laura Ingraham. Ibid.*, p. 1.

Laura Ingraham: I'm really excited that the Hollywood elite has lined up behind Wesley Clark . . .
Alan Colmes: . . . When you say Hollywood elite, it's interesting to me because why can't you apply that same term toward those supporting Arnold Schwarzenegger or does Hollywood elite only apply to someone when they're a Democrat . . .
Ingraham: . . . The elite is about a state of mind, if you believe in the goodness of the American people and you trust the overall common sense of the American people, then you're not an elite.
  —*"Hannity & Colmes,"* Fox News Channel, 10-1-03.

If I was still in office I would be raping and pillaging throughout the intelligence community to get to the bottom of this.
—*Retired Joint Chief of Staff Chairman Colin Powell*, testifying before the Senate Veterans' Affairs Committee about the exposure of U.S. troops to chemical weapons during the gulf war. "Powell: No warning of chemicals," *USA Today*, Washington section, 4-18-97.

I'm not going to defend bad ideas even if they're proposed or pursued by my own party.
—*Sean Hannity, Let Freedom Ring*. NY: Reganbooks, HarperCollins, 2002, p. 252.

Although he was very popular, Reagan evoked hostility in many liberals. He was shot two months after taking office. The would-be assassin was an upper-middle-class young man. He used explosive bullets, which are illegal and require criminal contacts to obtain. I have written articles for gun magazines, and I wouldn't know where to get them. So where did Hinckley get them? Why was this fact omitted from most media accounts? Why didn't commentators comment? Why didn't conspiracy theorists theorize? Why did I have to learn this from a medical journal that is rarely quoted in the media? The answer seems clear. The large majority of journalists and media moguls are liberals. If there were a conspiracy to assassinate Reagan, the only thing they might say would be, "Who planned it? Who supplied the explosive bullets? Who cares!" To conspiracy lovers, Oswald and Sirhan were "patsies," but not Hinckley. Why was there deep suspicion in the first two cases, placid credulity in the third? Perhaps what bothered many of these people was that Hinckley wasn't a better shot. There was no reason for journalists or media moguls to expend a drop of ink, an inch of film or a minute of airtime on considering who wanted Reagan dead. The answer was obvious. They did.
—*Columnist David C. Stolinsky*, "One-Sided Conspiracy Theories," NewsMax.com, 9-10-02.

I can tell you as a physician who has been in the operating room for thousands of days and hundreds of thousands of hours . . .
—*Sen. Bill Frist.* Timothy Noah, "Whopper of the week: They don't teach arithmetic in medical school," *Slate*, 1-23-03. Noah maintains that it would have been impossible for Frist to have spent even 100,000 hours in operating rooms, let alone hundreds of thousands of hours.

I would eliminate the payroll tax and institute a national sales tax to cover Social Security and Medicare. The sales tax would slide depending on need . . .
—*Bill O'Reilly, The No Spin Zone,* NY: Broadway Books, 2001, p. 175.

America loves pancakes! Pancake houses across the country are packed. But what are those syrup drenched, hot cakes doing to our bodies? Putting us on a fast track to weight gain, high cholesterol and adult onset diabetes.

But now there is hope for everyone who loves this early morning treat. Pat's very own Age-Defying Protein Pancakes! These delicious pancakes give you energy, help your heart and provide a substantial boost of muscle-building protein.

Pat's Age-Defying Protein Pancakes can:
* Combat the build-up of plaque in your blood vessels and arteries
* Provide complex carbohydrates to keep your system running at its best
* Provide an excellent source of energy and essential fatty acids, important for good heart health
* Help protect against breast, uterine and prostate cancer
* And Pat shares his cooking tips along the way to help make your pancakes light and fluffy.
—*Pat Robertson's miraculous pancakes,* described under the headline "Pat's Age-Defying Protein Pancake," CBN.org.

. . . And you have to have a reason to displace an incumbent
president, and I still think they're looking, the Democrats, all
ten of them, for that reason.

> —*George Will.* "News Night With Aaron Brown," CNN,
> 10-1-03.

I'm afraid, I wish there were, but there aren't weapons of mass
destruction so far, at least big numbers of them, in Iraq.

> —*William Kristol,* editor of *The Weekly Standard.* "On the
> Record," Fox News Channel, 10-1-03.

I used to pine away that my birthday wasn't April 13th. That
was Thomas Jefferson's birthday, and I loved Thomas Jefferson. I always wished I had a "1" in front of my "3,"—until I
discovered that April 3rd was the day Christ was crucified.

> —*Congressman Bob Dornan.* Lloyd Grove, "Out of the
> mouth of . . . Bob," *Washington Post,* 11-23-96.

There has been a huge problem with the political lopsidedness
of the debate. People in the opposition [to new media ownership rules] are part of a highly vocal and strenuous community.
They have relatively strong viewpoints, are very active and
mobile. On the other side, if you are in a fraternity watching
TV and drinking beer and happy, what are you going to do to
get in the debate?

> —*FCC Chairman Michael K. Powell.* Stephen Labaton,
> "F.C.C. Chief talks of Frustration and Surprise," *New York
> Times,* 9-22-03.

There was a time when Democrats like John F. Kennedy and
Franklin Roosevelt spoke with moral clarity about evil in the
world, and the responsibility of the United States to fight that
evil with all of the strength of a great and mighty nation. They
have allowed their cause to be bullied by people who believe

vandalizing Starbucks represents a legitimate foreign policy agenda.
> —*Tom DeLay* on his website: Majorityleader.gov.

Gay marriage should be between a man and a woman.
> —*Arnold Schwarzenegger*, during a radio interview with Sean Hannity. David Hinckley, "Jinx, 84, Joins Partner Tex," *New York Daily News*, 8-29-03.

I'm conservative because Milton Friedman is right and Karl Marx is wrong.
> —*Arnold Schwarzenegger* speaking to a state GOP convention in Los Angeles. Zachary Coile, John Wildermuth, "The California Recall: A day of division for GOP: Schwarzenegger bid for support fails to sway McClintock," *San Francisco Chronicle*, 9-14-03.

And when I am President, our men and women in our Armed Forces will know the president is his commander in chief—not Boutros Boutros Ghali, or any other U.N. Secretary General.
> —*Republican Presidential Candidate Bob Dole*, accepting the nomination at the Republican National Convention, 8-15-96.

Amuse your conservative friends and annoy your liberal neighbors with the brand new Ann Coulter Talking Action Figure. This incredibly lifelike action figure looks just like the beautiful Ann Coulter, and best of all . . . it sounds like Ann, too! Ann recorded these classic Coulter sayings especially for this action figure. Push the button on the figure, and you'll hear such "Coulterisms" as:
 * Liberals can't just come out and say they want to take more of our money, kill babies, and discriminate on the basis of race.
 * At least when right-wingers rant, there's a point.
 * Swing voters are more appropriately known as the "idiot voters" because they have no set of philosophical principles.

> By the age of fourteen, you're either a Conservative or a Liberal if you have an IQ above a toaster.
> * Why not go to war just for oil? We need oil. What do Hollywood celebrities imagine fuels their private jets? How do they think their cocaine is delivered to them?
> * Liberals hate America, they hate flag-wavers, they hate abortion opponents, they hate all religions except Islam, post 9/11. Even Islamic terrorists don't hate America like Liberals do. They don't have the energy. If they had that much energy, they'd have indoor plumbing by now.
>
> This highly collectible doll comes in a display box with information highlighting Ann's unique contributions to America's political discourse. If you can't get enough Ann Coulter, you'll want to order the Ann Coulter Talking Action Figure today!
> Don't forget to order replacement batteries!
> —*Conservativebookservice.com.*

The Declaration of Independence speaks of God-given natural rights, our founders clearly understood this, and what we're looking at is a conflict here with man-granted privileges. I don't know if I'm saying this well. You have your God-given rights, and I think there's a concerted campaign, a concerted effort to replace God-given rights with man-given privileges and they are not always accurate as evidenced by former court decisions, does that make sense?
> —*Sean Hannity* addressing a Caller to his radio program, 8-22-03.

. . . Despite Grammy and Emmy awards, best-selling books and a successful career as a political satirist, [Al] Franken doesn't have near the name recognition of [Bill] O'Reilly . . . Franken, meanwhile, gets credited for cleverness, if not hilarity, for his strategy of using more-famous people to sell his books. His 1996 book was titled "Rush Limbaugh Is a Big Fat Idiot: and Other Observations." Franken, relatively unknown by comparison, attached his byline to one of the best-known names in America and, voila, he's got a best seller.

—*Kathleen Parker*, "O'Reilly and Franken deserve each other," *Chicago Tribune*, 8-27-03.

Here is a small article from a paper last week that film legend Gregory Peck says there is no place for him in Hollywood any longer because today's movies are too full of sex and violence. . . . Peck said there is only one decent hero in recent movies: Babe the Pig. In every sense, I thought Babe was a beautiful young lady pig. He said he is in every sense an old-fashioned hero. Well, I would recommend to Mr. Peck that he see "Braveheart," the film which won Best Director for Mel Gibson and Best Movie of the Year. There, too, was a film where the hero was truly a hero who died with a beautiful word on his lips: freedom.

—*Rep. Bob Dornan. Congressional Record*, H3795, 4-24-96.

I'm sort of holding my nose and voting for the tax cut because I want to see him get reelected.

—*Rep. Ray LaHood (R-IL)* on the budget bill and George W. Bush. Jill Zuckerman, "President's appeal falls short in D.C.," *Chicago Tribune*, 5-12-03.

He'll probably be doing industrial training films in a couple of years and nobody will ever hear of him again.

—*Former Sen., now actor, Fred Thompson (R-TN)*, talking about Michael Moore's anti-war statement during the 2003 Academy Awards ceremony. Frank Rich, "Bowling for Kennebunkport," *New York Times*, 4-06-03.

We ought to be beating our chests every day. We ought to look in a mirror and get proud and stick out our chests and suck in our bellies and say: "Damn, we're Americans!"

—*Chief U.S. Administrator in Iraq, Lt. Gen. Jay Garner.* Laura J. Winter and Helen Kennedy, "Troops kill 2, wound 14 in anti-U.S. protest," *N.Y. Daily News*, 5-1-03.

I spend hours upon hours researching my beliefs and structuring the way I wish to say things so as precisely to be understood
... What I attempt to do is use reason and facts and even actual quotes from the people with whom I disagree. Everything I say to you is always grounded in truth.
   —*Rush Limbaugh*, 4-29-97.

Why should we hear about body bags and deaths and how many, what day it's gonna happen? ... It's not relevant. So why should I waste my beautiful mind on something like that?
   —*Barbara Bush* on "Good Morning America," the day before the Iraq war started. Frank Rich, "The Spoils of War Coverage," *New York Times*, 1-13-03.

The suggestion that male-only ordination implies a devaluation of women is as silly as the suggestion that a woman devalues women when she looks exclusively among men for a husband. The assertion that males and females both should be ordained without regard to their sex is akin to the assertion that same-sex relationships should be regarded as having equal legitimacy with heterosexual marriage.
   —*Judge James Leon Holmes*, nominated by the Bush administration on 1-28-03 to the U.S. District Court for the Eastern District of Arkansas. Leon and Susan Holmes, "Gender Neutral Language," *Arkansas Catholic*, 4-12-97.

Dick Armey speaks often about something very simple that I happen to believe is very profound. "Freedom works" is a slogan that he has coined, to some extent. It is a long [*sic*] way of saying "we hold these truths to be self-evident, that all men are created equal and endowed by their Creator with certain inalienable rights, that of life, liberty and the pursuit of happiness." It took a long sentence to get that out back in 1776, but today we can say it very simply as freedom works; freedom works in America, freedom works in our economy, freedom works in our workplace. Freedom may even work in Iraq. Freedom works in a lot of places,

in a lot of places that we call America, and Dick Armey has helped
bring freedom to our country.

> —*Rep. Jim Nussle (R-IA),* Chairman of the House Budget Com-
> mittee, in support of H. Res. 19 which would designate Room
> 236 in the House of Representatives as the Richard K. Armey
> Room. *Congressional Record,* H1710, 3-11-03.

. . . But, nonetheless, I do not for one minute believe that Lott
should go, nor do I believe that he is a racist, nor do I believe
that we should be characterizing his remarks as racist. But we
should be criticizing him for making them . . .

> —*Rep. Bill McCollum (R-FL).* "Lott under fire for com-
> ments," on "Crossfire," CNN.com, 12-12-02.

I have to admit, when I heard about the Democrat's proposal, I
almost forgot what year it was. I started looking around for
bell-bottom pants and aggressive chest hair. But, before I dusted
off my polyester, you will be happy to know, Mr. Chairman,
that I have come to my senses, because, despite the earnest wishes
of the Democrats, it is not 1977 anymore and hiking taxes to
pay for big government programs is as dead as disco.

> —*Tom DeLay (R-TX). Congressional Record,* H6524, 7-10-03.

I dismiss that as without merit. The prisoners in Guantanamo
are being treated humanely. They're receiving medical care.
They're receiving food. They're receiving far better treatment
than they received in the life that they were living previously.

> —*Ari Fleischer,* responding to the Amnesty International de-
> scription of the Guantanamo Bay prison camp as "a hu-
> man rights scandal," and Amnesty's demand that the de-
> tainees should be released or charged. Sarah Lyall, "Am-
> nesty Calls World Less Safe," *New York Times,* 5-29-03.

The problem with the French is that they don't have a word for
"entrepreneur."

> —*George W. Bush* to British Prime Minister Tony Blair. David
> Margolick, "Blair's Big Gamble," *Vanity Fair,* p. 226.

As a rule of thumb, all career government bureaucrats are liberal Democrats. (Children in Republican families do not grow up yearning to work for the government someday.) Republican presidents come in, make a handful of appointments to each department, and then the career bureaucrats go about gleefully denouncing the Republicans while allowing themselves to be described in the New York Times as "internal" whistleblowers.
> —*Ann Coulter,* "You Don't Say," Anncoulter.org, 6-19-03.

I thought he [Jesus Christ] was a free enterpriser . . . He was a carpenter's son and I thought he was doing well. He was able to change water into wine; now that to me is the classic definition of a guy in the entrepreneurial spirit.
> —*Gov. Tommy Thompson (R-WI)* responding to a reporter
> who asked him if Jesus was "a socialist." Madison *Capital*
> *Times,* 7-10-96, p. 3A.

Without trying to pick on Iowa, it was an eye-opener for me . . . Des Moines prides itself on low taxes, low this, low that. I'll tell you what else they're low in—they don't have any people. It's dead. Absolutely dead.
> —*Gov. Arne Carlson (R-MN)* on radio station WCCO-AM
> in Minneapolis. These remarks prompted calls in Iowa for
> a boycott of the Minneapolis Mall of America. Conrad
> deFiebre, "Carlson's Comments Are No Joke to Iowans,"
> *Minneapolis Star-Tribune,* 2-18-97.

Liberals have always loved him [Mike Royko] for championing the "little guy." But nowadays the little guy is just as likely to be a white middle-aged small-businessman harassed by OSHA or the EEOC, or otherwise bedeviled by do-gooders and busybodies.
> —*Andrew Ferguson,* "S.O.B., R.I.P." Ferguson praises Royko
> for not bowing to "political correctness," but also tells of
> an incident at the Billy Goat Tavern in Chicago when
> Ferguson went there for a drink. While Ferguson was in
> the bathroom, Royko sat down next to Ferguson's girlfriend
> and called him "a dork." *Weekly Standard,* 5-12-97.

So the next time you see "artists for" or "artists against" some cause, without reading any further, you can pretty much bet your mortgage that whatever it is they are for or against, they are morally wrong.
— *Dennis Prager*, "Much talent, little wisdom," Townhall.com, 4-22-03.

And I think Bush—I was thinking earlier today that I think he's kind of morphed from when we first met him about two and a half years ago. I remember his friend's nickname for him was Bombastic Bushkin. You know, he was sort of this peppery, maybe slightly Harry Trumanesque, was a kind of a peppery, sports-speaking, business-speaking, plain-spoken sort of fellow.

And I think he's—he has really evolved, as presidents do over time, since September 11, 2001, and since this war, into something like old backbone . . .
— *Peggy Noonan*. "Hardball," MSNBC, 4-11-03.

Don Wade: Passover's not just a Jewish observance, Christians also observe Passover, and so then the angel of death flies over your resort?
Roma: It does.
Wade: And if your first born son is conceived at the resort during the time the angel of death is flying over your luxury resort then is that how it worked in the bible? I'm trying to recall.
— *A discussion about a report that some resorts now offer Passover holiday packages.* "Don Wade and Roma," WLS-AM 890, Chicago, 4-16-03.

Don Wade: Should George W. Bush accept a French Kiss from Jacques Chirac?
— *A question prompted by a phone call made by the French president to Mr. Bush. Ibid.*

Roma: Well, it's great to see a summit going on though, isn't it? A little meeting there to establish a new government. It's like

something that would have happened here hundreds of years ago.
  —*A comment on a meeting in Nasiriyah, Iraq, organized by the Bush Administration. Ibid.*

I structured my life to be a concert musician. That was all I wanted to do. And it fell apart on me.
  —*National Security Advisor Condoleezza Rice.* Kathleen Rountree, "Musicians by any other name," *American Music Teacher*, Jun/Jul 2002.

I can't pay my bills.
  —*Nicholas E. Calio*, announcing his resignation as George W. Bush's assistant for legislative affairs. He had served Bush's father in the same capacity. Calio lives in a $1.5 million home, wears monogrammed French-cuffed shirts, and keeps 1000 bottles of wine in his cellar. Susan Ager, "A man who just can't live on $145,000," *Detroit Free Press*, 1-9-03.

When I was a kid and this was a free country, we were free to debate our country's history. Because of the frantic efforts of the notorious rat John Dean, we almost lost that right.
  —*G. Gordon Liddy, When I Was a Kid This Was a Free Country*, Washington D.C.: Regnery, 2002, p.167.

Question: You said that the war in Iraq was not just about weapons of mass destruction, but is part of the overall fight against terrorism. Given that profound statement, what are your feelings about criticism of President Bush that because we've found no weapons of mass destruction in Iraq, it suggests the president misled our country, and we had no business going to war there?
Gen. Franks: That's a fair question. I'll give you an answer on two levels. First off, with respect to the whole discussion of what was known that caused our government to decide to go into Iraq and how that was tied to the war on terrorism, and so forth: my first comment is, Ain't this a great country! The people who crafted our Constitution more than 200 years ago saw fit

to enable America to be informed, saw fit to enable both nega-
tivists and positivists to make their points forcefully. Ain't this a
great country? The fact that there is negativism and questioning and political debate and discussion and sniping, and so forth,
satisfies me just fine. I'm OK with that.

> —*Gen. Tommy Franks (Ret.)* in an interview, *Cigar Aficio-
> nado*, 12-03, pp. 85–86.

... Of all the people who were poor during the entire period of
'96–'99, one out of 17 people who were ever poor were poor
for the whole period.

> —*Grover Norquist*, President of Americans for Tax Reform,
> citing census bureau statistics on poverty. NPR, "Fresh Air,"
> 10-2-03.

CIVIL WARS & SORE LOSERS

I view Rush Limbaugh as entertainment. I view him like I view a circus clown. He makes people laugh, he makes fun of me all the time, and that's fine. I don't pay attention to it.
> —*Sen. John McCain (R-AZ)*. George Rush and Joanna Molloy, "Limbaugh Lambast," *New York Daily News*, 11-22-02.

I regret that statement, because my office has been flooded with angry phone calls from circus clowns all over America. They resent that comparison, and so I would like to extend my apologies to Bozo, Chuckles, and Krusty.
> —*Sen. John McCain.* Joe Conason, "Rush's Defenders Ignore His Venom," *New York Observer*, 11-27-02.

She's a liar. The whole thing stinks to high heaven . . . What beat me was more homosexual money than in any race in history, including from a group called Lesbians for Motherhood . . . She lied her way into office . . . She played the Hispanic card to the utmost.
> —*Rep. Bob Dornan* on his loss to Loretta Sanchez. Christopher Georges, "Liars, Gays, Aliens, Hispanics, Women: It's All Their Fault," *Wall Street Journal*, 11-20-96.

You are a disgrace to your baptism! You are a poor excuse for a Marine. You are a pathetic, senile old man. You are a slimy coward. Go register in another party.
> —*Bob Dornan* berating William Dougherty, a member of the Orange County Republican Central Committee, for working against him in the election. Associated Press, 11-19-96.

You know many years ago when you and I were young, we used to have a gag button that said "Support mental health or

I'll kill you." And this is what this reminds me of. "You better volunteer." The problem is you get the government and these fat cat corporations and good old Pa and George Bush and all the usual witnesses up in Philadelphia saying "We are going to insist on having citizen servants." Did you hear the president? I don't want to be anybody's servant. The problem is this is part of the whole conspiracy of government against the freedom of the American people and that's something that politicians don't use any more—the word "freedom." None of them, not even the Republicans.
    —*Robert Novak*, on President Clinton's Philadelphia summit on volunteerism. "Capital Gang," CNN, 4-26-97.

The Republican revolution my father began is by most appearances dead, sacrificed on the altar of civility by party leaders more interested in making friends and being liked than in fulfilling the mandate they were given by voters . . . In case after case, today's Republicans seem content to simply slow creeping socialism rather than reverse it. This retreat from bedrock principles is why I am breaking ranks with the Republicans. When Republicans come back to grass-roots America, then I'll come back to the Republican Party.
    —*Michael Reagan*. USA Today, Forum section, 4-17-97.

Newt Gingrich is one of the oddest men in modern American politics.
    —*Kate O'Beirne*, Washington editor of the conservative *National Review*. "Time for Newt to go?" *Chicago Sun-Times* op-ed, 11-12-96.

As road kill on the highway of American politics, Newt Gingrich cannot sell the Republican Agenda . . . He should be replaced as speaker . . . he is killing us . . . [He has] a public approval rating a few points shy of the Ebola virus.
    —*Rep. Peter King (R-NY)*, in the conservative *Weekly Standard*. *Chicago Tribune*, 3-25-97.

All of them ought to err on the side of less flamboyance. They should turn down the ideological thermostat just a tad. I saw her [Ann Coulter] on TV once calling Clinton a `scumbag.' Frankly, that's not needed. She has a good lawyer's mind. Her book was very helpful to me in writing about all that stuff. I'm just not sure that the skills necessary to litigation in a combative way are the same skills for political analysis, least of all on TV.

  —*George Will. Hartford Courant, 6-25-99.*

At the very least, I could get him to spend it all [his campaign funds] so the next person who runs against him might be able to actually win. I really want to hurt him. I want him to feel pain.

  —*Ann Coulter* talking about running for Congress against Rep.
  Christopher Shays (R-CT), to punish him for voting against
  Clinton's impeachment. *Hartford Courant*, 6-25-99.

It's time to stop the madness. We're destroying ourselves here.

  —*Rep. Peter King (R-NY),* one of five Republicans who op-
  posed all four articles of impeachment, after the impeach-
  ment/sex scandal involving President Clinton led to revela-
  tions of sexual affairs by Rep. Bob Livingston (R-LA), House
  Judiciary Committee Chairman Henry J. Hyde (R-IL) and
  Reps. Dan Burton (R-IN) and Helen Chenoweth (R-ID).
  Livingston resigned. Jonathan Weisman, "Sex scandals leave
  House shell-shocked; Developments bring cry of 'sexual
  McCarthyism'," *Baltimore Sun*, 12-20-98.

If there was ever a point where [members] have to come to-gether before this place melts down, it's now. Somebody new needs to emerge and bring consensus and peace.

  —*Rep. Zach Wamp (R-TN)* talking about Congress in the
  aftermath of Rep. Livingston's resignation and the sex scandals. *Baltimore Sun*, 12-20-98.

Much to the chagrin of millions of conservatives who fought tooth and nail to see him elected, President George Bush made it apparent early on in his administration that he would abide by the mainstream media's unwritten rule placing Bill and Hillary Clinton above the law. When, on the day before his inauguration, Independent Counsel Robert Ray cut a deal with Bill Clinton that allowed him to escape prosecution on an airtight perjury rap that has cost the government $70 million to bring, Bush was uncritical.

> —Carl Limbacher, *Hillary's Scheme: Inside the Next Clinton's Ruthless Agenda to Take the White House*. NY: Crown Forum, 2003, p. 57.

Judy Woodruff: Gentlemen, Trent Lott made those comments. He's now apologized for them. The Black Caucus is still upset. Some Democrats are still upset, but so are some conservatives. Let me just read quickly what Ken Conner with the Family Research Council said. "Such thoughtless remarks—and the senator has an unfortunate history of such gaffs—simply reinforce the suspicion that conservatives are closet racists and secret segregationists." Is there a problem for Trent Lott among conservatives, Bob Novak?

Robert Novak: Well, I think it is with *The Weekly Standard* and the editorial page of *The Wall Street Journal* and the other la-di-da conservatives inside the Beltway. It just shows how far political correctness has gone. This is really one of the silliest stories I have ever seen. The idea that Trent Lott is a segregationist is just absolutely nonsense. He made a mistake. He says he made a mistake. Tom Daschle says, "OK, you made a mistake." It is really ridiculous for conservatives to join the P.C. bandwagon.

> —*"Crossfire,"* CNN, 12-10-02. See Thomas B. Edsall and Darryl Fears, "Lott Has Moved Little On Civil Rights Issues/Senator's Record Consistent With Remarks," *Washington Post*, 12-13-02.

There are a lot of people here who have tried to be a strong supporter of this administration, doing everything they possibly could. But you bump up against a degree of arrogance over and over again . . . I want the president to do well, but it's important that you be open when members of Congress on either side, on either party, try to get information. Pride goeth before the fall.

> —*Rep. Frank Wolf (R-VA)*, Chairman of the House Appropriations subcommittee for the Commerce and Justice Departments. David Firestone, "Plan for Iraq to Repay U.S. Aid Is Rejected," *New York Times*, 10-30-03.

I think the underlying fact is you have Bill Clinton's generals designing a campaign that is not very creative, and it's not very clever, and it's very worrisome.

> —*Newt Gingrich*, current member of the Defense Policy Board. Peter J. Boyer, "The New War Machine," *The New Yorker*, 6-30-03

They hate him. I mean it, they hate him. He's lucky he hasn't gotten fragged.

> —*A senior deputy to Secretary of State Colin Powell*, describing how "many Senior Army leaders" feel about Secretary of Defense Donald Rumsfeld. Peter J. Boyer, "The New War Machine," *The New Yorker*, 6-30-03.

We've got a conservative, evangelical Christian, Republican governor trying to get a massive turnout of black voters to pass a tax increase so he can raise taxes on Republican constituents . . . Alabama needs to raise some revenue; there's no question about that. But this is not a tax increase any longer. This is a massive redistribution of wealth. We are the Republican Party— of *Alabama!* If a Democrat had proposed this, we would be burning down cities.

> —*Alabama GOP Chairman Marty Connors*, talking about Gov. Bob Riley's tax plan, which was eventually overwhelmingly rejected in a referendum, causing the state to cut back drastically on all services. Dale Russakoff, "Alabama tied in knots by tax vote," *Washington Post*, 8-17-03.

... Ashcroft is even more intractable than his predecessor, Janet Reno, in refusing information to the legislative branch. He is currently stonewalling requests by Rep. James Sensenbrenner, Republican Chairman of the House Judiciary Comitteee, about Justice's administration of the anti-terrorist Patriot Act ...
> —*Robert Novak*, "FBI's bullying tactics are growing tiresome," *Chicago Sun-Times*, 8-29-02.

Lying about Michael Savage's ratings is not "fair and balanced." A phony conservative is trying to put a knife in my back while I am on the ground. It is bad enough when the Liberals lie. Now a legion of so-called conservatives are creating false statements, publishing half-truths, and trying to rewrite the history of my ratings on television.
> —*Michael Savage.* MichaelSavage.com. Homestead.com, 8-14-03.

At any rate I can now announce that the worst book of 1996 was the vulgar and repellent, *Bare Knuckles and Back Rooms* [by Ed Rollins]. ... the hundreds of pages of trite thoughts, vulgar sentiments, and coarse language expose Rollins as an ass, a stupid ass, and a spectacularly dishonorable ass.
> —*R. Emmett Tyrrell, Jr.* "The Worst Book of the Year," Editorial section, *The American Spectator*, 5-97. Rollins is a well-known Republican conservative campaign adviser, a devoted admirer of Ronald Reagan.

The result is structurally unsound, constitutionally dubious, and—in overstating the degree of institutional independence—disingenuous.
> —*Independent Counsel Kenneth Starr,* addressing a 1999 Senate Governmental Affairs Committee on flaws in the Independent Counsel Act, under which he investigated Bill Clinton for over four years. Senate.gov, 4-14-99.

[T]hey are thinking about defeat, and wishing for it, and they will take pleasure if it should happen. They began by hating the neo-conservatives. They came to hate their party and this president. They have finished by hating their country.

—*David Frum*, White House speechwriter, attacking Robert Novak, Patrick Buchanan and others. Novak's column, *Chicago Sun-Times*, 3-24-03.

As Governor, Mr. Schwarzenegger would be a darker villain than any he has faced in his movies. And when it comes to the moral issues that Californians really care about—he gives us inaction not action.

—*Rev. Louis P. Sheldon*, Chairman of TVC, the Traditional Values Coalition. "How is Schwarzenegger Different From a Democrat?" NewsMax.com, 8-8-03.

Hear me now and believe me later, my friends: all these conservative orgasms over Arnold Schwarzenegger are—like the "Gorbasms" liberals experienced over Mikhail Sergeevich Gorbachev—fake. I know that R. next to Schwarzenegger's name excites the White House, but his own words prove he's not a conservative.

—*Rush Limbaugh. Ibid.*

It's a criticism you wouldn't expect to hear, like . . . Shaquille O'Neal is too small, or the Fox News Channel is just too detached and objective. Today, William F. Buckley's magazine, *The National Review*, says the Republican Party isn't conservative enough. They cite recent Supreme Court rulings on affirmative action and gay rights, which, they argue, Republicans have not done enough to decry. And they point to the explosion in federal spending since the GOP took over Congress.

—*Former Rep. Joe Scarborough (R-FL).* "Scarborough Country," MSNBC, 7-10-03.

The White House has made it known they don't want it [the 9-
11 investigation] to go into the election period.
　—*Former Gov. Thomas H. Kean (R-NJ).* Scot J. Paltrow,
　"White House Hurdles Delay 9/11 Commission Investiga-
　tion," *Wall Street Journal*, 7-8-03.

While I don't want to believe such a basic lack of cooperation
was intentional, it nonetheless creates the appearance of bureaucratic stonewalling. Excessive administration secrecy on
issues related to the Sept. 11 attacks feeds conspiracy theories
and reduces the public's confidence in government.
　—*Sen. John McCain (R-AZ). Ibid.*

I think it is nothing short of unbelievable that the governor of a
major state running for president thought it was acceptable to
mock a woman he decided to put to death.
　—*Gary Bauer*, GOP presidential candidate on George W.
　Bush's mocking impersonation of Karla Faye Tucker. Ben-
　nett Roth and R.G. Ratcliffe, "Republican foe says Bush
　mocked woman who was put to death," *Houston Chronicle*,
　8-11-99.

HE SAID/HE SAID

1. Eighteen months ago, this building came under attack. From that day to this, we have been engaged in a new kind of war—and we are winning.

> —*George W. Bush.* "President to Submit Wartime Budget; Remarks by the President on the Wartime Supplemental," USembassy.state.gov, 3-25-03.

2. Today, we lack metrics to know if we are winning or losing the global war on terror. Are we capturing, killing or deterring and dissuading more terrorists every day than the madrassas and the radical clerics are recruiting, training and deploying against us? Does the US need to fashion a broad, integrated plan to stop the next generation of terrorists? The US is putting relatively little effort into a long-range plan, but we are putting a great deal of effort into trying to stop terrorists. The cost-benefit ratio is against us! Our cost is billions against the terrorists' costs of millions.

> —*Defense Secretary Donald Rumsfeld* in a memo dated 10-16-03. *USA Today* website, 10-22-03.

---

1. John Ashcroft: The truth of the matter is that if the law's been violated, we should be able to ascertain that. We can if we have an independent person without a conflict of interest. And if there's been a violation that can be prosecuted—there's a whole range of additional questions that you might want to ask . . .

Rowland Evans: Well, that's what I want to get to. The Attorney General [Janet Reno] has shaved down all the allegations [against] Vice President Gore apparently down to one single allegation—which telephone he used to make these fundraising calls from. Do you really think that alone is worthy of a special prosecutor?

Ashcroft: Well, whether—you know, a single allegation can be most worthy of a special prosecutor. If you're abusing government property, if you're abusing your status in office, it can be a single fact that makes the difference on that. So my own view is that there are plenty of things which should have caused her [Att'y Gen. Janet Reno] a long time ago to appoint a special prosecutor, an independent investigator. We asked for that on March the 13th of this year in letters from Republican members on the Judiciary Committee. And she's in a bad position.

. . . The man who signs her check is the man that she's investigating, and she hasn't been very aggressive about it.
—*Sen. John Ashcroft,* "Evans & Novak," CNN, 10-4-97.

2. The prosecutors and agents who are and will be handling this investigation are career professionals with extensive experience in handling matters involving sensitive national security information and with experience relating to investigations of unauthorized disclosures of such information.
—*Attorney General John Ashcroft* announcing that the Justice Department, not a special prosecutor, would investigate the leak of information about CIA agent Valerie Plame, Joseph Wilson's wife, to columnist Robert Novak and other journalists. Richard W. Stevenson and Eric Lichtblau, "President orders full cooperation in leaking of name," *New York Times,* 10-1-03.

---

1. [Joe] Wilson never worked for the CIA, but his wife, Valerie Plame, is an Agency operative on weapons of mass destruction. Two senior administration officials told me Wilson's wife

suggested sending him to Niger to investigate the Italian report. The CIA says its counter-proliferation officials selected Wilson and asked his wife to contact him. "I will not answer any question about my wife," Wilson told me.
  —*Robert Novak*, "Mission To Niger," *Chicago Sun-Times*, 7-14-03.

2. I didn't dig it out, it was given to me. They thought it was significant, they gave me the name and I used it.
  —*Robert Novak*. Timothy M. Phelps and Knut Royce, "Columnist Blows CIA Agent's Cover," *Newsday*, 7-22-03.

3. Nobody in the Bush administration called me to leak this. There is no great crime here.
  —*Robert Novak*. "Crossfire," CNN, 9-29-03.

4. I'm only saying something I have written in print before, that I said that the person who told me was not a political gunslinger. I mean that literally. And that indicates that this was not a—some kind of a plot to discredit Ambassador Wilson, that it came about almost incidentally. And that's about all I can say.
  —*Robert Novak*. "Crossfire," 1-3-04.

---

1. . . . the sanctions exist—not for the purpose of hurting the Iraqi people, but for the purpose of keeping in check Saddam Hussein's ambitions toward developing weapons of mass destruction. . . . That purpose is every bit as important now as it was ten years ago when we began it. And frankly they have worked. He has not developed any significant capability with respect to weapons of mass destruction. He is unable to project conventional power against his neighbors. So in effect, our policies have strengthened the security of the neighbors of Iraq, and these are policies that we are going to keep in place, but we are always willing to review them to make sure that they are being carried out in a way that does not affect the

Iraqi people but does affect the Iraqi regime's ambitions and the ability to acquire weapons of mass destruction . . .
—*Secretary of State Colin L. Powell* after his meeting with Egyptian Foreign Minister Amre Moussa, 2-24-01. USembassyisrael.org.il.

2. Our conservative estimate is that Iraq today has a stockpile of between 100 and 500 tons of chemical weapons agent. . . . Saddam Hussein has chemical weapons . . . And we have sources who tell us that he recently has authorized his field commanders to use them.
—*Secretary of State Colin Powell* addressing the U.N. on 2-5-03. Charles J. Hanley, "Powell's case hasn't held up very well," *Wisconsin State Journal*, 8-11-03.

3. A sinister nexus [exists] between Iraq and the al Quaeda terrorist network, a nexus that combines classic terrorist organizations and modern methods of murder. Iraq today harbors a deadly terrorist network headed by Abu Musaab al-Zarqawi, an associate and collaborator of Osama bin-Laden and his al-Qaeda lieutenants . . . Iraqi officials deny accusations of ties with al-Qaeda. These denials are simply not credible.
—*Colin Powell* addressing the U.N. on 2-5-03. Christopher Marquis, "Powell admits no hard proof in linking Iraq to al Qaeda," New York Times, 1-9-04.

4. I have not seen smoking-gun, concrete evidence about the connection [between Hussein and al Qaeda].
—*Colin Powell* at a news conference, 1-8-04. *Ibid.*

---

1. **Tim Russert:** Do we have evidence that he's [Saddam Hussein] harboring terrorists?
V.P. Dick Cheney: There is—in the past, there have been some activities related to terrorism by Saddam Hussein. But at this stage, you know, the focus is over here on al Qaeda and the

most recent events in New York. Saddam Hussein's bottled up, at this point, but clearly, we continue to have a fairly tough policy where the Iraqis are concerned.

Russert: Do we have any evidence linking Saddam Hussein or Iraqis to this operation?

Cheney: No.

—*"Meet the Press,"* NBC, 9-16-01.

2. . . . We know that Iraq and the al Qaeda terrorist network share a common enemy—the United States of America. We know that Iraq and al Qaeda have had high-level contacts that go back a decade. Some al Qaeda leaders who fled Afghanistan went to Iraq. These include one very senior al Qaeda leader who received medical treatment in Baghdad this year, and who has been associated with planning for chemical and biological attacks. We've learned that Iraq has trained al Qaeda members in bomb-making and poisons and deadly gases. And we know that after September the 11th, Saddam Hussein's regime gleefully celebrated the terrorist attacks on America . . .

—*President Bush Outlines Iraqi Threat.* Remarks by the President on Iraq; Cincinnati Museum Center, Cincinnati Union Terminal, 10-7-02. Whitehouse.gov.

3. The battle of Iraq is one victory in a war on terror that began on Sept. 11th, 2001—and still goes on.

—*George W. Bush,* 5-1-03. Bob Kemper, "Bush: No Iraqi link to Sept. 11," *Chicago Tribune,* 9-18-03, p. 1.

4. **V.P. Dick Cheney:** If we're successful in Iraq, if we can stand up a good representative government in Iraq, that secures the region so that it never again becomes a threat to its neighbors or to the United States, so it's not pursuing weapons of mass destruction, so that it's not a safe haven for terrorists, now we will have struck a major blow right at the heart of the base, if you will, the geographic base of the terrorists who have had us under assault now for many years, but most especially on 9/11.

—*"Meet the Press,"* NBC, 9-14-03.

5. We've had no evidence that Saddam Hussein was involved with the September 11th.

—*George W. Bush*, press conference, 9-17-03. Whitehouse.gov.

6. We have never claimed that Saddam Hussein had either direction or control of 9-11.

—*National Security Adviser Condoleezza Rice*, discussing the public's perception that Saddam Hussein was somehow personally involved with the Sept. 11th attacks. "Nightline," ABC, 9-16-03.

---

1. With a great sense of purpose, I present to the Congress my budget. It offers more than a plan for funding the Government for the next year; it offers a new vision for governing the Nation for a new generation . . . It will retire nearly $1 trillion in debt over the next four years. This will be the largest debt reduction ever achieved by any nation at any time. It achieves the maximum amount of debt reduction possible without payment of wasteful premiums. It will reduce the indebtedness of the United States, relative to our national income, to the lowest level since early in the 20th Century and to the lowest level of any of the largest industrial economies . . .

—*President G.W. Bush's first budget plan*. "A Blueprint For New Beginnings: A Responsible Budget for America's Priorities," section I, "President's message," 2-28-01. Whitehouse.gov.

2. . . . The priority was properly placed on getting the economy back to growth. And if that meant larger deficits in the short run, well, if there ever was a time to run deficits, this is it.

—*Budget Director Joshua Bolten*. "The $5.6 trillion surplus once predicted for the ten years ending in 2011 is now a 2.3 trillion cumulative deficit . . . under the best-case prediction issued by the Congressional Budget office two weeks ago." David Firestone, "Dizzying Dive to Red Ink Has Law-makers Facing Difficult Budget Choices," *New York Times*, 9-14-03.

---

1. We know that Saddam Hussein has chemical and biological weapons, and we know he has an active program for development of nuclear weapons.
   —*Donald Rumsfeld*. Associated Press, 11-15-02.

2. Well, there's no question that we have evidence and information that Iraq has weapons of mass destruction, biological and chemical, particularly.
   —*White House Press Secretary Ari Fleischer*, 3-21-03. Molly Ivins, "Utter nonsense: Open Mouth, insert foot," *Chicago Tribune*, 9-4-03.

3. We know where they are. They are in the area around Tikrit and Baghdad.
   —*Defense Secretary Donald Rumsfeld*, 3-30-03. *Ibid.*

4. I never believed that we'd just tumble over weapons of mass destruction in that country.
   —*Donald Rumsfeld*, 5-4-03. *Ibid.*

5. They may have had time to destroy them, and I don't know the answer.
   —*Donald Rumsfeld*, 5-27-03. *Ibid.*

6. I have so many things to do at the Department of Defense. I made a conscious decision that I didn't need to stay current every 15 minutes on the issue [the search for WMD]. I literally did not ask . . . I'm assuming he'll [David Kay] tell me if he'd gotten something we should know.
   —*Donald Rumsfeld*. Dana Priest, "Rumsfeld Is Muted On Weapons Hunt," *Washington Post*, 9-9-03.

7. . . . sometimes I overstate for emphasis . . . And I said, "We know they're in that area." I should have said, "I believe we're in that area. Our intelligence tells us they're in that area," and that was our best judgment. And we were being pressed to find them while the war was still in its earliest, earliest days. And it seemed to me a somewhat unrealistic expectation.
   —*Donald Rumsfeld.* "Remarks at National Press Club Luncheon," 9-10-03.

---

1. We have no intention of breaking the [1972 Anti-Ballistic Missile] treaty. Trust me.
   —*Secretary of Defense Donald Rumsfeld.* "Rumsfeld: 'No intention of breaking' ABM treaty," Jamie McIntyre, CNN, 7-11-01.

2. Today, I have given formal notice to Russia, in accordance with the treaty, that the United States of America is withdrawing from this almost 30 year old treaty.
   —*George W. Bush.* Press Conference. U.S Department of State transcript, 12-13-01.

---

1. I can't say if the use of force would last five days or five weeks or five months, but it certainly isn't going to last any longer than that.
   —*Donald Rumsfeld* on the impending war with Iraq. Associated Press, 11-15-02.

2. You say we didn't plan for when the war was over. The problem is, the war isn't over.
   —*Deputy Defense Secretary Paul Wolfowitz*, in a September 9th Senate Armed Services Committee hearing. Vince Crawley, "U.S. seeks foreign aid in postwar Iraq," *Army Times*, 9-22-03. The war began in March.

---

1. I will never take money from the special interests, from Indian gaming, from unions or anything like that.
   —*Arnold Schwarzenegger*, during campaign stops on Labor
   Day, '03. "State disclosures show [Schwarzenegger] has collected more than $1 million from companies and individu-
   als with business before the state": Dean E. Murphy, "Recall campaigning is no picnic," *Chicago Tribune*, 9-2-03.

2. . . . I get donations from businesses and individuals absolutely, because they're powerful interests who control things.
   —*Ibid*.

---

1. No, absolutely not. No, the force flow is something that you
   put in motion months ago and it has been proceeding exactly
   as planned and there isn't an hour or a day that goes by that
   there aren't an increased number of troops in Iraq in one or
   more locations. In any given day, they go up by a non-trivial
   number, and they will continue to do until it's done and it
   will be done at some point.
   —*Donald Rumsfeld*, responding to a question about whether
   his Iraq war plan was "going wrong." "PM," Australian
   Broadcasting Corporation program, John Shovelan, "US
   sending an extra 30,000 troops to Iraq," 3-27-03. ABC.net.

2. It is continuously under review. I spoke with the Deputy Secretary of Defence this morning. He had just completed a call
   with the military commanders in Iraq and they reiterated their
   belief that the size of the forces in Iraq is appropriate—you
   need to provide security where it's possible to provide it, but
   it's not possible to provide it on every street corner.
   —*Donald Rumsfeld*, "The World Today," Australian Broadcasting Corporation program, John Shovelan, "Rumsfeld
   says US troops in Iraq are appropriate for security," 8-21-
   03. ABC.net

3. I am advised that current analysis by the Joint Chiefs of Staff indicates that at the present time we have sufficient active and reserve forces to conduct and execute successfully the missions that have been assigned.
   —*Donald Rumsfeld* speaking to the Veterans of Foreign Wars, 8-25-03. USAtoday.com.

4. Should the total number go up for security? Yes, I think so. But I think it's going to be on the Iraqi side and on the international side more than on the U.S. side.
   —*Donald Rumsfeld*. E.A. Torriero, "U.S. seeks international forces," *Chicago Tribune*, 9-5-03.

---

1. But, hey, as I said before, it's a film that speaks about faith, hope, love, and forgiveness. That's the basic message. And that's what we need to get back to, I think. And if everybody practiced a little more of that, there would be a lot less friction in the world.
   —*Mel Gibson* describing his film, *The Passion*. "The O'Reilly Factor," Fox News Channel, 1-14-03.

2. I want to kill him. I want his intestines on a stick . . . I want to kill his dog.
   —Mel Gibson on Frank Rich, the *New York Times* critic who criticized Gibson's *The Passion*, "Mel Gibson's Martyrdom Complex," 8-3-03. Peter J. Boyer, "The Jesus War," *The New Yorker*, 9-15-03.

---

1. . . . Your magazine [*Southern Partisan*] also helps set the record straight. You've got a heritage of doing that, of defending Southern patriots like [Gen. Robert E.] Lee, [Gen. Stonewall] Jackson and [Confederate President Jefferson]

Davis. Traditionalists must do more. I've got to do more. We've all got to stand up and speak in this respect, or else we'll be taught that these people were giving their lives, subscribing their sacred fortunes and their honor to some perverted agenda.

—*John Ashcroft,* interviewed in the *Southern Partisan* magazine, 2nd Quarter, 1998. Templeofdemocracy.com.

2. On the magazine, frankly, I can't say that I knew very much at all about the magazine [*Southern Partisan*]. I've given magazine interviews to lots of people. *Mother Jones* has interviewed me. I don't know if I've ever read the magazine [*Southern Partisan*] or seen it. It doesn't mean I endorse the views of magazines. It's a telephone interview. And I regret that speaking to them is being used to imply that I agree with their views.

—*John Ashcroft* during his January 2001 Senate confirmation hearings for the position of Attorney General. Fair.org.

---

1. Mr. Offner, do you have the same sexual preference of most men?

—*Gov. of Missouri John Ashcroft* asked health-care expert Paul Offner this question during a job interview in 1985 when Offner was applying to head the Missouri Department of Social Services. David A. Vise and Dan Eggen, "Job Applicant Says Ashcroft Queried Him on Sexuality," *Washington Post,* 1-25-01.

2. Sexual orientation has never been something that I've used in hiring in any of the jobs, in any of the offices, I've held. It will not be a consideration in hiring at the Department of Justice.

—*John Ashcroft* during Senate confirmation hearings in January 2001 on his nomination for Attorney General. *Ibid.*

---

1. The people in this room stand for the right principles and the right philosophy. Let's take it in the right direction and our children will be the beneficiaries.
   —*Senate Majority Leader Trent Lott* giving the keynote address to the Council of Conservative Citizens, a white supremacist group, in 1992. Thomas B. Edsall, "Lott Renounces White 'Racialist' Group He Praised in 1992," *Washington Post*, 12-16-98.

2. This group [Council of Conservative Citizens] harbors views which Senator Lott firmly rejects. He has absolutely no involvement with them either now or in the future.
   —*John Czwartacki*, spokesman for Sen. Lott. *Ibid*.

-----

1. April 14, 1997

    Mr. Kenneth Lay
    2121 Kirby Drive
    Houston, Texas 77019

    Dear Ken:
        One of the sad things about old friends is that they seem to be getting older—just like you!
        55 years old. Wow! That is really old.
        Thanks goodness you have such a young, beautiful wife.
        Laura and I value our friendship with you. Best wishes to Linda, your family, and friends.

    Your younger friend,
    George W. Bush

    —*Thesmokinggun.com*

2. Q: When was the last time you talked to either Mr. Lay or any other Enron official, about the—about anything? And did discussions involve the financial problems of the company?

The President: I have never discussed, with Mr. Lay, the financial problems of the company. The last time that I saw Mr. Lay was at my mother's fundraising event to—for literacy, in Houston. That would have been last spring. I do know that Mr. Lay came to the White House in—early in my administration, along with, I think 20 other business leaders, to discuss the state of the economy. It was just kind of a general discussion. I have not met with him personally.

Q: —to inoculate you and your administration politically from the fallout?

The President: Well, first of all, Ken Lay is a supporter. And I got to know Ken Lay when he was the head of the—what they call the Governor's Business Council in Texas. He was a supporter of Ann Richards in my run in 1994. And she had named him the head of the Governor's Business Council. And I decided to leave him in place, just for the sake of continuity. And that's when I first got to know Ken, and worked with Ken, and he supported my candidacy . . .

—*Remarks by the President*, 1-10-02. Whitehouse.gov.

---

1. **Tim Russert:** . . . Do you still believe there is no evidence that Iraq was involved in September 11?

Dick Cheney: Well, what we now have that's developed since you and I last talked, Tim, of course, was that report that's been pretty well confirmed, that he [9/11 hijacker Muhammed Atta] did go to Prague and he did meet with a senior official of the Iraqi intelligence service in Czechoslovakia last April, several months before the attack. Now, what the purpose of that was, what transpired between them, we simply don't know at this point. But that's clearly an avenue that we want to pursue.

—*Vice-President Dick Cheney.* "Meet the Press," NBC, 12-9-01. A congressional report published in the summer of

2003 on the attacks states, "The CIA has been unable to
establish that [Atta] left the United States or entered Europe in April under his true name or any known alias."
Dana Milbank and Claudia Deane, "Hussein Link to 9/11
Lingers in Many Minds," *Washington Post*, 9-6-03.

2. With respect to 9/11, of course, we've had the story that's
been public out there. The Czechs alleged that Mohamed Atta,
the lead attacker, met in Prague with a senior Iraqi intelligence official five months before the attack, but we've never
been able to develop anymore of that yet either in terms of
confirming it or discrediting it. We just don't know.
   —*Vice President Dick Cheney.* "Meet the Press," NBC, 9-14-
   03. *Chicago Tribune*: "Czech officials disputed that story in
   December 2001 and intelligence officials have said that Atta
   was actually in the U.S. at the time of the alleged meeting."
   Bob Kemper, "Bush: No Iraqi link to Sept. 11," 9-18-03, p.1.

Homeland Security

. . . I mean this town is a—is a town full of people who like to leak information. And I don't know if we're going to find out the senior administration official. Now, this is a large administration, and there's a lot of senior officials. I don't have any idea. I'd like to. I want to know the truth. That's why I've instructed this staff of mine to cooperate fully with the investigators—full disclosure, everything we know the investigators will find out. I have no idea whether we'll find out who the leaker is—partially because, in all due respect to your profession, you do a very good job of protecting the leakers . . .

> —*George W. Bush*. "President Discusses National, Economic Security in Cabinet Meeting; Remarks by the President After Meeting with Cabinet Members," 10-7-03. He is discussing the possibility of discovering who leaked the information to Robert Novak that Joseph Wilson's wife was an undercover CIA agent. Whitehouse.gov.

Kate O'Beirne: I think an awful lot of people are playing awfully loose with the facts, as we know them, it seems, in news stories, I look at the same set of facts, and I don't see any reason to believe that any mention of her [Valerie Plame] was specifically done with the intent of discrediting Joe Wilson. First of all, the guy discredits himself by having such a left-wing agenda . . . I will say, I'm perfectly open to the proposition that it's a terribly serious thing that happened—if not criminal, serious, although maybe inadvertent—if Joe Wilson himself were not having the time of his life. Now, I—he argues that his wife's career is in—has been shattered, but boy, is he enjoying more than his five minutes of fame. And the photo spread in *Vanity*

Fair—who wouldn't recognize his wife? She was in a very thin disguise.

Mark Shields: . . . reason there's a photo spread in *Vanity Fair* is because of this leak. That's the only reason . . . That's the only reason anybody knows Valerie Plame.

O'Beirne: Her picture had not appeared until she posed for *Vanity Fair*!

Margaret Carlson: But it doesn't matter! Her picture can be out there now.

Bob Novak: Again, I'm only saying things that I have written before, and that is that I was told, reporting the story, by the press person at the CIA that it was unlikely that she would ever make another overseas trip on business for the CIA.

— *"Capital Gang,"* CNN, 1-3-04

Even though I'm a tranquil guy now at this stage of my life, I have nothing but contempt and anger for those who betray the trust by exposing the name of our [Intelligence] sources. They are, in my view, the most insidious of traitors.

— *George H.W. Bush* at the dedication ceremony for the George Bush Center for Intelligence, 4-26-99.

Our concern is that enemies who hate America do not get information which could help them attack America.

— *White House Communications Director Dan Bartlett*, defending the Administration's successful attempts to delay the investigation of 9-11.

It [North Korean possession of nuclear weapons] doesn't help an economy in need. It doesn't feed anyone. It doesn't scare anyone.

— *Secretary of State Colin Powell*. Bob Kemper and William Neikirk, "Bush offers agreement on North Korea," *Chicago Tribune*, 10-20-03.

If your idea of a vacation is two weeks in a terrorist training camp in Afghanistan, you might be a target of the Patriot Act. If you have cave-side dinners with a certain thug named bin Laden and if you enjoy swapping chemical weapons recipes from your Joy of Jihad cookbook, you might be a target of the Patriot Act.
—*Attorney General John Ashcroft* speaking in Minneapolis. Elizabeth Stawicki, "Ashcroft Defends Patriot Act," Minnesota Public Radio, 9-19-03.

America is freer today than at any time in the history of human freedom.
—*John Ashcroft*, 9-19-03. Greg Gordon, "Whistle-blower Rowley pulls no punches in critique of Ashcroft," *Minneapolis Star-Tribune*, 10-12-03.

V.P. Cheney: . . . It's very important we make that transition in understanding that we're at war, that the war continues, that this is a global enemy that struck in not only New York and Washington but in Bali and in Djakarta, in Mombasa, in Casablanca, Riyadh since 9/11, that this is an enterprise that is global in scope and one we've had major success against it. And the fact of the matter is there were thousands of people that went through those training camps in Afghanistan. We know they are seeking deadlier weapons—chemical, biological and nuclear weapons if they can get it. And if anything, those basic notions that developed in the early days after 9/11 have been reinforced by what we've learned since.
Tim Russert: There's grave concern about surface-to-air missiles shooting down American commercial aircraft. Should we not outfit all U.S. commercial airliners with equipment to detect and avoid that?
Cheney: Well, there are technologies available. They are extremely expensive if you're going to put them on every airliner. You've got to make choices here about, you know, when you're dealing with a risk, there may be certain aircraft flying into certain locales that

are especially vulnerable that you may want to deal with. But I
wouldn't automatically go to the assumption that we need to put
the most sophisticated system on every single airplane.
—*"Meet the Press,"* NBC, 9-14-03.

This is Secretary Tom Ridge of the Department of Homeland
Security. Congratulations, you've taken an important step towards surviving in an emergency. Here at the Dept. of Homeland Security we're working hard to prepare our nation, but
each of us must be ready to make it on our own, at least for a
period of time, no matter where we are when disaster strikes.
Stay on the line to receive our free brochure with simple tips
that could save your life or go to www.ready.gov. You can do
something to protect your family and yourself against the threat
of terrorism. The time to prepare is now. The fight against
terror begins at home. With a little planning and some common sense you can be better prepared. The first step is to
begin a process of learning about potential threats so you are
able to react during an emergency. Be prepared to assess the
situation and to use whatever you have on hand to take care
of yourself and your loved ones. Now depending on your circumstances and the nature of the attack, you might do better
by staying put. Or it might be better to get away. You should
understand and plan for both possibilities. Think about fresh
water, food, and clean air. You will need a gallon of water per
person per day and food that won't go bad. Keep basic emergency supplies like a radio, flashlight, batteries, and a first aid
kit. Store heavy-weight garbage bags and duct tape to seal
windows doors and air vents from outside contamination.
While there is no way to predict what will happen or what
your personal circumstances will be, there are things you can
do now. To learn more about how to get ready now go on line
to www.ready.gov. Thanks for calling the Dept. of Homeland
Security. Terrorism forces us to make a choice. We can be
afraid or we can be ready.
—*Sec. of the Dept. of Homeland Security Tom Ridge*, voice
    message at 1-800-BE-READY. Promoted in a full-page *New
    York Times* advertisement, 4-9-03.

Those folks who had the emergency kits when the lights went out a couple of weeks ago in Detroit and Cleveland and New York probably said, "Hey, it's a pretty good thing I had those batteries and those flashlights." And in a couple of those cities, "Probably a good thing I had an extra stash of water."
   —*Tom Ridge*. Frank James, "Ridge: Terror precautions may help in storm," *Chicago Tribune*, 9-17-03.

Obviously, I think there's been some political belittling of duct tape . . . But the Centers for Disease Control and professionals will tell you that duct tape and a secure room and a couple of gallons of water to tide you over for a day or two is precisely what you might have to do in the event something occurs . . . I don't worry so much about the negative commentary from elected officials, because I think most Americans get it.
   —*Tom Ridge*. Frank James and Rick Pearson, "Ridge Defends Duct Tape Tip," *Chicago Tribune*, 2-14-03.

Stash away the duct tape, don't use it!
   —*Tom Ridge*, quoted by Pete Williams, MSNBC, 2-19-03.

My legislation will prevent a Communist Chinese beachhead at the naval station.
   —*Rep. Duncan Hunter (R-CA)* introducing a bill to prevent the city of Long Beach from building a new cargo terminal on the site of the naval station which had been shut down by the Pentagon. The city planned to lease the terminal to Cosco, the China Ocean Shipping Company, which has been a tenant at the port since 1981. Jeff Leeds, "Congressman Tries to Sink Plan for Long Beach Port Economy: City officials denounce effort to block lease to Chinese company," *Los Angeles Times*, 3-21-97.

Giving complete control of a former national security asset to a Communist country is wrong. They are going to have intelligence agents here. They are going to ship arms in. They are going to possibly ship chemical weapons here.

—*Rep. Randy Cunningham (R-CA).* Laura Mecoy, "Stormy Sailing in Long Beach," *Sacramento Bee,* 4-13-97

Al Qaeda is on the run. That group of terrorists who attacked our country is slowly, but surely being decimated. Right now, about half of all the top al Qaeda operatives are either jailed or dead. In either case, they're not a problem anymore.

—*George W. Bush* at a Little Rock press conference a week before the al Qaeda attack in Riyadh that killed 34 people and injured 200. Maureen Dowd, "In-a-Gadda Da-Vida We Trust," *New York Times,* 5-28-03.

PART VII

A CHICKEN IN EVERY POT

"When I see someone who's making anywhere from $300,00 to $750,000 a year, that's middle class."

—REP. FRED HEINEMAN (R-NC)

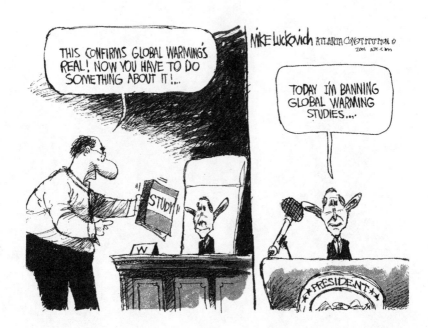

A Balanced Budget
or The Dive to Red Ink

[Balancing the budget] has nothing to do with our pay . . . No, I would not, I am not a federal employee. I am a constitutional officer. My job is in the Constitution of the United States, I am not a government employee, I am in the Constitution.
> —*House Majority Whip Tom DeLay (R-TX)*, when asked if he would support congressional pay cuts during a government shutdown. "Talk Back Live," CNN, 12 -19-95. In "Don't Touch Our Pay, House Republicans Say," 1-2-96, the *Washington Post* pointed out that House members made $133,600 per year, that those in leadership positions made even more, that on three occasions the Senate unanimously approved language preventing U.S. representatives, senators and the president from getting paid during a government shutdown, and that five times Rep. (now Sen.) Richard J. Durbin (D-IL) tried to get the House to consider the proposal and was rebuffed by Republicans, especially in the leadership-controlled Rules Committee.

Isn't it time we hold Congress accountable for how much they spend—and for what? The American people demand responsibility from Congress. The spending madness must stop. Our Contract with America begins with fiscal responsibility. Just as every American sits at the kitchen table and balances his or her budget, Congress must begin balancing our nation's budget—now. That's why in the first hundred days of a Republican House we will vote on the Fiscal Responsibility Act . . .
> —*Contract with America, etc.* NY: Times Books, 1994, p. 23.

A chimpanzee, banging away at a typewriter, would type out the entire *Encyclopedia Britannica* before the Clinton budget balances.
   —*Sen. Chuck Grassley (R-IA). Congressional Record*, S2796, 3-25-96.

Mr. Speaker, House Democrats, searching vainly for an issue to sidetrack the Contract With America, have now decided to attack the Speaker regarding a book he has not written yet. Instead of attacking Republicans for writing books, I suggest the Democrats write their own book. The suggested title might be "The Gang That Wouldn't Shoot Straight." After all, Democrats are not being straight with the American people regarding their own agenda. They are not being straight on why they do not want to pass the Balanced Budget Amendment. In fact, they want to spend more money. They are not being straight with the American people on why they opposed the unfunded mandates bill. In fact, they like unfunded mandates . . .
   —*Rep. Bob Barr (R-GA). Congressional Record*, H308, 1-18-95. The Speaker, Newt Gingrich, had signed a book contract with Rupert Murdoch's HarperCollins publishing house at a time when various legislation affecting Murdoch's interests was pending.

Mr. Chairman, today is a great day in America. As you all know, it is Fall. Back in my hometown of Mariposa in California it is also Fall, and what appears about this time of year is something that is known as a face fly. Why they call it a face fly is because if you are outside and you try to do some work, you are trying to get something done, you get this tiny bunch of flies that are in your eyes, in your mouth and buzzing in your ears, and they are a major distraction.
   This budget gives that face fly a good swat. It gives freedom to the American people and freedom from a body in this Congress for the last 40 years that has tried to be America's mother,

tried to be America's father, tried to be America's pastor, tried to be America's employer. We are giving freedom back to the American people to live their own lives.

    I would imagine that I have got working poor in my district and their message to you [the Democrats] is, get out of my face.
    —*Rep. George P. Radanovich (R-CA)*, arguing in favor of
        H.R.2491, the Seven Year Balanced Budget Reconciliation
        Act of 1995. *Congressional Record*, H10881, 10-26-95.

I would love to see like four Lee Iacocca's. I'd like to see a president with the cajones that said, "You know what we're gonna do, gang? We're gonna get four guys who are just not involved in politics and have made it so, so big in their life and are almost at their death bed so they don't really care about making any favorites with anybody . . . They're gonna go in a room, they're gonna take the budget and they're gonna cut 30% . . . and you have these guys just sit around a room and go "What is this? What do you mean it's a museum for frogs in Mississippi? What the hell are we doing with a museum for frogs?"
    —*Radio Talk Show Host Glenn Beck.* 570 KLIF, Dallas,
        4-16-03.

. . . The federal government has operated in the black for the last two years and is now projected to run a surplus of nearly $5 trillion over ten years. That wasn't magic. It took honesty and guts from a Congress that manages the nation's purse strings. Over a five year period, as surpluses continue to grow, we will return half a trillion dollars to the taxpayers who really own it, without touching the Social Security surplus. That's what we mean by our Lock-Box: The Social Security surplus is off-limits, off budget, and will not be touched. We will not stop there, for we are also determined to protect Medicare and to pay down the national debt. Reducing that debt is both a sound policy goal and a moral imperative. Our families and most states are required to balance their budgets; it is reasonable to assume the

federal government should do the same. Therefore, we reaffirm our support for a constitutional amendment to require a balanced budget.
> —*Republican Party Platform 2000*, "Renewing America's Purpose Together. RNC.org.

The President's Budget commits to using today's surpluses to reduce the Federal Government's publicly held debt so that future generations are not shackled with the responsibility of paying for the current generation's overspending. It commits to an historic amount of debt retirement and will retire $2 trillion in debt over the next 10 years. This is all the debt that can be retired without using taxpayer dollars to make bonus payments to investors in order to induce them to give up their bonds.
> —*From President George W. Bush's first budget plan*: "A Blueprint For New Beginnings: A Responsible Budget for America's Priorities," Section IV, "An Unprecedented Moment in History," 2-28-01. Whitehouse.gov.

We ought not to hyperventilate about this. By any historical measure, these are manageable deficits.
> —*Mitchell E. Daniels, Jr.*, then Bush's budget director, on his own projections of a $200 billion deficit in 2003 and one over $300 billion in 2004, taking into account Bush's proposed tax cuts, but not the cost of the Iraq war. David E. Rosenbaum and Edmund L. Andrews, "Bush Aide Sees Deficit in 2003 of $200 Billion," *New York Times*, 1-16-03.

. . . how can we ever cut government down to size? I believe there is one and only one way: the way parents control spendthrift children, cutting their allowance. For government that means cutting taxes . . . Resulting deficits will be an effective—I would go so far as to say, the only effective—restraint on the spending propensities of the executive branch and the legislature.
> —*Republican Economist Milton Friedman. Wall Street Journal*, 1-15-03.

Anything that will help us stop spending money, I'm in favor of. This place is set up to spend money; you know it's just the nature of the beast. And we've tried to say, hey, we don't have to spend so much of it. And if there's a deficit, that may help us.

> —*Rep. Sue Myrick (R-NC)*, Chair of the Republican Study Committee. David Firestone, "Washington Talk; Conservatives Now See Deficits as a Tool to Fight Spending," *New York Times*, 2-10-03.

People refer to the sham in this budget. The sham is when we do not pass the budget . . . I strongly support any effort we have to cut taxes. I don't think our tax cut package is big enough, considering how big our gross domestic product is. It really needs to be more to stimulate the economy.

> —*Sen. Wayne Allard (R-CO)*, on the $350 billion tax cut in the reduced Republican budget resolution for 2004. *Congressional Record*, S5298, 4-11-03. President Bush had originally proposed a $726 billion tax cut.

While our economy is growing today, it is growing slowly. Too many companies struggle and too many Americans look for work. There's wide agreement on the need to promote growth, but fundamental disagreement on how to achieve it. Count me among those who believe the best way to promote economic growth is to further reduce marginal income tax rates. I say this with respect for serious critics of tax-rate reduction, who believe that a balanced budget should trump tax relief. I respect them because I once sincerely subscribed to the same fiscal theology. But I was wrong. That's why I often refer to myself on this issue as a "reformed drunk." The success of the tax-rate reductions we achieved during President Reagan's two terms in office in the 1980's sobered me up.

> —*James A. Baker III.* "A 'Reformed Drunk' on Tax Relief," *Wall Street Journal*, 4-18-03.

. . . but this tax cut, there is no tax cut that needs to be paid for. That, please shelve that. Please sweep that from your lexicon. Tax cuts do not need to be paid for. If, if, if any of you continue to look at tax cuts that way you may as well be under the Svengali mind-control of the Democrats. Tax cuts don't need to be paid for . . .
—*Rush Limbaugh*, 5-23-03.

This ain't the end of it—we're going to have some more. Our budget says we're going to have $1.3 trillion in tax cuts, and you bet we're coming back for more.
—*Tom DeLay (R-TX)*. David Firestone, "With Tax Cut Bill Passed, Republicans Call for More," *New York Times*, 5-24-03.

We would have had deficits with or without tax cuts.
—*George W. Bush*, 7-30-03 press conference. Bob Kemper, "Bush: Nuclear claim my fault," *Chicago Tribune*, 7-31-03.

There's no question that annual federal deficits have been the only effective check on congressional spending in the modern era.
—*Rep. Mike Pence (R-IN)*. David Firestone, "Dizzying Dive to Red Ink Has Lawmakers Facing Difficult Budget Choices," *New York Times*, 9-14-03.

Let Them Eat Cake
or Leave No Millionaire Behind

Slowly, but surely, they're taking away your liberty to mutually make employment decisions. I dare say that's socialism. It's government paternalism at its worst.

  —*Mark Wilson* of the Heritage Foundation, on the minimum wage law. Peter T. Kilborn, "A Minimal-Impact Minimum Wage," *New York Times*, 4-6-97.

You and I are driving cars. Why should we pay for Amtrak?

  —*Rep. Jay Kim (R-CA)*, a member of the House Transportation and Infrastructure Committee, objecting to the Clinton Administration transportation bill (the National Economic Crossroads Transportation Efficiency Act) for its provision to use some Highway Trust Fund money for Amtrak. Asra Q. Nomani, "Highway Bill's Amtrak Funds Upset Many," *Wall Street Journal*, 3-13-97.

Who is this guy, back on the streets after doing time for dealing drugs? He's got a nice rent-controlled apartment to come home to, courtesy of you.

  —*Voice-over on an ad aired in upstate New York*—not in New York City—by the Community Housing Improvement Program, a landlords' lobbying group. The screen showed a man walking through Times Square to make a drug deal. This ad campaign was part of an ongoing effort to eliminate rent controls. Dan Morton, "Landlord Ads Sour Big Apple Upstate," *Newsday*, 5-3-97.

On June 16th, the rent control laws and rent-stabilization laws in this city will no longer exist. We are going to liberate the city.
—*State Senate Majority Leader Joe Bruno (R-NY)*, vowing to "sweep aside decades of state laws limiting rent hikes." Kimberly Schaye and Michael Finnegan, "Bruno Ready to Raise Living Costs by Killing Control, Stabilization," *New York Daily News*, 12-6-96. Even Republicans like New York Mayor Ralph Giuliani, and Gov. George Pataki attempted to distance themselves from Bruno's statements, although Pataki received large campaign contributions from landlords.

. . . In 1999, there were 127 million tax filers, 94.5 million of whom showed an income tax liability. That is, 26% had no liability at all. The actual number of people filing without paying comes to 16 million (after subtracting those getting earned income tax credits and thus, presumably, still somewhat sensitive to tax rates). So almost 13% of all workers have no tax liability and so are indifferent to income tax rates. And that doesn't include another 16.5 million who have some income but don't file at all.

Who are these lucky duckies? They are the beneficiaries of tax policies that have expanded the personal exemption and standard deduction and targeted certain voter groups by introducing a welter of tax credits for things like child care and education. When these escape hatches are figured against income, the result is either a zero liability or a liability that represents a tiny percentage of income. The 1986 tax reform, for example, with its giant increase in the personal exemption and standard deduction, took six to seven million people off the tax rolls . . .
—*Wall Street Journal* editorial, "The Non-Taxpaying Class; Those Lucky Duckies!" 11-20-02.

Last Fall, the *Wall Street Journal* ran an editorial entitled "The Non-Taxpaying Class." The editorial, which dubbed those too poor to pay taxes "lucky duckies," won the *Journal* widespread

ridicule from big-hearted egalitarians throughout the world of media and punditry. But the *Wall Street Journal* was right. There are now more than 16 million Americans who file tax returns but pay no taxes. And that's not because we're getting poorer. America is getting richer. Fewer people are paying taxes because more and more politicians are succumbing to class warfare, and granting more and more exemptions to an increasingly complex tax code. The tax burden is climbing higher and higher up the income ladder . . .
>   —*Radley Balko.* "Tax the Poor," FoxNews.com, 4-9-03.

You know, we in our party believe growth is very important to the American economy. I always point out the most beautiful words Mom and Dad ever hear in their life is, "Mom, Dad, I got the job." And your youngsters get jobs in a growing economy. An across-the-board capital gains tax reduction will generate those jobs for those youngsters so Mom and Dad can hear those golden words.
>   —*Dick Armey.* "Late Edition," CNN, 2-2-97.

. . . we basically created a lawsuit mentality in the area of the workplace relative to overtime pay questions. In fact, this is the fastest growing area of lawsuits for trial lawyers. This is sort of the new oil field they have struck. You know how sometimes we strike oil fields in Kansas, or in Saudi Arabia or in the North Slope. Well, this is the new oil field that the trial lawyers have struck, which is the inconsistency, the confusion, of the overtime law. It has become the new gusher for one element of the bar.
>   —*Sen. Judd Gregg (R-NH)* in defense of the Republican proposal to limit overtime pay. *Congressional Record*, 9-9-03, S11203–04.

Mike Ozanian, *Forbes* Senior Editor: And we're implementing a lot of the technology that we can put in place the last 10, 15 years from companies like Cisco.

David Asman, Host: But that just means that folks lose their jobs, they're out on the unemployment lines.
Ozanian: That's just now, that's just now. As profits continue, they're going to start to hire. This means our companies have it right, we're not like France, Japan, and Germany—excuse me—preoccupied with jobs. We're preoccupied with profits, where we should be.
    —*"Forbes on Fox,"* Fox News Channel, 9-6-03.

But the first thing we ought to say is, you know, to the three million people who have lost their jobs during the Bush administration, we're sorry, we know that's horrible, we know that's terrible. And yet, if you're an investor in a company, you want your company to make things, make products for as cheap as possible so that the company can thrive.
    —*Dennis Kneale*, Managing Editor, *Forbes* magazine. *Ibid.*

When I see someone who is making anywhere from $300,000 to $750,000 a year, that's middle class.
    —*Rep. Fred Heineman (R-NC). Washington Post, 10-25-96.*
    Rep. Heineman defended his comments by attacking the Democratic Party, and saying that his remarks "were accurate for me and others like me." *Congressional Record,* H10754, 10-25-95.

Now if the gentleman really seriously was concerned about the children of America he would remember that the children in Head Start are not the only children in America. All of the children of America, roughly 100 million, are the future of America . . . This cut is meaningless, and for these people to say the world is coming to an end when all we are doing is trimming back a measly 2.9 percent, $.1 billion out of $3.5 billion, then it seems to me this is much ado about nothing. We are speaking about how many angels can dance on the head of a pin . . . It is

time to say no. It is time to make a trim. It is time to make the
cuts. It is time to pass this bill.

> —*Rep. Bob Livingston (R-LA)*, in support of Bill H.R.2127,
> the 1996 Appropriations Act for the Departments of La-
> bor, Health and Human Services, Education, and Related
> Agencies. Rep. David Obey (D-WI), commented that the
> bill cut 55,000 children from the Head Start program. *Con-*
> *gressional Record*, H8320, 8-3-95.

And to have these kids in Maryland—to have these kids in
Maryland they can't get a high school diploma unless they put
in a 120 hours of community services,that's like a Fascist state.

> —*Robert Novak*, objecting to the Summit on Volunteerism
> held by President Clinton in Philadelphia in 1997. "Capi-
> tal Gang," CNN, 4-26-97.

I really feel strongly that we ought to find some way to convince the people that there ought to be some volunteerism at
home. Those people overseas in the desert they're not getting
paid overtime . . . I don't know why the people working for the
cities and counties ought to be paid overtime when they're responding to matters of national security.

> —*Sen. Ted Stevens (R-AK)*, Chairman of the Senate Appro-
> priations Committee. Robert Hardt, Jr., "Pol Urges Unpaid
> Cop Overtime," *New York Post*, 4-02-03.

Of all the barriers to opportunity imposed by government, I
can think of few more onerous than the minimum wage law,
for it arrests the natural development of young people at a crucial stage.

> —*Republican vice-presidential candidate Jack Kemp*, from
> his 1979 book, *An American Renaissance. A Strategy for*
> *the 1980's*, quoted in *New York Times*, 8-11-96.

We can sympathize with those who've lost everything. If it is possible to tap some of the millions made by management who unfairly sold their stock and give it to employees prohibited from selling theirs, this should be done. But people who were seduced by the prospect of unending riches were ultimately responsible for what they did with their money. In an age when everyone is a victim and no one is responsible for making bad decisions—whether about the consequences of cigarette smoking or financial behavior—most of those suffering from the Enron disaster put themselves at risk.

It may sound cruel, but they were done in by their own greed. For the Stevenses, $720,000 in a relatively safe retirement account was not enough. They wanted more—fast—and what they got was much less. It's very sad, even tragic, but the real tragedy is that this could have been prevented if their decisions had been based on sound financial principles rather than emotion and greed. Some Enron investors were given that advice but ignored it. Is that Enron's fault or their own?

> —*Cal Thomas.* "Enron and personal responsibility," Tribune
> Media Services, 1-29-02.

Emotional appeals about working families trying to get by on $4.25 an hour are hard to resist. Fortunately, such families do not exist.

> —*House Majority Whip Tom DeLay (R-TX). Congressional
> Record,* H3706, 4-23-96. Rep. DeLay defended his position on the minimum wage: ". . . any parent who is earning
> the minimum wage is eligible for food stamps and the earned
> income tax credit" and if you add these things together, a
> married couple with one child would end up making
> "$13,134 amounting to $6.31 an hour."

The Proposition to raise the minimum wage is fools' gold. It appeals to the naked eye, but upon closer inspection it is fraud, pure and simple.

> —*Ibid.,* H3713, 4-23-96.

We recommended terminating the low-income home energy assistance program beyond fiscal year 1995. Now we are being accused of causing low-income people to freeze to death, but this is just one more example of a temporary program far out-living its time. Energy costs are far below the pre-1980 levels in real terms. If low-income people need an income supplement, then a reason other than energy cost needs to be used.
—*Bob Livingston (R-LA). Congressional Record*, H3194, 3-15-95.

You will hear people say, "Well, you cannot change this. You are going to harm children." Folks, look at all the welfare payments, AFDC [Aid to Families With Dependent Children], SSI [Supplemental Security Income], on down the list. How many of those benefits get paid directly to the children? How many of them? The answer is none. A child in this country does not get any money paid directly to them. It all goes to parents. They all go to parents.
—*Sen. Rick Santorum (R-PA). Congressional Record*, S4679, 3-28-95.

[Medicare] is not necessarily a good program. It helped some people but at a huge cost to the government.
—*Pat Robertson.* "700 Club," CBN, 9-20-95.

I am tired of the nonsense we are hearing about the minimum wage and how we can increase it and how we are going to do wonderful things for people.
—*Jim Longley (R-ME)* in a one-minute address to the House. *Congressional Record*, H1167, 2-3-95.

I will resist an increase in the minimum wage with every fiber of my being.
—*House Majority Leader Dick Armey (R-TX). Boston Globe*, 1-29-95. A minimum wage increase passed in both the House and Senate, 8-2-96.

My bill, the Student Loan Privatization Act of 1995 (H.R. 1501), calls for a phase-out of the Federal Direct Student Loan Program . . . Direct lending is nothing more than a government-run, multi-billion dollar consumer loan program.
> —*Rep. Ernest Jim Istook, Jr. (R-OK). Congressional Record,*
> E1212, 6-9-95.

Heeding the outcry from the nation's campuses, we will end the Clinton Administration's perverse direct lending program.
> —*Republican Party Platform*, adopted 8-12-96, p.23.

Where did this idea come from that everybody deserves free education? Free medical care? Free whatever? It comes from Moscow. From Russia. It comes straight out of the pit of hell.
> —*State Rep. Debbie Riddle (R-TX)* during a political commit-
> tee meeting. "Perspectives" column, *Newsweek,* 5-26-03.

We're poor people.
> —*Newt Gingrich,* describing his wife and himself. Bill
> Tammeus, "The Year of Talking Dangerously: Next time,
> folks, consider silence," *Denver Post,* 12-29-95.

It's a little difficult to give tax relief to people who don't pay taxes. It's a spending program.
> —*House Majority Leader Tom DeLay (R-TX)* defending the
> last-minute removal from the budget bill of a tax credit for
> families making from $10,500 to $26,625, while overlook-
> ing the fact that these working families pay payroll taxes.
> Jill Zuckman, "GOP scrambles on tax credit," *Chicago
> Tribune,* 6-4-03.

The distinguished Senator from Massachusetts, and those who support this concept, believes that an increase in the minimum wage is the quick, painless way to help the disadvantaged in our society. They believe that a minimum wage hike is absolutely costless, and they believe that it has no adverse impact

whatsoever. I can only wonder, then, why they have not offered
an amendment raising the minimum wage to $15 an hour or
$20 or $25 or $30, because if it has no impact and it really is
going to benefit people, why not do that. In fact, if raising Senators' salaries $1.50 an hour over the last year is right, why not
give everybody whatever the amount of money the Senators
make—$100,000, $130,000, or whatever it is to even things up
and make everybody equal in our society? I am sure the Senator
is not arguing that so I do not mean to raise that type of ridiculous argument.

. . . I think instead of having minimum wages we ought to
have minimum taxes. But where do we get the help from the
other side on that? We don't get much of it. If you cut taxes,
you actually give people an increase in wages, because they actually take more money home.

—*Sen. Orrin Hatch (R-UT). Congressional Record,* S10692,
9-22-98.

. . . I mean, to me, it's obvious that if somebody doesn't pay
taxes, they shouldn't get a tax cut. They shouldn't get anything.

—*Robert Novak* discussing the 350 billion dollar tax cut that
passed both Houses of Congress. "Meet the Press," NBC,
6-1-03. At the 11th hour, a provision giving a tax credit to
low-income Americans was removed from the bill, which
was then signed into law by George W. Bush.

. . . Today, of 100 American families, 50 of them paid 96.1 percent of the taxes before the last tax cut, and in the last tax cut, we
gave Americans back their own money. And what the Democrats
have proposed is taking Americans' money, your money, America,
and we are giving it to someone else, and that is not a tax credit.
That is welfare. Let us be honest with the American people. We
are turning our Tax Code into a welfare system . . .

—*Rep. Spencer Bachus (R-AL),* arguing against the child tax
credit for low-income working families. *Congressional
Record,* H5321, 6-12-0.

When we talk about the death tax, it is truth in labeling, because under the current scheme, in the current lexicon, people talk about estate taxes as if this were some sort of palatial gains. It does not tell us the truth. It is a tax literally upon people who die, there is a penalty for dying . . .
—*Rep. J.D. Hayworth (R-AZ)*. *Congressional Record*, H873, 3-11-97.

Ultimately, the rich do not pay because the rich have salted away enough already. The people that pay are the ones who pay with their jobs. If we have a death tax that literally causes the business, their place of employment, to be busted up, of course they lose their jobs. Of course they pay a 100-percent rate of tax. Of course they are the ones bearing the entire burden on their shoulders.
—*Rep. Christopher Cox (R-CA)* attempting to convince working people that estate taxes are taking away their jobs. *Congressional Record*, H872, 3-11-97.

I cannot help but think what Meriwether Lewis or Thomas Jefferson would have thought had they realized that this country had come to the point where the U.S. Government is taking away wealth from not even the rich, I mean this is middle-class stuff here, and that they are actually into income redistribution.
—*Rep. George P. Radanovich (R-CA)* in the debate over estate and capital gains taxes. He appears to be opposed to any taxation at all. *Congressional Record*, H870, 4-11-97.

I favor a zero tax on savings and job creation. We're for zero tax on death benefits.
—*House Speaker Newt Gingrich* arguing for the elimination of estate and capital gains taxes. Jerry Gray, "Gingrich Suggests Removing Capital Gains and Estate Tax," *New York Times*, 4-10-97. Gray writes, "two-thirds of all capital gains taxes" collected by the Federal Government "come from the wealthiest 1% of taxpayers." Estate taxes can be as high as 55%, but "are imposed only on the part of inheritances that exceed $600,000."

As a result of the higher education market distortion, administration staffs have become bloated. Faculties and staff have seen
their compensation rising sharply in modern times. New technology is not used aggressively to reduce labor costs. Universities "rent-seeking" activity—that is, getting payments beyond
the amount needed to provide goods and services—is strong.
Price discrimination in the form of scholarships has facilitated
the cost explosion as well . . . As universities become more tu-
ition-driven, many of their inefficiencies will be squeezed out of
the system as they struggle to survive. Universities may then be
forced into meaningful reforms such as ending tenure, increasing teaching loads, paring administrative staffs, slashing costly
enrollment programs, increasing distance learning, addressing
high student attrition rates, contracting out more services, cutting costly non-educational programs of dubious worth, and
altering affirmative action. Vedder suggests even more dramatic
and fundamental changes, including moving to a student-based
funding model (voucherization) and even privatization of state
universities.

> —*Jacket copy* for Richard Kent Vedder, *Going Broke by De-
> gree, Why College Costs Too Much*, Washington, D.C.: AEI
> Press, 2004.

Grover Norquist: Well, social security, the good news is, that
there's an emerging consensus in the United States that we need
to do what President Bush recommended in the last campaign
and that is to take, begin the process of moving it from a Ponzi
scheme, a pay-as-you-go scheme where you pay your social security fica taxes this week and next week it goes to pay for
somebody who's retired and there is no savings for you, there is
no account for you, there is just debt, to one where you take
your fica tax of the equivalent of your fica tax and put part of
it, and I would like eventually to phase in all of it, into a 401k
an IRA, a personal saving account . . .
Terry Gross: First of all, unless you have money to put into
these 401k's you're not going to get much back, and you know

there was this kind of guarantee of social security for working people. The stock market can fall, you can make bad investments and end up with little or nothing in the alternate scheme to social security. You're not concerned about this?

Norquist: I am concerned the demagogues of the left will trot that out again, I'm less concerned because they've done it before and nobody's buying.

    —*Grover Norquist,* President of Americans for Tax Reform.
    "Fresh Air," NPR, 10-2-03.

We've been extending, extending, extending [unemployment benefits]. Now that the economy is improving, the jobs picture is looking a little bit brighter, I think we need to hold fast.

    —*Rep. Jim McCrery (R-LA),* senior member of the House Ways
    and Means Committee. Sheryl Gay Stolberg, "House votes,
    Fights, and Then Adjourns," *New York Times,* 12-9-03.

Mark Shields: I just don't think that the rising stock market or economic growth means anything if jobs aren't created.

Robert Novak: Let me set you correct, Mark, a little bit, because you guys play that class warfare, you're way out of date. Oh, boy, jobs, jobs, jobs, you know, there's a lot of people in this country—you don't like it—but the middle class has stocks, they have 401(k)s, and they're very interested in the stock market.

    —*"Capital Gang,"* CNN, 11-1-03.

FUZZY MATH

We are at a point now where we are now paying taxes at the highest rate in the history of this republic.
—*Sen. John Ashcroft.* "Springfield Boys and Girls Club Gymnasium, Transcript of Remarks," 1-5-99. GWU.edu.

Did the Reagan tax cuts cause the deficits of the 1980's? Not at all. In fact, government revenue nearly doubled during the Reagan years.
—*Sean Hannity, Let Freedom Ring*, NY: Reganbooks, HarperCollins, 2002, pp. 222–223.

One negative influence on the rate of new hires in every recovery is the distorting effect of unemployment insurance. The increase in the maximum duration of unemployment benefits that Congress enacted last year has delayed the current employment recovery even more than usual.
—*Martin Feldstein*, Harvard Professor and Chairman of the Council of Economic Advisors under President Reagan. "There's No such Thing as a 'Jobless' Recovery," *Wall Street Journal,* 10-13-03.

Yes, the price tag may be very high. Freedom is priceless.
—*National Security Advisor Condoleezza Rice,* defending the $87 billion supplemental spending request for Iraq and Afghanistan announced by President Bush on 9-7-03. Thomas E. Ricks and Vernon Loeb, "$87 billion request spurs Iraq Debate," *Washington Post,* 9-10-03.

Tim Russert: Is the $87 billion the end of it? Will the American people be asked for any more money?
V.P. Dick Cheney: I can't say that. It's all that we think we'll need for the foreseeable future for this year.
   —*"Meet the Press,"* 9-14-03.

Did everybody understand everything that was in the Contract? No. Did I understand everything that was in the Contract? No.
   —*Rep. Gil Gutknecht (R-MN)*, on the Contract with America that he had voted for 100 percent. "GOP Congressman Votes Perfect Score," *St. Paul Pioneer Press*, 3-4-96.

One would think from the rhetoric of the liberal Democrats that balancing the budget means Draconian cuts in the budget. Actually, all we have to do is slow the rate of spending to an additional 2 trillion instead of 3 trillion in the next 7 years.
   —*Rep. Steve Chabot (R-OH)*, on the Balanced Budget Amendment. *Congressional Record*, H2232, 2-27-95.

. . . there's 15 billion dollars that can be reduced from the state budget without in any way affecting the vital services and, in fact, in many cases, improving the vital services available to the people of California.
   —*Tom McClintock,* Republican candidate for governor in the 2003 California recall election. "Talk of the Nation," NPR, 8-12-03.

Very simply, this has been going on for 50 years. Jobs have been sucked overseas, and as a result we create two new jobs here, usually better-paying jobs. It's called globalization, it works. Trust the market. Now, what you're—you guys, when millions of steelworkers' jobs went overseas you didn't really care too much, but now that some of your classmates and neighbors are losing their jobs, you're getting very excited about it. But it's

still the same trend that's been going on, and if you trust the market—which you gotta do—it's a beneficent trend.
—*Jim Michaels*, Editorial Vice-President, *Forbes* magazine. "Forbes on Fox," Fox News Channel, 9-6-03.

Caller: I usually agree with your views, but I had one point about the taxes, which I don't understand, and I think maybe you're making a mistake.
Sean Hannity: What is it?
Caller: OK, you were saying that 10 percent of the tax payers pay 65 percent of the taxes?
Hannity: Whatever the final numbers are. Those are the IRS numbers.
Caller: OK, there's another perspective to it as well. The top 10 percent of wage earners also, probably, rake in about 65 percent of the income.
Hannity: Why would they be raking in more, to use your term, why would people rake in more money then other people? Because maybe they work harder? Longer hours? Greater sacrifice?
—*Sean Hannity*, 8-25-03.

With all of these actions [tax cuts] we are laying the foundation for greater prosperity and more jobs across America so every single person in this country can realize the American dream.
—*George W. Bush*. Deb Riechmann, "Bush's Two-Day Texas Trip pushes campaign war chest over $40 million," Associated Press, 7-20-03.

Our failure to call it a tax in the bill doesn't mean that it is not a tax. It just means that it is a tax that we will not admit is a tax. They say if it walks like a duck and squawks like a duck, if it quacks like a duck and acts like a duck, it is probably a duck. Well, this is a higher price that is charged for these cigarettes. It is collected from the people. It gets transmitted to the Govern-

ment and the Government spends it on Government programs. Now, I think that walks like a duck and squawks like a duck. I think it acts like a duck and quacks like a duck. I think it is a duck or it is a tax, if you want to use that word.
> —*Sen. John Ashcroft (R-MO)*. *Congressional Record*, S5153, 5-20-98.

Nothing is more important in the face of a war than cutting taxes.
> —*Tom DeLay (R-TX)* in a speech to bankers, cited by Rep. George Miller (D-CA). *Congressional Record*, H1779, 3-12-03.

The Fair Tax Act of 2003 would repeal the individual income tax, the corporate tax, capital gains taxes, all payroll taxes, the self-employment tax and the estate and gift taxes in lieu of a 23 percent tax on the final sale of all goods and services. The eradication of these taxes will not only bring about equality within our tax system, it will also bring about simplicity.
> —*Sen. Saxby Chambliss (R-GA)*. *Congressional Record*, S10269, 7-30-03.

I'm concerned about deficits, but this nation has got a deficit because we have been through a war. And I told the American people we would spend what is necessary to win the war. But I know we can grow out of the deficits with wise policy.
> —*George W. Bush*. Bob Kemper, "Bush Touts 'robust' tax cut as a cure for lean times," *Chicago Tribune*, 4-25-03.

The only reason God put Republicans on earth is to cut taxes.
> —*President of Club for Growth Stephen Moore*. "Realtime with Bill Maher," HBO, 4-25-03. Club for Growth is a political fundraising group dedicated to electing "Reaganite" Republicans to office.

Well, this is why his tax cut package is so important. Reagan understood when he dropped the top margin of rates from 90 to 28 percent, as you know, we doubled revenues in eight years. We went from over 500 billion to over a trillion dollars in revenues. This is what the President's trying to do here, stimulate the economy. Look, he's had a very tough time. He inherited the Clinton/Gore recession. We had to deal with the corporate scandals that Clinton created for us in the 90's. We had 9/11, and we fought two wars, and his economic plan has only been in place a year, a little over a year and a half. I mean, the fact that he got us out of the recession, we're in a period of economic growth, albeit anemic, in my view, it's somewhat phenomenal.

—*Sean Hannity.* "700 Club," CBN, 6-6-03.

We committed ourselves to help get the economy started moving again, and since the House passed the President's Jobs and Growth Package, wealth has been created, losses recovered, consumer confidence has risen and jobless claims have fallen.

—*Tom DeLay (R-TX). Congressional Record,* H5717, 6-24-03.

We have had one of the shallowest recessions in our nation's history as a result of the tax relief plan.

—*George W. Bush* to small business owners in Elizabeth, N.J. David E. Sanger, " In speech Bush reiterates threat Hussein posed but makes no mention of weapons search," *New York Times,* 6-17-03.

. . . For an incremental benefit of 1%, we should only have to pay an incremental cost of 1% or less. Nowhere else but in the Federal Government do people spend $1 million to get $100 worth of benefit, and we must end this practice. The Clean Air Act refinery MCAT rule is a perfect example. As proposed, the rule would cost approximately $10 million and only save less than half of one life.

—*Sen. James Inhofe,* speaking about the Environmental Protection Agency and regulatory reform. *Congressional Record,* S9829, 7-13-95.

Campaign Strategies

I think that the mother killing the two children in South Carolina vividly reminds every American how sick the society is getting and how much we need to change things . . . The only way you get change is to vote Republican.

> —*Newt Gingrich* on the case of Susan Smith, who drowned her two sons. Associated Press, 11-8-94.

We need to find new issues that polarize in our favor. We should not fight things that are clearly popular. It makes us look Draconian.

> —*Anthony Fabrizio*, Republican pollster. Richard Benedetto, "GOP Poll," *USA Today*, 2-26-97.

Heard the one about Republicans "cutting" Medicare? The fact is Republicans are increasing Medicare spending by more than half. I'm Haley Barbour, and I'm so sure of that fact I'm willing to give you this check for a million dollars if you can prove me wrong.

> —*Republican National Committee 1995 newspaper ad* with a picture of Haley Barbour, then RNC Chairman, promoting the "Million Dollar Medicare Challenge," to counter Democratic claims that the Republicans would cut Medicare. The eighty people who entered the contest were told that their responses were incorrect. One of the contestants, Robert Shireman, filed a lawsuit in Washington D.C. Superior Court to claim the million dollars he said he was owed by the Republican Party.
>
> Haley Barbour responded to this by filing an action of his own in U.S. District Court in Mississippi. All eighty

people who responded to the advertisement received "a summons notifying them that if they wanted to claim they deserved the $1 million prize, they would have to respond to the court in Mississippi." Dan Balz, "After One 'Medicare Challenge' Entrant Goes to Court, Party Sues Them All," *Washington Post*, 1-30-97.

Mr. Speaker, I am again introducing legislation to repeal the National Voter Registration Act of 1993, the so-called "motor-voter" bill . . . While voter apathy under motor-voter is unsettling, there is another, more compelling reason to rethink the soundness of the law. It has allowed for voter fraud on a national scale.
—*Rep. Bob Stump (R-AZ). Congressional Record*, E7, 1-7-97.

Unless George W. steps in front of a bus or some woman comes forward, let's say some black woman comes forward with an illegitimate child that he fathered within the last 18 months, or some other scenario that you could be equally creative in thinking of, George W. Bush will be the nominee.
—*Sen. Bob Bennett (R-UT)*. Paul Foy, "Bennett apologizes for remark," Associated Press, 8-24-99.

George understands what a great President must understand. The first three words of America's most sacred document are, "We the People"—not "Us vs.Them"! George rejects the old-style politics of false choices. He believes that a leader can be for the environment and jobs, for tax cuts and fiscal discipline, for public schools—and parental choice. George wants to win—but he won't divide us to do it.
—*Pennsylvania Gov. Tom Ridge* speaking to the Republican National Convention, 8-3-00. PBS.org.

But I will defend my record at the appropriate time, and look forward to it. I'll say that the world is more peaceful and more

free under my leadership, and America is more secure. And that will be the—that will be how I'll begin describing our foreign policy.
>   —*George W. Bush*, press conference, White House Rose Garden, 10-28-03. Whitehouse.gov.

I have been a longtime supporter of President Bush and the Republican Party and am committed to helping Ohio deliver its electoral votes to the President next year. Because of this, on Friday, September 26th my wife Patricia and I are opening our home for an event featuring Governor Bob Taft and Ohio Senators Mike DeWine and George Voinovich to benefit the Ohio Republican Party . . . Your help is greatly needed if we are to reach our financial goals through this event. As a member of the host committee, you will be asked to commit to donate or raise $10,000 for the Ohio Republican Party.
>   —*A letter signed by Wally O'Dell*, CEO of Diebold, Inc., one of the largest makers of electronic voting machines: "The letter went out the day before Ohio Secretary of State Ken Blackwell, also a Republican, was set to qualify Diebold as one of three firms eligible to sell upgraded electronic voting machines to Ohio counties in time for the 2004 election . . ." Julie Carr Smyth, "Voting Machine Controversy," *Cleveland Plain Dealer*, 8-28-03.

Hey, hey folks, get this: The Democratic field gets crowded. Retired Army General Wesley Clark has told friends that he is likely to become the 10th Democratic Presidential dwarf. It is a move that could shake up the crowded field just four months before the first ballots are cast. These people actually think that Wesley Clark is going to reorder all this and he's going to become the automatic front runner. Wesley Clark may not know what day it is, during a given week. And he may not know certain historical facts, but that's par for the course. It was in-

teresting that Nikita Dean, Howard Dean, sent a little [vice-residential] feeler out to Wesley Clark this week.
    —*Rush Limbaugh*, 9-11-03.

But politically, the constant refrain about the need for more jobs and that tax cuts will generate growth, that level of engagement will have a significant political payoff whether it has a significant economic payoff or not.
    —*A prominent Republican advisor.* Richard W. Stevenson, "In Bush Math, Economy Equals Votes," *New York Times*, 5-25-03.

I will promise you when I go up to Sacramento, I will pump Sacramento up.
    —*Actor and professional body-builder Arnold Schwarzenegger* announcing his candidacy for California governor in the recall election. *Detroit Free Press*, 8-7-03.

One thing's for sure, the Speaker of the House will be able to bring home a lot more bacon than a freshman.
    —*Newt Gingrich,* shortly before his re-election. *Marietta Journal,* 10-23-94. He had made a commitment to end the practice of pork barrel politics.

Heh, heh, heh. Yeah, that's the one we want. How come no one is cheering for Dean? Come on everybody! Go, Howard Dean!
    —*Karl Rove* encountering a dozen Dean supporters at a Fourth of July parade in Washington, D.C. Juliet Epstein, "Rove Spends the Fourth Rousing Support for Dean," *Washington Post*, 7-5-03.

Americans spend more on yogurt than we do on campaign spending.
    —*Rep. John P. Doolittle (R-CA),* speaking against campaign finance reform, and against reducing the influence of money on politicians. *New York Times*, 7-26-96.

You know, if you take the presidential campaign of last year and combine both campaigns, we spent less money on those campaigns—something that's vitally important to American family today—than we spend on potato chips.

—*Tom DeLay* arguing against campaign finance reform. "Late Edition," CNN, 4-6-97.

Limits on campaign giving and spending are limits on political expression.

—*George Will. Chicago Sun-Times*, 10-15-95. Will, a television personality and newspaper columnist, also acts as a Republican consultant. His wife worked for the Bob Dole presidential campaign in 1996.

It's not necessary to tell people where their checks went. There is nothing wrong with that. We don't have an obligation to tell people. Money is fungible.

—*Sen. Alphonse M. D'Amato (R-NY)*, on his practice of depositing campaign donation checks made out to the National Republican Senatorial Committee into two bank accounts supporting Republican candidates for state office. The donors were not told of this sleight-of-hand, which served to skirt campaign finance disclosures. Leslie Wayne, "D'Amato Converted Donations to Help New York Candidates," *New York Times*, 2-18-97.

His [Russ Feingold's] prescription is the same prescription the Democrats have had for the last ten years, which is designed to put the government in charge of the political speech of individuals, candidates, parties, and groups . . . This whole issue is about the First Amendment. . . .

The Republican National Committee, the Republican Senatorial Committee, the Republican Congressional Committee, and 95 percent of Republican members of Congress are against the bill. That by definition does not make it bipartisan. So, that bill has got about as much chance of passing as the Patriots do, . . . unfortunately, of winning today. That bill's not going to pass.

> —*Sen. Mitch McConnell (R-KY)*. "Late Edition," CNN, 1-26-97. Sen. McConnell also opposed the gift ban, which eventually passed both houses as did the McCain-Feingold bill, later upheld by the Supreme Court.

Campaign finance reform—especially in the guise of S.27, the McCain-Feingold legislation that passed the Senate in April—is a direct killing attack on every individual American's First Amendment right to use political speech to protect the entire Bill of Rights.

> —*James O.E. Norell*. NRA website, "Campaign Finance Reform: Silencing Freedom to gain power," posted 7-11-01.

Andrew: In regards to delivering the message. Would you be in favor of networks granting free air time in exchange for a severe tightening of campaign finances?

Kayne Robinson: The nice thing about living in America is that it's a free country. The networks are private businesses. Having government use the force of law to seize their property and turn it over to government is against our free traditions in America. And forcing the networks to put free airtime on for candidates would be exactly that. If the writer of the question would read the Constitution you'd see that we enjoy freedom of speech and so putting a candidate in the penitentiary because they bought airtime to speak to the people of their state or nation, would be un-American.

> —*Robinson was chairman of the Iowa Republican Party* during this question-and-answer session from the "Iowa Straw Poll Preview," ABC News, 8-13-99. While the networks are private businesses, the airwaves are not their exclusive property. Kayne Robinson is now president of the National Rifle Association.

Sen. John F. Kerry has been citing his valorous Vietnam record
more often than Gen. George Patton cursed. It's a good theme
for him. With Bush rounding up al-Qaeda and clearing out the
terrorist swamps, the greatest danger now facing the nation is
that liberals could somehow return to the White House. Whenever America is threatened from outside, Republicans have a
lock on the Oval Office. No matter how secure the world seems,
after 9-11 you have to vote for the better man on national defense. That is always the Republican.
        —*Ann Coulter*, "American women to Kerry: We don't think
        you're so hot," Townhall.com, 5-8-03.

Now let me tell you, I think we got a little bit off-step (since the
GOP took control of the Congress) because our vision last year
was anti-regulation. Well . . . if you think about it, anti-
regulation's not exactly a big battle cry. I mean, it may mean a
lot if you're the one being regulated, but if you're an average
American, you don't—you somehow don't go, "Okay, why am
I supposed to get excited about anti-regulation?" . . . Now I
think "pro-small business" works. I think "pro-family farm"
works. "Pro-family ranch" works. I think you can explain that.
        —*House Speaker Newt Gingrich* addressing the U.S. Cham-
        ber of Commerce in Washington, D.C. EWG.org, 6-18-96.

I think one of the great problems we have in the Republican
Party is that we don't encourage you to be nasty. We encourage
you to be neat, obedient and loyal and faithful and all those
Boy Scout words, which would be great around the campfire
but are lousy in politics.
        —*Newt Gingrich*. *Congressional Record*, H10528, 10-11-98.

We affirm the right of individuals to voluntarily participate in
labor organizations and to bargain collectively. We therefore
support the right of states to enact Right-to-Work laws. No one
should be forced to contribute to a campaign or a candidate, so

we will vigorously implement the Supreme Court's Beck decision to stop the involuntary use of union dues for political purposes. We will revoke the illegal executive order excluding millions of workers from federal contracts, and safeguard the unemployment compensation system against the diversion of its funds for political purposes.

—*Republican Party Platform 2000*. RNC.org.

I think George Bush is going to win in a walk. I really believe I'm hearing from the Lord it's going to be like a blowout election in 2004. The Lord has just blessed him, I mean, he could make terrible mistakes and come out of it. It doesn't make any difference what he does, good or bad, God picks him up because he's a man of prayer and God's blessing him.

—*Pat Robertson*. "700 Club," CBN. *New York Times*, 1-3-04. Rev. Barry Lynn commented, "Maybe Pat got a message from Karl Rove and thought it was from God."

. . . tax-hiking, government-expanding, latte-drinking, sushi-eating, Volvo-driving, *New-York-Times* reading, body piercing, Hollywood-loving, left-wing freak show.

—*A TV commercial by the Club for Growth attacking Howard Dean* during the Iowa Caucuses campaign. *Chicago Tribune*, 1-19-04.

It's all very funny! Even the political thing, all the things you have to do to make an initiative pass, it's hilarious. You have to call the head of the California Fire Association and can you endorse my initiative and then the guy says, Oh, yeah, it's great. It is funny, the whole system itself, so you have to be able to sit back and look at the whole thing as kind of like a big stage play.

—*Arnold Schwarzenegger*. Jeanne Marie Laskas, "The Amazing Ahhnold! Part One," *Esquire*, 7-03.

PART VIII

BIRDS DO IT, BEES DO IT

"Still, if we aren't having sex on a daily basis, we are thinking about it all the time. I mean all the time."

—BILL O'REILLY

SexSexSex

Ann Coulter: That seems like a lot of words to explain that she's [Hillary Clinton] in it for the power. And it's interesting—
Geraldo Rivera: For the power?
Coulter: Yeah. I mean, why do prostitutes turn tricks? Of course, she's in it for the power.
Rivera: Are you comparing the first lady of the United States to a prostitute?
Coulter: Oh, yeah. Yeah. I mean—
Rivera: You are?
Coulter: There's always been some women who will take the easy path to glory. But what I think is interesting about it is a lot of the president's bimbos, as his campaign called them, appeared to have actually loved him. That is to say Monica, Dolly Kyle Browning, Gennifer Flowers. Hillary's the only woman in his life who's in it for the power.
> —*Ann Coulter* on "Rivera Live." David Daley, "Spin On The Right Ann Coulter: Light's All Shining On Her," *Hartford Courant,* 6-25-99.

[Clinton] masturbates in the sinks.
> —*Ann Coulter.* "Rivera Live," 8-2-99. "The Wisdom Of Ann Coulter," *Washington Monthly,* 10-01.

During routine systems checks conducted on staff office computers during the first week of June 1999, certain inappropriate material was discovered. This resulted in immediate and appropriate disciplinary actions being taken against those involved. In deference to legitimate privacy concerns, our office plans no further comment.
> —*Gary Hoitsma,* spokesman for Sen. James Inhofe (R-OK).
> Three male staffers in the Senator's office downloaded so

many porno files, the computer system malfunctioned. Hoitsma would not say if the staffers had been fired. Ed Henry, "Pornography Problem, Heard on the Hill Column," *Roll Call*, 6-14-99.

. . . yet another revolting example of such [pro-homosexual] propaganda and "tolerance"—some readers might want to skip the paragraph that follows—occurred in Newton South High School in Newton, Massachusetts in 2001. A teacher there told the *Boston Globe* that he had subtly introduced "bisexual, gay, lesbian, and transgendered" subjects in class. He distributed the novel *The Perks Of Being A Wallflower* by Stephen Chbosky and instructed the class to write an essay on it. The book features such subjects as bestiality (between boy and dog), man-boy sex, anal sex between boys, male masturbation, and female masturbation using a hot dog. When a parent objected, school officials treated her as an ignorant pest.

    —*David Limbaugh, Persecution—How Liberals Are Waging War Against Christianity,* Washington, D.C.: Regnery, 2003, p. 78. Limbaugh's source for this story (note 31 in his book) is an article from the right-wing online magazine, *Insight on the News*, John Haskins, "It's 1984 in Massachusetts—And Big Brother Is Gay," 12-17-01. A Proquest search failed to turn up the *Boston Globe* article mentioned here. There was a piece in the *Boston Herald,* Jack Sullivan, "Miffed Mom Says teach assigned porn book," 7-20-01. The book received a positive review in the respected library journal *Kirkus Reviews.* While the book does frankly discuss sex, Limbaugh's description is inaccurate and greatly exaggerated.

Bill Clinton is gonna give the commencement speech at the U.S. Military Academy. Kind of strange, you know, a few years ago the military didn't even wanna know Bill Clinton, and now, with all the, you know, sex stuff going on, suddenly, he's their man.

    —*Don Wade*, referring to sex scandals in the military at the time. "Don Wade and Roma," WLS talk radio 890-AM, Chicago, 5-14-97.

One of the most memorable aspects of this entire proceeding was the solemn occasion wherein every Senator in this chamber took an oath to do impartial justice under the Constitution. But I must say, despite massive and relentless efforts to change the subject, the case before you, Senators, is not about sexual misconduct, infidelity, adultery. Those are private acts and are none of our business.

> —*Rep. Henry Hyde (R-IL).* "Lead House manager Hyde gives final summation of case against president," CNN.com, 1-16-99.

We are deeply troubled by recent media reports indicating that certain individuals may be engaged in a systematic attempt to intimidate Judiciary Committee Chairman Henry Hyde and other elected members of the House from doing their constitutional duty by promoting prurient allegations about their personal lives to the media. If these reports are true, the actions of the individuals responsible are pure and simple intimidation— no different than threatening jurors to change their verdicts in organized crime trials. Therefore, we urge you to investigate these reports in an effort to determine whether any individuals—inside or outside of the White House—have made efforts to undermine the lawful and constitutional work of the Judiciary Committee.

> —*From a letter written by House Republicans leaders and sent to FBI Director Louis Freeh.* Steve Lash, "GOP: White House smearing party/FBI asked to look into sex disclosures," *Houston Chronicle,* 9-18-98.

This is about lawbreaking, This is not about sex. This is not about gossip. This is not about soap operas. This is about lawbreaking.

> —*Newt Gingrich* on President Clinton. Alison Mitchell, "Gingrich Says Attacks On Clinton About Lawbreaking," *Cleveland Plain Dealer,* 4-30-98.

We live in an age characterized by the maxim "if it feels good do it, regardless of the consequences." It's a sex-drenched culture—from movies, music, and magazines to TV, radio and the internet—that glorifies premarital sex, promiscuous sex, extramarital sex, kinky sex, rough sex, and gay sex. You name it, you can find it, and without looking that hard.
> —*Sean Hannity, Let Freedom Ring*, NY: Reganbooks, HarperCollins, 2002, p. 286.

Ms. Lewinsky testified that her physical relationship with the President included oral sex but not sexual intercourse. According to Ms. Lewinsky, she performed oral sex on the President; he never performed oral sex on her. Initially, according to Ms. Lewinsky, the President would not let her perform oral sex to completion. In Ms. Lewinsky's understanding, his refusal was related to "trust and not knowing me well enough." During their last two sexual encounters, both in 1997, he did ejaculate.

According to Ms. Lewinsky, she performed oral sex on the President on nine occasions. On all nine of those occasions, the President fondled and kissed her bare breasts. He touched her genitals, both through her underwear and directly, bringing her to orgasm on two occasions. On one occasion, the President inserted a cigar into her vagina. On another occasion, she and the President had brief genital-to-genital contact.
> —*The Starr Report*, "Narrative," section I.C.2, "Ms. Lewinsky's Account," 9-9-98.

The evidence suggests that the president, acting in a premeditated and calculated fashion, deceived the American people on Jan. 26 and on other occasions when he denied a relationship with Ms. Lewinsky.
> —*Kenneth W. Starr*, Independent Counsel, listing one of 10 examples of "misuse of presidential authority" by Bill Clinton, CNN.com,11-19-98.

Nevertheless, our society has played a terrible trick on many women. It has told them that equality means acting the same as men. That is how you have the utterly false spectacle of women acting thrilled to have anonymous men strip and rub themselves on them. It is also a function of anger. Many women are not thrilled at the prospect of soon-to-be-husbands getting all aroused with naked strippers on their laps. So here's their response: "See, men, we can do it, too." But they really can't. The false attempt to act like males also explains the current phenomenon of the female sexual predator—whatever men can do, women can do better. But such behavior, like the bachelorette party, is all pretend, created by a generation of women deliberately confused about their sexual identity by feminism and the university.

    —*Dennis Prager.* "Women pretending to be men," TownHall.com, 5-20-03.

It is sickening what is going on in Hollywood. But what was my rationale for Cary Grant? Here it was, I remember it vividly, I was in my teens. I said when you have too much money, and you can have any beautiful woman in the world, and you start going to wild Hollywood parties and drinking too much—we did not know about drugs much in those days—and you start drinking too much, and you are at an orgy, whatever moves, I guess. It is all a mortal sin. It is all promiscuity. It is all flesh. Flesh is flesh, so you experiment with everything. So I do not think Cary Grant was a homosexual or a bisexual. He just got carried away at those orgies. That was my rationale so I could like Sergeant McChesney of *Gunga Din* with McLaglen and with Sergeant Ballentine Douglas Fairbanks, Jr . . . My teenage rationale for Cary Grant. We are in advanced moral decay, Mr. Speaker, and I am going to stay in the Presidential race as long as I can, because there is not anyone in the race like Congressman Robert K. Dornan at age 62.

    —*Rep. Bob Dornan (R-CA) on moral decay in America. Congressional Record,* H8719 and H8720, 9-8-95.

Sen. Rick Santorum: Every society in the history of man has upheld the institution of marriage as a bond between a man and a woman. Why? Because society is based on one thing: that society is based on the future of the society. And that's what? Children. Monogamous relationships. In every society, the definition of marriage has not ever, to my knowledge, included homosexuality. That's not to pick on homosexuality. It's not, you know, man on child, man on dog, or whatever the case may be. It is one thing. And when you destroy that, you have a dramatic impact on the quality—

Lara Jakes Jordan: I'm sorry, I didn't think I was going to talk about "man on dog" with a United States senator, it's sort of freaking me out.

Santorum: And that's sort of where we are in today's world, unfortunately . . . And if you make the case that if you can do whatever you want to do, as long as it's in the privacy of your own home, this "right to privacy," then why be surprised that people are doing things that are deviant within their own home?

—*Excerpts from an AP interview with Sen. Rick Santorum (R-PA), 4-7-03. CNN.com, 4-22-03.*

We are a sick people with weak, ineffectual families. The United States Center For Disease Control reported recently that 43 million of our citizens (nearly one in five) are infected with an incurable sexually transmitted virus. Some will die of it. Others will suffer for the rest of their lives. Can anyone doubt that sexual liberation has been a social, spiritual, and physiological disaster!?

—*Dr. James Dobson, When God Doesn't Make Sense,* Wheaton, Ill.: Tyndale House, 1993, p. 189. A call to the Sexually Transmitted Diseases Division of the CDC on 9-5-03, revealed that there are now 45 million people (one in five) infected with genital herpes, a non-fatal condition.

God in his great mercy has blessed America, and made this a haven for Christians and Jews alike. But we've gone away from

our Christian heritage. And God has little obligation at the present time to spare America, because we are polluting the world with our television programs, our movies and so forth, our books. We are polluting the whole world. We've made the world drunk, if you will, with the wine of our fornication. The whole world has been affected by Hollywood.
　　—*Pat Robertson.* "700 Club," CBN, 17-7-95.

Last night was socialist night . . . Last night was Harold Ickes sticks-it-in-an-orifice-or-two of Dick Morris.
　　—*Rush Limbaugh* criticizing the Democratic National Convention, 8-28-96.

Following are selected points from a complaint filed by Kansas State Sen. Susan Wagle against a sex education class, 4-16-03:
　　Point 2.) It is reported that inappropriate "street" language and obscene gestures are a regular part of the class. Dr. Dailey usually substitutes the "F" word for the word "sex." Dr. Dailey makes groping motions with his hands when discussing women's breasts. "Butt f . . . ing" is one of the many sexual acts students are told they will learn about, and although they might not choose such acts for their own sexual expression, they will accept these behaviors before the class is completed. Dr. Dailey and his 20 -year-old teaching assistant, Teresa Scalise, hug each other inappropriately at times in front of the class. Ms. Scalise is currently the primary defender of Dr. Dailey in newsprint.
　　Point 5.) During the class that was scheduled to study the female anatomy, Dr. Dailey started by explaining the different parts of the female anatomy. Then he progressed to show close-up slides of female genitals, however, before he started the slide show, he told the girls in the class they would see themselves in the slides. During the viewing of the slides, Dr. Dailey commented on one picture, the brunette with the large lips, being very beautiful. Many side comments were made about the photos. Then upon seeing another photo, Dr. Dailey ex-

claimed this one "looks like an aberration, we have just seen the Virgin Mary." After numerous slides, Dr. Dailey, without transitioning into the subject matter of human development, showed the genitals of a five-year-old girl, then the genitals of a ten-year-old girl.

Point 6.) During the female anatomy day, Dr. Dailey told the class during his discussion of the G-spot that it was his goal to find this spot on women and name it the "Dailey Spot."

Point 7.) During the female anatomy day, Dr. Dailey told the females in the class that their homework assignment was to spread their legs. He told them to take a flashlight and a mirror, spread their lips, and explore.

Point 8.) During one class, Dr. Dailey stated that if he were Chancellor, he would require empirical evidence from the females who desire to graduate from K.U. to prove they are orgasmic. He stated that evidence could be in the form of a videotape.

Point 9.) During the day that was scheduled to discuss masturbation, explicit discussion ensued and films of females and males masturbating were shown. A female student got up to walk out of the room. Dr. Dailey questioned where she was going with the implication that she could not contain her sexual urges after being exposed to his comments. The girl turned and blurted out "I'm going to the bathroom." Dr. Dailey said that was good because you can't do it on a full bladder. After the films, Dr. Dailey asked the students personal questions about their masturbatory habits and had students respond by raising hands. After seeing their answers, he called the students in the classroom "horny devils."

—*Lawrence Journal-World*, 4-16-03. Sen. Wagle inserted a provision in the budget that would in effect ban the appropriation of money for the popular class which had been taught at the University of Kansas by Professor Dennis Dailey for the last 20 years. The allegations were based on statements by Jessica Zahn, a student who attended the class and has served as an intern in Sen. Wagle's office. Gov. Kathleen Sebelius (D) used her line-item veto on this ban.

Susan Wagle: Well, I carried the amendment. I was so upset after I talked to a lot of students and found that this professor has a very widespread reputation for having heavy porn. He goes to porn night in the fraternities. He goes to porn night in the dormitories. He advertises his class. Everybody knows what's going on. The department had bought him his videos, and I believe they are what I would consider pornography. They are full sexual acts, all different kinds, and he shows them constantly in his class.

Bill O'Reilly: So the school knows—the school knows what he's doing, and they sanction it. So what are you going to do in . . .

Wagle: Absolutely.

O'Reilly: . . . the legislature? We've got 20 seconds. What are you going to do?

Wagle: I carried an amendment—it passed—to de-fund that college, and the governor vetoed it.

> —"*The O'Reilly Factor,*" 4-29-03. On 4-30-03, O'Reilly once more aired Sen. Wagle's allegations, attacking the university and Gov. Kathleen Sebelius for letting Daily "go wild in the classroom."
>
> On 5-13-03, the university released a report on the controversy created by Sen. Wagle and her former intern: "A thorough month-long investigation by the University of Kansas' chief academic officer has found no validity to allegations against Professor Dennis Daily by State Sen. Susan Wagle, R-Wichita, regarding his teaching of a human sexuality course." David Shulenburger, "Provost responds: Dailey charges baseless," *Lawrence Journal-World*, 6-29-03. For comments of Daily's students praising his class, see Dave Ranney, "Senator lodges complaint against professor," *Lawrence Journal-World*, 4-16-03.
>
> On 5-5-03, Professor Daily received the Del Shankel Teaching Excellence Award. He was nominated by KU athletes and selected by an advisory committee. "Sexuality Professor wins KU Award," *The Wichita Eagle*, 5-7-03.

Still, if we aren't having sex on a daily basis, we are *thinking* about it all the time. I mean *all* the time.
> —*Bill O'Reilly, The O'Reilly Factor.* NY: Broadway Books, 2000, p. 29.

I had the most astonishing thought last Thursday. After a long day of hauling the kids to play dates and ballet, I turned on the news. And there was the president, landing on the deck of the USS Abraham Lincoln, stepping out of a fighter jet in that amazing uniform, looking—how to put it?—really hot. Also presidential, of course. Not to mention credible as commander in chief. But mostly "hot," as in virile, sexy and powerful . . .
> —*Lisa Schiffren,* "Hey Flyboy! Women Voters agree: President Bush is a hottie!" *Wall Street Journal* editorial page, 5-9-03.

Chris Matthews: What do you make of this broadside against the USS Abraham Lincoln and its chief visitor last week?
Gordon Liddy: Well, I—in the first place, I think it's envy. I mean, after all, Al Gore had to go get some woman [Naomi Wolf] to tell him how to be a man. And here comes George Bush. You know, he's in his flight suit, he's striding across the deck, and he's wearing his parachute harness, you know—and I've worn those because I parachute—and it makes the best of his manly characteristic. You go run those, run that stuff again of him walking across there with the parachute. He has just won every woman's vote in the United States of America. You know, all those women who say size doesn't count—they're all liars. Check that out. I hope the Democrats keep ratting on him and all of this stuff so that they keep showing that tape.
> —"Hardball," 5-8-03. Dailyhowler.com

Down & Dirty

Lying Chicken-shit! . . . Gutless Chicken (expletive)!
—*Rep. Tom DeLay (R-TX)*, then House Majority Whip, swearing at Rep. David Obey (D-WI) and shoving him in a dispute over a newspaper report that lobbyists wrote legislation in DeLay's office. John Mercurio, "House's Road to Civility Takes Detour After DeLay-Obey Fight, Members Say," *Roll Call,* 4-14-97.

Al Franken: Clinton's military did pretty well in Iraq, huh?
Paul Wolfowitz: Fuck you.
—*Humorist Al Franken and Deputy Secretary of Defense Paul Wolfowitz* exchanging words at the annual White House Correspondents' Dinner. Karen Croft, "The Fix," Salon.com, 4-27-03.

That's not policy, that's bullshit.
—*Steve Largent,* former Congressman and gubernatorial candidate (R-OK), during a televised interview on Oklahoma City's Fox affiliate, KOKH. Largent objected to news anchor Andrew Speno's questions about his whereabouts during George W. Bush's first State-of-the-Union address. Largent claimed to have been in Washington when in fact he had been filming a commercial for the NRA in New Mexico. Chuck Ervin, "Largent foe takes aim at remark," *Tulsa World,* 10-16-02.

I asked [Newt], "What is she like?" He said, "Mother, she's a bitch."
—*Newt Gingrich's mother* talking about Hillary Clinton. Bill Tammeus, "The Year of Talking Dangerously: Next time, folks, consider silence," *Denver Post,* 12-29-95.

Kick their asses out.

—*Gov. Jeb Bush (R-FL)*, to staffers during a sit-in staged by two African-American legislators at the Florida state capitol. Gary Fineout, "Jeb Bush enters his toughest year yet," *Sarasota Herald Tribune*, 12-25-00. State Democrats Sen. Kendrick Meek and Rep. Tony Hill were demonstrating against Bush's "One Florida" plan to repeal affirmative action. Gov. Bush later said that he was referring to reporters covering the sit-in, not to the lawmakers themselves.

My wife, she always calls him a slut, that's her term, and I will not disagree with my wife publicly.

—*Rep. Darrell Issa*, speaking about President Clinton. Marsha Mercer, "Clinton Back On Track In Bid To Confound His Opponents," *Richmond Times-Dispatch*, 4-12-98.

Texas Lieutenant Gov. Bob Bullock: I'm sorry, [Gov. Bush], but I'm going to have to fuck you on this one [by backing a bill Bush opposed].
Gov. George Bush: [Grabbing Bullock by the shoulders, pulling him forward and kissing him] If you're going to fuck me, you'll have to kiss me first.

—*Tucker Carlson*, "Devil may care." *Talk Magazine*, 9-99, p. 104.

He used to say "fuck" alot more before all this started.

—*A Bush advisor during the presidential campaign. Ibid.*, p. 108.

Part IX

Put Not Your Faith in Judges

"Please God, no more Souters."
—ALABAMA ATT'Y GEN. WILLIAM PRYOR

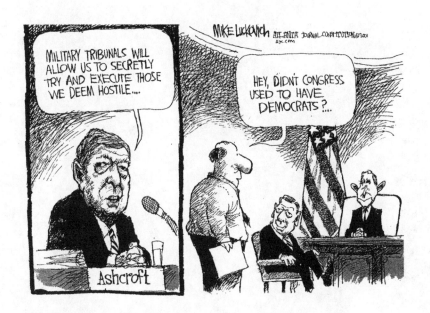

JUDICIAL ACTIVISM

Judicial activism results from the enlistment of judges on one side of the culture war in every western nation. Despite denials by some that any such conflict exists, the culture war is an obtrusive fact. It is a struggle between the cultural or liberal left and the great mass of citizens who, left to their own devices, tend to be traditionalists. The courts are enacting the agenda of the cultural left. There is a certain embarrassment in choosing a name for this group. I will sometimes refer to these faux intellectuals as the "New Class," . . . [which] consists of print and electronic journalists; academics at all levels; denizens of Hollywood; mainline clergy and church bureaucracies; personnel of museums, galleries, and philanthropic foundations; radical environmentalists; and activist groups for a multiplicity of single causes.

It is able to exercise influence in many ways, but when cultural and social issues become sufficiently clear, the intellectual class loses elections. It is, therefore, essential that the cultural left find a way to avoid the verdict of the ballot box. Constitutional courts provide the necessary means to outflank majorities and nullify their votes. The judiciary is the liberals' weapon of choice. Democracy and the rule of law are undermined while the culture is altered in ways the electorate would never choose.

—*Robert Bork, Coercing Virtue*. Washington D.C.: The Aei Press, 2003, pp. 5-6.

When I laid my hand on the Bible to take the Oath of Office, I made my pledge to our Constitution. And as long as I have a voice and a vote in the U.S. Senate, I will fight the judicial despotism that stands like a behemoth over this great land.

At its best, the Court is the guardian of the Constitution, a body to which all Americans look for the ultimate protection of their rights. At its worst, it is home to a "let-them-eat-cake elite" who hold the people in the deepest disdain. By guiding the judicial selection process, we can begin to reestablish the constitutional balance envisioned by the Framers.

It is also time for us to take a broader, comprehensive look at the alarming increase in activism on the Court. As Chairman of the Senate Subcommittee on the Constitution, I intend to convene hearings in the months ahead to examine this disturbing trend. Americans should not sit idly by as our individual rights are surrendered. We should enlist the American people in an effort to rein in an out-of-control Court.

> —*Sen. John Ashcroft*, CPAC Annual Meeting, 3-6-97.
> Freerepublic.com.

All these so-called culture wars reflect this incredible disconnect between an out-of-control, despotic, high-handed elite in the courts and the two other branches, which still seem to have some responsiveness and some accountability to the electorate.

> —*Mary Parker Lewis*, chief of staff to Alan Keyes. Abby
> Goodnough, "Victory in Florida Feeding Case Emboldens
> the Religious Right," *New York Times*, 10-24-03.

Finally, a governor and legislature had the courage to stand up to judicial despots because of an overwhelming call by the public.

> —*Randall Terry*, praising Gov. Jeb Bush and the Florida legis-
> lature for passing a bill to prevent the death of Terri Schiavo
> who had been in a vegetative state for thirteen years. *Ibid.*

I believe Judge White's opinions have been and, if confirmed, his opinions on the Federal bench will continue to be, procriminal and activist, with a slant toward criminals and defendants against prosecutors and the culture in terms of maintaining order; he will use his lifetime appointment to push law in a pro-criminal direction, consistent with his own personal political agenda, rather than defer to the legislative will of the people and interpret the law rather than expand it or redirect the law . . . These opinions, and particularly his dissents, reflect a serious bias against a willingness to impose the death penalty . . .

> —Sen. John Ashcroft (R-MO) speaking in opposition to the nominaton of State Supreme Court Judge Ronnie White to the United States District Court for the Eastern District of Missouri. Congressional Record, S11872, 10-4-99. Said Sen. Patrick Leahy (D-VT), "I just note that Justice Ronnie White is far more apt to affirm a death penalty decision than to vote as one of many members of the Supreme Court to reverse it. He has voted to affirm 41 times and voted to reverse only 17 times." Congressional Record, S11874, 10-4-99.

The federal judiciary is out-of-control . . . Congress is not utilizing four constitutional tools already at their disposal. Presently, Congress has the constitutional authority for a rigorous judicial selection process, impeachment, restricting appellate jurisdiction, and reducing or redistributing the number of judicial positions . . . There have been times in recent memory when the actions of the federal judiciary have caused such outrage that the American people have called for impeachment . . . But, out of the 16 federal judges impeached in our history, no federal judge has ever been impeached for the tyranny of judicial activism. There are however, many constitutional experts who agree that attempts to subvert the Constitution and rendering unconstitutional opinions constitute "high crimes and misdemeanors." It is clear the Framers of the Constitution wanted judicial independence, however, it is just as clear they included impeachment as a powerful check on judicial tyranny. The Congress must restrain an out-of-control judiciary if it cannot or will not restrain itself.

. . . Congress should simply remove the ability of federal judges to decide cases on a particular subject matter if they refuse to render restrained constitutional decisions in that area of the law.

. . . Congress ought to refuse to replace or redistribute the positions of liberal activist judges if they insist on rendering decisions based on their own personal policy.

> —*Judicial Selection Monitor,* a publication of a right-wing coalition set up by the Free Congress Research and Education Foundation. "GOP Battles Clinton Over Court Nominees," *Congressional Quarterly,* Dec 1996/Jan 1997.

The impact of Clinton Supreme Court appointees Ruth Bader Ginsburg and Stephen Breyer is best seen in decisions such as *Romer v. Evans* and *Virginia v. United States.* In *Romer,* the Court struck down a Colorado constitutional provision prohibiting quota preferences for homosexuals. Though the Court in1986 allowed states to criminalize homosexual conduct, it now concluded that the voters of Colorado may not prohibit the state from bestowing special protections upon homosexuals.

Justice Antonin Scalia, joined by Chief Justice William Rehnquist and Justice Clarence Thomas, dissented: "No principle set forth in the Constitution, nor even any imagined by this Court in the past 200 years, prohibits what Colorado has done here." They explained that laws against polygamy and homosexuality both represent society's effort to preserve sexual morality. The Court's majority, led by Justice Anthony Kennedy, apparently believes that homosexuals are entitled to more rights than polygamists.

> —*Judicial Selection Monitor,* 7-96.

The judges need to be intimidated. They need to uphold the Constitution. [If they don't behave] we're going to go after them in a big way.

> —*Tom DeLay (R-TX).* Joan Biskupic, "Hill Republicans Target 'Judicial Activism'; Conservatives Block Nominees, Threaten Impeachment and Term Limits," *Washington Post,* 9-14-97.

. . . Just think what five unelected judges have done to our nation's moral framework.

In 1962, they ruled prayer out of the public schools.

In 1963, they ruled the Bible out of public schools.

In 1973, they applied a "right of privacy" not found in the Constitution as the basis for opening the door to the slaughter of more than 43,000,000 innocent unborn children.

Subsequent federal courts have ruled the Ten Commandments were illegal in schools, that statues of Jesus were illegal in public parks, that prayers on a map in North Carolina were illegal, and that it was illegal for little elementary school children to give thanks over their milk and cookies at snack time.

Now, the Supreme Court has declared a constitutional right to consensual sodomy and, by the language in its decision, has opened the door to homosexual marriages, bigamy, legalized prostitution, and even incest.

The framers of our Constitution never intended anything like this to take place in our land . . . Just think, five unelected men and women who serve for life can change the moral fabric of our nation and take away the protections which our elected legislators have wisely put in place . . . Would you join with me and many others in crying out to our Lord to change the Court? If we fast and pray and earnestly seek God's face, then He will hear our prayer and give us relief. One justice is 83 years old, another has cancer, and another has a heart condition. Would it not be possible for God to put it in the minds of these three judges that the time has come to retire? With their retirement and the appointment of conservative judges, a massive change in federal jurisprudence can take place. We can have a court that no longer legislates from the bench the wishes of The New York Times and The Washington Post, but which will earnestly seek to interpret the Constitution as it is written and to give meaning to the centuries of moral standards which have under girded this wonderful country called the United States of America.

Please join us in prayer to support a massive prayer offensive that we are going to call Operation Supreme Court Freedom . . .

—*Pat Robertson*. PatRobertson.com, 2003.

When I am president, only conservative judges need apply.
—*Bob Dole*, 5-28-96, quoted in the Republican Party Plat-
    form, adopted 8-12-96, p.13.

God has chosen this time and this place so that we can save our
country and save our courts for our children . . . I will never
forget Jan. 22, 1973, the day seven members of our highest
court ripped the Constitution and ripped out the life of millions
of unborn children.
—*Alabama Attorney General Bill Pryor*, at a 1997 Christian
    Coalition rally. President Bush has nominated him to sit as
    a judge on the 11th U.S. Circuit Court of Appeals. Bill
    Rankin, "Bush judicial nominee a conservative activist,"
    Atlanta Journal-Constitution, 5-25-03.

While I, the people of Alabama and especially Alabamans who
know him best agree that Gen. Pryor is an excellent, well-quali-
fied nominee, the radical left and its Beltway sympathizers believe he has already disqualified himself. Why? Because the left
is trying to enforce an anti-religious litmus test. It appears that
nominees who openly adhere to Catholic and Baptist doctrines,
as a matter of personal faith, are unqualified for the federal
bench in the eyes of the liberal Washington interest groups. Period. No exceptions for Carolyn Kuhl or Leon Holmes, and
certainly not for Gen. Pryor.
—*Sen. Orrin G. Hatch (R-UT)*, Chairman of the Judiciary
    Committee. David G. Savage, "Fight Gets Political Over
    Religion," *Los Angeles Times*, 7-24-03.

We are receiving nominations from all across the country [for
judges] that could be a prime candidate for impeachment under
our approach.
—*House Majority Whip Tom DeLay (R-TX)*. Rep. Henry Hyde,
    Republican Chairman of the House Judiciary Committee has
    spoken against this approach. Mike Dorning, "New GOP tar-
    get: Liberal Judges," *Chicago Tribune*, 5-16-97.

Everyone on the right agreed in 2000 that judicial nominations were the single most important reason to be for Bush.

> —*Clint Bolick,* former Reagan Justice Dept. official. E.J. Dionne, Jr., "Payback in Judges," *Washington Post,* 1-10-03.

The Constitution just sets minimums, most of the rights that you enjoy go way beyond what the Constitution requires.

> —*Supreme Court Justice Antonin Scalia,* speaking at John Carroll University in Cleveland. He refused to allow any radio or television coverage of this speech. The next day he accepted an award at Cleveland's City Club for his support of free speech. "Justice Bans Media from Free Speech event," Associated Press, 3-19-03.

Do you believe that Bill Clinton should have to obey the law and respect the United States Constitution? . . . Make no mistake, if we allow Bill Clinton's EXECUTIVE ORDER 13061 to go unopposed, there may be no end to his lawbreaking in the future. You see, through this dangerous Executive Order, Clinton is trying to make himself America's "Dictator-In-Chief."

This is an outrageous and UN-CONSTITUTIONAL power grab! Bill Clinton is trying to enact his liberal agenda as a one-man dictator—accountable to no one. And if his scheme succeeds, not even Congress will be able to stop his socialist programs and his shameful abuses of power.

I know what you're thinking: "How can Bill Clinton get away with this?" Well, he shouldn't be able to. That's why I'm suing Bill Clinton in federal court. Someone has to stop Clinton . . . But he's got Janet Reno's Justice Department on his side, fighting tooth-and-nail against me. And I have run up against some liberal judges who support Clinton and his big-government plans. One federal judge—a Clinton appointee—threw out my case, saying that Members of Congress don't have the right to sue the President . . . even when he is trashing the Constitution!

> —*Rep. Helen Chenoweth (R-ID)* in a letter attacking the American Heritage Rivers Initiative, an executive order issued by President Clinton "that designates certain rivers,

TAKE THEM AT THEIR WORDS

like the Mississippi and Colorado Rivers, as nationally protected resources. Included in the letter is a solicitation for
donations to Mountain States Legal Foundation, a prop-
erty-rights organization, and a request to sign a petition
opposing Executive Order 13061. Throughout the letter
she avoids mentioning the actual content of the American
Heritage Rivers Initiative, instead focusing her attention
on Bill Clinton." "Right Wing Watch Online," PFAW.org,
11-12-99.

Diane Sawyer: Massachusetts Supreme Court said that they were
not, they did not feel the law was in a position to block gay
marriage. When you talk about the sanctity of marriage between a man and a woman, are you saying you will absolutely
support a constitutional amendment against gay marriage and
against gay civil unions?
President Bush: If necessary, I will support a constitutional
amendment which would honor marriage between a man and a
woman, codify that, and will—the position of this administration is that whatever legal arrangements people want to make,
they're allowed to make, so long as it's embraced by the state or
[?] start at the state level. Let me tell you, the court I thought
overreached its bounds as a court. It did the job of the legislature. It was a very activist court in making the decision it made.
As you know, I'm a person who believes in judicial restraint, as
opposed to judicial activism that takes the place of the Legislative Branch.
  —*ABC-TV News Interview,* 12-16-03.

We are heirs to a mind-numbing bureaucracy; subject to a level
of legalization that cannot avoid being arbitrary, capricious,
and discriminatory. What other outcome is possible in a society
in which no adult can wake up, go about their business, and
return to their homes without breaking several laws? There are
of course many reasons for our present difficulties, but some of
our troubles can be laid at the feet of that most innocuous

branch—the judiciary . . . From the 1960s onward we have witnessed the rise of the judge militant.

> —*Judge Janice Rogers Brown*, Bush nominee for D.C. Appeals Court. Speech to California Lincoln Club Libertarian Law Counsel, 12-11-97.

The Declaration of Independence and the Constitution of the United States are rooted in a Christian perpective of the nature of government and the nature of man. The challenge of the next millenium will be to preserve the American experiment by restoring its Christian perspective.

> —*Alabama Attorney Gen. William Pryor*, Bush Administration nominee for a seat on the Federal Appeals Court in Atlanta. The nomination was dropped after a Democratic filibuster. PFAW.org.

Tragically, the courts have turned your individual rights into group rights as the aggrieved rush to our least representative branch in search of entitlement . . . Over the last half century, the federal courts have usurped from school boards the power to determine what a child can learn; removed from the people the ability to establish equality under the law; and challenged God's ability to mark when life begins and ends. The courts have made liars of Hamilton, Madison, and Morris, confirming our forefathers' worst fears. For what the Framers intended to be the weakest branch of government, the judiciary, has become the most powerful.

> —*Sen. John Ashcroft*, CPAC Annual Meeting, 3-6-97. Freerepublic.com.

Some members of the federal judiciary threaten the safety, the values, and the freedom of law-abiding citizens. They make up laws and invent new rights as they go along, arrogating to themselves powers King George III never dared to exercise.

> —*Republican Party Platform*, adopted 8-12-96, p. 13.

INDEX